D1407210

Sparks

New Writing from Bath Spa

With an introduction by
Gerard Woodward

And an interview with
Mo Hayder

Sulis Press, Bath

All enquiries regarding contributors, as well as any requests for permission to make copies of any part of the work, should be sent to the publisher:

Sulis Press
c/o Bath Spa University
Newton Park
Newton St Loe
Bath
BA2 9BN
www.sparksanthology.co.uk

British Library Cataloguing in Publication Data.
A catalogue record for this book is available from the British Library.

ISBN 0-9545648-3-9

10 9 8 7 6 5 4 3 2 1

Slipcase design © Emily Reeves and Tom Frost
emily_reeves@yahoo.com
tom.frost@btinternet.com

Cover and text design © Oliver Hayes
dartmouth04@hotmail.co.uk

Text set in Helvetica and Times
Printed and bound in Great Britain by Antony Rowe Ltd, Chippenham, Wiltshire
Slipcase printed in Great Britain by APB Colour Print Ltd, Bristol

First edition

With special thanks to

Tim Middleton and Tessa Hadley, for their editorial advice and support
Emily Reeves, for her time and commitment with the slipcase design
Oliver Hayes, for cover and text design and layout
Paul Meyer, for his assistance, advice and tireless enthusiasm
Gerard Woodward, for his inspiring introduction
Mo Hayder, for her enlightening interview
Nikky Twyman, for proofreading
Peter Frost, for his help with the production of the slipcase
Nik Grigoriadis, for IT support
The School of English and Creative Studies at Bath Spa University, for
its financial support

Contents

MA Writing for Young People

Introduction

I first decided I wanted to be a novelist at the age of eleven. I sat down with a Black Prince pencil and a scuffed exercise book and began to write a story about a robbery in a pet shop. This robbery is witnessed only by a talking mynah bird, whose endless reiteration of a phrase spoken by one of the thieves provides the detectives with their one lead – or at least it would do if they could catch it! The bird flies all around London, pursued by the detectives, and ends up at Battersea fun fair where there's a climactic, clambering chase on the big wheel.

When I think about this story now I'm suddenly struck by its absurd aptness as a subject for an embryonic writer – the desperate pursuit of an exotic bird whose only utterance is a fragment of incomprehensible language, repeated endlessly. I sometimes feel I've been chasing this mynah bird all my life, that it's always perched on a twig just out of reach, preening itself and chuckling at me. That's what the writing life can seem like at times. The solitary hunt for the uncatchable, the journey without maps.

MA courses in creative writing provide an alternative (at least temporarily) to this type of existence. I have never attended a course myself but I imagine the experience must be rather similar to discovering there's a party going on in a room of the empty house you've always lived in. You wonder where these people have been all your life, and now here they are, full of conversation and ideas, laughter and dancing, and you can actually understand what they are saying. Writing is suddenly a social activity and friendships are formed that outgrow the year-long course that nurtured them. At Bath Spa University it is said that workshop groups still meet informally in the town a decade after graduation. And each year brings its new cohort of writers, many of whom will settle permanently in the area. By such sedimentary accumulation Bath should eventually fill with writers to the brim.

An anthology such as this, then, representing as it does the work of the Bath Spa students of 2004–5 (including those on the newly formed MA in Writing for Young People), is much more than simply a showcase of new writing (though it is an outstanding one of those); it is a captured moment in time of the creative lives of forty or so people. Forged in the intense heat of our seminar workshops these are not just novel extracts, stories, poems and scripts; they are arguments, friendships, squabbles, jokes and rambling conversations in the pub.

As for the quality of the work, I can only let it speak for itself. Bath Spa has an outstanding track record of producing writers who go on to achieve publishing or broadcasting success, and this year's students will add substantially to that tally.

Now hand me my shotgun. I've just spotted that bird again.

Gerard Woodward

MA Creative Writing

The First Englishman

Jenni Mills

from a novel

Look at this. A sea urchin, so close we could snog each other. My eyes are crossing with the excitement, not to mention the proximity. I feel like calling to Martin to get his fat arse down here, so I'd have someone to share it with. But Martin couldn't care less, and neither could the sea urchin.

I'd guess it's been dead for a hundred million years or so. When it was pottering about, doing whatever sea urchins do in the warm shallow sea, dinosaurs tramped the shore. It looks like a bun, doughy white, slightly heart-shaped. The stuff of life, turned to stone.

I'm lying on my back. Stone is digging painfully into bone, nodules of chalk and outcrops of flint, none of them dovetailing with the knobbles on my spine. My nose is a couple of inches away from a white chalky ceiling with the sea urchin in it. Until I saw it, I was trying to turn over, to wriggle back the way I came in – feet first, because there isn't room to turn round. This is a fairly delicate moment. I don't think the entire lot is going to come crashing down on me, but it's always possible. The tunnel's hardly more than body width. Even by Neolithic standards, this is poky.

'You OK?'

Martin is at the end of the passage where it opens into the main gallery: a luxurious four feet high, so he can crouch on hands and knees, and turn round, lucky bugger. He's too big to crawl any further, so, being the woman, as usual I get all the shit jobs.

'Happy as a sunbeam,' I hiss. We rarely shout underground, unless it's 'Get the fuck out, quick.' I've perfected a penetrating whisper that seems to travel down tunnels. Martin's heard me, because he grunts. It's hard to know who are the sparkier conversationalists: archaeologists or mining engineers.

This wouldn't be most people's idea of Saturday afternoon fun, but I've lost count of the years we've been doing this. Martin's favourite archaeology happens underground. It's dirty and it's dangerous, and you can't have much more fun than that. We'll probably go on doing it as long as our joints hold out, or our luck.

Luck shouldn't come into it. Being the engineer, I'm the guardian of the luck, the one who understands stresses and loads and how water seeps through stone, and can therefore take an educated guess as to whether we are going to die today, entombed in a flint mine.

These galleries were dug out between five and six thousand years ago, by people who had only recently discovered farming. They're amazing: they have proper airshafts, and pillars to support the roof. The light of my head-torch picks out five-thousand-year-old carbon stains on the walls, from the oil lamps the miners worked by. This passage is a dead end, never properly dug out, a speculative tunnel that either failed to produce any decent flint, or perhaps was one of the last to be opened before stone tools were superseded by bronze. *Sorry, mate, no call for flint axeheads any more. Ever thought of re-skilling in metalwork?* The thought of a Neolithic Arthur Scargill pops disconcertingly into my head.

Sea urchin apart, I don't like this place. There's something claustrophobic about it, even for someone who makes a living out of going underground. The side galleries nip and pinch spitefully as you crawl down them. I keep thinking I should have brought a ball of string to make sure we find the way out again.

We'll look bloody silly if we can't. Particularly as no one knows we're in here. I say goodbye to the sea urchin and succeed in shuffling on to my stomach, so I can start slithering backwards down the tunnel. It seems much further when you can't see where you're going, and it's with enormous relief that I feel Martin grasp my ankles to let me know I've made it out to the main gallery.

'Whew. Don't ask me to do that again in a hurry.' I flip over on to my bottom, and bang my hard hat on the tunnel roof. 'Next time, it's your turn to wriggle up the miners' back passages.'

Martin giggles, easing back on to his haunches. He may be six foot four and built like a bear, but he's as camp as a Boy Scout jamboree. He's had my arse in his face more times than I care to count, crawling through underground tunnels, and never shown the slightest interest, which suits me fine.

'So what do you think?' he asks, offering me a swig of water. It tastes of chalk dust.

'Well, it's going to be expensive to dig. You'll need to prop it to make it safe.' I look around, my head-torch casting wild wobbling shadows over the walls. 'And I think you should steer clear of the side galleries altogether.'

'Which are the most interesting from an archaeological point of view. Most of the main shafts were worked over thoroughly in the nineteenth century. Damn...' Martin is chewing it over. I can see his heavy jaw grinding away as he nibbles the inside of his cheek. '...And bugger. And fuck. If I had the money to employ diggers who knew what they were doing, I might risk it, but I'm going to have to take on students and anoraks. Ooh, duh, Dr Wintle, I seem to have brought down the ceiling with one blow of my mighty trowel.'

'Don't joke. It's that delicate.'

Martin frowns. 'I suppose the insurance will be prohibitive.'

'And there's one tiny technicality,' I remind him.

'Ah. Yes.'

We don't actually have permission to be here. Martin picked the padlock on the shaft cover. We broke in and we're trespassing. An unofficial recce saves paperwork, but the drawback is that, if anything happens to us down here, we'll be waiting a hell of a long time for the rescue party.

'Quarter to four,' he says. 'Better get a move on, or it'll be dark before we get back to the jeep.'

We hands-and-knee it back towards the central shaft. I have a prickling feeling between my shoulder blades, and fight the temptation to keep twisting round to look behind. For God's sake, what am I expecting to see? A flare of light far down in the passage?

There's an iron ladder back to ground level. My arms are killing me by the time we reach the top. I could swear my belly is on fire, too. While Martin's on his way up, I unzip my fleece to take a look. I was in such a hurry to get out, my sweater must have ridden up as I stomached over the chalk floor, and there are ugly red grazes across my abdomen. An icy wind flicks across the hollow in the hillside, and I quickly zip up again.

Martin swings the trapdoor shut over the shaft, and crouches down to padlock it. The sun is almost touching the metal rim of the sea, and there's a tiny sliver of moon in the sky, no more than a nail paring. Back in the Neolithic age, the hillside was probably cleared right to the entrance of the mine. Those old miners liked a spectacular view when they came up from below. Martin's theory is that flint mines were as much sacred sites as industrial estates, the underworld being the realm of the ancestors.

'You didn't like it much in there, did you?' he asks. He has the unnerving habit of reading my thoughts.

'No.'

'It's funny, I don't like that one, either,' he says. 'Some of those side galleries feel... spooky.'

'I just got a bit claustrophobic. It was very tight.'

'Sorry. Get fatter. Then I wouldn't send you in.'

'You'd still send me in and I'd get stuck like a chimney sweep's boy.'

'If only you were.' Martin sighs, and starts to undo the chin strap on his helmet.

My nose is beginning to run in the freezing air, so I reach into my pocket for my tissues.

'Ah, shit.'

There's nothing in my pocket. My tissues have gone. But I've got a bigger problem than a dripping nose.

Martin looks up, his face ghostly with chalk dust. 'What's the matter?'

'We've got to go back. My car keys have fallen out of my pocket.'

He rolls his eyes. Yeah, well, I don't feel like it either. But the spare keys are three hundred miles away in Cornwall.

'Do you even know where they are?' he asks.

'That last tunnel. I'm sure.'

'Better be quick. I want to be gone before dark. If the landowner sees a light, we're stuffed.'

Something coughs behind me, and I swivel in sudden panic, just in time to see a huge black bird flap out of the beech trees, swooping across the clearing.

'Jesus!' There's always something numinous about places like this, entrances to the underworld. 'That must be the biggest bloody crow I saw in my life.'

'Not a crow,' says Martin, uncoupling the padlock. 'Raven.'

'Raven? Here? Come on.'

'Definitely. Right size, right croak.' Martin is the kind of bloke who knows these things.

'I thought they hung around mountains and wild Welsh cliffs.'

'Not exclusively,' says Martin. He peers towards the frost-tipped clump of bramble where the bird disappeared. 'It's unusual, I admit. Might have been a pet.' The bird is hopping about near a deadfall, getting excited about the smell of rotting rabbit or something equally whiffy. It doesn't look much of a pet to me.

'Perhaps it's the shade of a flint miner, come back to moan about us disturbing his nap.'

Martin throws back the cover with a crash loud enough to wake the dead. I sit on the edge of the shaft, feet dangling.

'Get on with it,' he says.

'I'm just thinking; maybe I should ring the AA instead.'

'Are you woman or are you wimp?'

'Wimp.' I stretch out one leg, feeling for the rungs of the ladder. Coal miners sometimes spat for luck before they got into the cage that took them underground to their shift. Gods live in the tunnels, and they can turn on you just like that. But there's instinct, too, a sense that some miners develop for where the danger lies, a feel for the state of the rock. As I start climbing down, I try spitting, but it's pathetic, just a *phhttt* of moisture off the end of my tongue, not a good rounded gob.

'Hi ho,' says Martin, from the top of the shaft. 'Hi bloody ho.'

There are good holes in the ground and there are bad holes in the ground. As I come off the ladder on to the chalk floor of the flint mine, this has turned into one of the bad ones. I know it from the way the shadows bounce and weave round the light of my head-torch; I smell it in the musty dead scent of the air.

Martin jumps down beside me.

'You didn't have to come down,' I tell him.

'Don't be daft.'

'No point in us both getting killed.'

'Ha bloody ha.'

I can tell he's feeling it, too. The place wasn't exactly welcoming the first time, but now it's positively chilly. That's not physically possible, of course, because underground is warmer in winter than up top. We're a couple of uninvited guests, tolerated out of politeness when we first came to call, now unmistakably being given the cold shoulder when we presume to pop back for a second visit.

'I don't want to sound stupid,' I say, 'but which gallery was it we went down?'

'That one.'

It would be. It's the smallest and the darkest, out of a set of very small, very dark, openings.

This time the gallery seems interminable. My knees have stiffened; they hurt, hurt, hurt, but I have to go on putting them down over and over again on the hard knobbled floor. There's still a hell of a lot of razor-sharp flint in this mine.

How could I have been so stupid as to leave my pocket unzipped? I can hear Martin behind me muttering 'Fuck,' softly with every breath, a mantra to get us through this ordeal. 'Fuck, fuck, fuck.' It bounces off my bum, matching the rhythm of the pain in my knees.

Chalk is made up of masses and masses of tiny, hard shells. When I was a student we had to take a piece of it and rub it with a nailbrush – abrade it, my geology textbook said; the same thing the chalk is now doing in revenge to my knees – then look at it under the microscope. The surface twinkled with minute shells belonging to foraminiferans, single-celled creatures that drifted aimlessly in their billions through sunlit Cretacean seas.

The Cretaceous follows the Jurassic, and is followed in its turn by...

The entrance to the side passage. I stop. Martin's head butts my bottom.

'Do you want me to go in?' he asks. Generous, but—

'My keys, my problem.' I take a deep, wavering breath. 'Right. Ready or not...'

I wriggle in on my stomach. As Martin's breathing fades behind me, I can hear the hush, hush, hush of my trousers against the rock. I start counting the movements of my elbows against the walls. I reckon the keys must have fallen out near the spot where the sea urchin floated above me, when I rolled over to examine the ceiling.

'Found them?' Martin's voice sounds hollow, distorted by echoes in the passage.

'No, but I just met Fungus the Bogeyman.'

Martin laughs. The echoes turn it into a creak that sets my teeth on edge.

Now, where is that blessed sea urchin? I turn over on to my back, feeling my hip bones scrape the sides of the tunnel. The head-torch shows a featureless stretch of chalk ceiling. I start pulling myself along slowly. For some unknown reason Martin is laughing again – I can hear the creak of it coming down the tunnel.

A creak: that sudden. It's not Martin laughing, and it's not funny.

Ah, shit.

The creak turns into a crack and then a rushing, pattering sound, just as my nose draws level with the sea urchin. Chalky rubble and stones begin to rain down over my legs! The ceiling's going, somewhere down the tunnel, and once one bit collapses there's nothing to hold the rest up.

I should have phoned the AA.

There's a swirl of dust fogging the head-torch, and I start to cough. As it darkens I imagine the thousands of tons of earth and rock that lie between me and the sky, and brace myself for the crushing weight of it all on my chest.

JENNI MILLS has been a radio presenter, a documentary maker and a television director. She presented *Woman's Hour* and *You and Yours*, and wrote a book (published in 2004) teaching broadcasters to use their voices effectively. But those aren't nearly enough careers for one lifetime; now she wants to write novels, too. This is the opening of the novel she wrote for the course.

Contact: jenni.mills@sparksanthology.co.uk

Paris–Rome Express

Ian Breckon

from *No Future*

The train leaves Paris after dark, pulling out of the Gare de Lyon and south through the suburbs, gathering speed across the flatlands of the Seine. In the dining car, alone at her table, Nina turns to the window and sips her dry gin soda. The night is filled with fleeting rain, and the reflections of the other tables in the dining car hang suspended within it, yellow and blurred by the water streaming across the glass. Now and again a station passes and Nina tries to read the nameboards in their little puddles of gaslight beneath the awnings, but the train is an express and moves too fast. This is the same train that she used to take years ago, on her trips to Paris with Amedeo.

There are a few people left in the dining car, lingering over late suppers, the duck terrine and the veal cutlets. All are men, and Nina watches them reflected in the window. One man seated across the aisle, neatly dressed with shining pomaded hair, lifts his wineglass every time Nina takes a drink, as if he hopes that he might catch her eye and smile at the coincidence, then perhaps ask to join her at her table. Perhaps he would be charming and a little suggestive, mentioning the hours that lie ahead, the difficulties of sleeping, the opportunities for discreet amusement in his compartment...

On the other side of the window the water beads and breaks, making fast diagonals across the black glass, cancelling the faces of the men in the dining car, all those other potential encounters. The train powers southwards, the locomotive, streamlined and bullet-nosed, shovelling smoke back over its shoulder. Paris is far behind in slumbering dusk and the winter chill, and Nina is going home.

She arrived in Paris in early October, the last flushes of cold bright sun lightening the grey stone of the city. Two weeks beforehand her life had fallen apart. Her husband Amedeo sent the note telling her that he was gone – not just *leaving* but already *gone*, with a finality that implied the pointlessness of further enquiry. Three days later, her lover Bianchi died in a motorcycle crash – it happened an hour after dawn on the road to the airfield, a patch of oil spilled on the tarmac; he lay unconscious for an hour before he was found, and was dead before he reached the hospital. Amedeo left her an annual allowance of twelve

thousand lire, an apartment in Milan, a house in the country near No-
vara and arrangements for the schooling of their son Marco in Geneva.
Bianchi left her pregnant with his child.

Paris was her first and best option. Deciding that if she was going
to be unhappy she would at least be comfortable, she took a suite in the
most expensive hotel she could afford, with high windows overlooking
the Luxembourg Gardens. For ten days she delayed. In the park, she
walked between the bare trees, watching the children playing, and in
the evenings she drank until she was drunk enough to cry, then wept for
all the lost love, all the bad luck, all the false morality and unfairness
of the world. She told herself that if her husband had not left she would
have kept the child. Amedeo would have understood; they would have
come to some arrangement. But with him gone, and Bianchi gone, she
had no choice. Or so she told herself. She thought of her son Marco far
away in Geneva; she saw him growing smaller and fainter, as he was
shrinking back into a distant infancy, into a memory, into an idea.

On the eleventh day she could put it off no longer. She took the
metro to Passy and found the address in a respectable residential street.
After the operation she walked beside the Seine feeling cold and sick,
then went back to the hotel and drank brandy from the bottle until she
could vomit. She tried not to think about Bianchi. She tried not to let
herself think that she had just killed the last remaining part of him.

She took a cheaper room at a hotel in Montparnasse, on Rue Notre-
Dame des Champs. She went to the famous bars and the cafés – the
Dôme, the Select, the Rotonde, the Bal Negre – and found them jammed
to the doors with Americans, a few third-rate artists sitting at tables
amidst the throng, doodling sketches on napkins and selling them to
pay their bar bills. Everyone told everyone else that they should have
been there ten years ago, or five years ago, or last summer; any time
but now. Everyone agreed that Montparnasse was dead, that Paris was
dead, that the whole of Europe, most likely, was dead. Probably the
only life remaining was in Soviet Russia, or the jungles of the Congo,
or between the canals of Mars.

'The only real artists left in Paris are the surrealists,' a woman told
her at the Select, 'and they're all communists and hate everybody!'

Nina went shopping. She bought clothes by Patou and Chanel,
perfumes by Guerlain, jewellery by Hermès. She went to cabarets and
theatres, she danced to live jazz at Le Grand Ecart and the Boeuf sur le
Toit, she got herself noticed. She got invited to gallery openings,
cultural salons and the Vicomte de Noailles house parties. She was

congratulated on having escaped the tyranny of Mussolini's Italy. One woman – the daughter of a textiles magnate – showed Nina the portrait of Leon Trotsky she wore in a brooch. 'Some nights I kiss it before I go to sleep,' the woman said.

In an attic in Saint-Germain she attended a private screening of Eisenstein's *Battleship Potemkin*. It was an illegally imported uncut copy of the film, but she had been up all the previous night dancing, and fell asleep halfway through. She only awoke at the end, when the red flag was raised – half the audience stood up and began singing the Internationale.

She took lovers: a Japanese lithographer, an Algerian saxophonist, a disgraced American tennis star. She had dinner with a Romanian grand duke in full military regalia, whose chest blazed with medals and decorations. 'The world, my dear, is clearly going to the dogs,' he told her, 'so we have a duty to enjoy ourselves while we can,' and he iced the rim of her cocktail glass with cocaine.

At the Gaumont Studios in December, she was an extra in a costume epic, standing shivering in a flimsy robe, pretending to cheer charioteers. That evening she went home with a Polish photographer called Tadeusz, who was connected with the surrealists and claimed to know everybody. 'You want to be an art whore?' he asked her. 'In Paris, it's easy. You want to meet Picasso? You want to meet Stravinsky?'

'Not really,' she said, lying on the bed naked, and lit another cigarette.

But she detested Paris in winter: the dripping black streets, steeped in nineteenth-century morbidity, the damp stewing languor of the cafés, the stumpy and harassed-looking prostitutes on the street corners. It snowed, and grey slush froze in mounds in the gutters. Nina stayed in Tadeusz's studio, injecting cocaine. 'Always into the vein,' he told her, guiding her hand. 'With coca, if you spike the muscle tissue you paralyse it.' She imaged herself paralysed, turned to cold hard white marble, numbed to all pain. She guided the needle in.

Tadeusz had no money to pay for his addiction – she lent him cash that he could never repay. He sold her one of his cameras – a Contessa Nettel – and all his darkroom equipment, and she taught herself how to develop photographic prints. The drug made him impotent but they would rush out together into the windy streets, crashing through the cafés, ranting in cemeteries, hating and loving each other erratically, like flickering electric bulbs. One night he did not come home – the next morning, she heard from the concierge that he had been arrested and was in jail. He had tried to rob two American tourists at knifepoint on the Boulevard St Michel. She packed her bags.

The *Paris–Rome Express* is not as popular as it once was, and Nina is the only passenger in her sleeping compartment. Returning from the dining car she finds the bed already made, blankets and crisp white sheets embroidered with the monogram of the Paris–Lyon–Mediter-ranée railway company. In the washing cubicle she wipes her face, cleans her teeth and gazes in the mirror, the harsh light glaring at her and plunging her eyes into black.

In Paris she was surrounded by mirrors. Her own reflection had stalked her through the bars and the cafés, staring back from stainless steel and glass, from the dark convexity of a lens. She became accus-tomed to seeing herself as others saw her, to seeing her own image as somebody separate from herself. She has left that person behind her now. All the dead matter of the past is left back in Paris; she is clean and free from it and the train is speeding her into the future, through the mountains and across the wide plains of Italy in morning sunshine. These are the things she tells herself, and leans closer to her reflection until her forehead touches the mirror pane.

Sleep holds her lightly, carrying her for an hour or two, then leaving her to wake, uneasy, the train rocking side to side, moving fast in dark-ness. Swinging her legs from the bed she sits up, puts on shoes and pulls a coat over her pyjamas. She thinks about opening the window in the compartment, but the rain is still streaming against the glass

Small blue bulbs light the corridor outside. Nina walks slowly, feel-ing her way in the dim glow, still drowsy from sleep and long silent thoughts, passing the closed doors of other compartments with the blinds pulled down to seal in the speeding dreams of others. At the end of the carriage she yanks down the window and the breeze rushes at her. She pulls the lapels of the coat tight, leans into the angle of the door and the carriage bulkhead and lights a cigarette, one of the last of her Gauloises. The air comes in flavoured with rain and wet green and engine smoke, and the noise of the rails is huge in the dark.

Nina gazes out into the night, wanting to stay like this, awake and alert, for the whole journey and not let sleep bury her again. Stations pass in the small hours, the deserted platforms and the spreading steel deltas of railyards empty under the moon: Macon, Lyon, Chambéry, the train ghosting slowly through, breathing steam, a slow wail of brakes.

A little after dawn, in the grey cold of the mountains, the train halts at Modane, the last French town before the Mont Cenis tunnel and the border. The bags are searched, the passports checked, the Italian police-men going through their lists of banned items, banned books, banned people. The passengers stand shivering on the platform, sleepy-eyed, threaded with the drifting steam. Nina stands a little apart from the others, wrapped in her coat with a hat pulled down low, the packet of cocaine and the syringes safely hidden in her inside pocket.

With the checks complete, the passengers pile back on to the train for breakfast and the last run under the mountains and out into the Italian sunrise. Before arriving at Turin a pair of Blackshirts pass along the carriages, opening the compartment doors and gazing into the faces of the passengers, silent and unsmiling. Nina hears them coming along the corridor, the swish and bump of the doors. When they arrive at her compartment, she glances up; the man framed in the open doorway is young, barely older than twenty, and wears his authority heavily. She manages a tired smile, and he pauses for a moment.

'Welcome to Italy, Signora,' he says.

IAN BRECKON was born in 1970 and has been writing for several years. The novel he is currently working on concerns a group of artists in 1920s Italy and their attempts to maintain personal and political integrity in a society increasingly dominated by Fascism.

Contact: ian.breckon@sparksanthology.co.uk

Selected Poems

Harry Man

The Communion of Hail

Angela had an unusually large tongue. She enjoyed rolling it into 'O's on Monday mornings in the coffee shop (right beside the espresso machine). There was little else to do when it was quiet. Occasionally she threaded biros and pencils into her hair. Just to achieve twists. For the sake of twisting. But one morning the hail came.

It burst over the street in white balls. Like caterpillar cocoons. Or, so she thought, like those absolutely tiny seashells.

It blasted at the shop front. Riding by, a cyclist was scattered from her seat. People ran for cover. Under battered newspapers. In under the awning.

David, Mary, Lucy and Matt. They met in the hail. David married Lucy. Mary dreamed about David. She kept his number until the area codes changed. Reluctantly she married a restaurateur. Angela ran an art workshop for the deaf. She was shot in 1997 during a failed local shop robbery. Matt never had the courage to ask Lucy out. This was good. She would have said no anyway. Both died without knowledge of each other's whereabouts in the same city, Aberdeen.

Pterophobia

In my fingers I pressed on her mittens
like finding the corners
of a duvet through the covers.

The fine hair of 'Goodbye'
wouldn't lift from my throat
and I walked the gullet of the bus to Heathrow,

felt its Richter shudder
and stepped off the coach.
And in the road,

in my flightlessness, I waved,
waved and waved,
her face and one hand

an ever-diminishing crescent
– and was jolted
an empty shopping bag grasping at my shins.

Photograph of New Year's Day in Davidson, Saskatchewan

Here is a photograph you sent with an email
to say among other things
that the snow is simply everywhere.

The Davidson ice has accreted
and become flattened into a plateau
for badly parked beaters; a van, a car, an SUV.

On the left, outside 'Kwok's Kitchen'
you are blue in the digital frieze;
genderless as an astronaut.

You have written that your grandma
was in her eight pink layers gripping the camera
like a teller inspecting a watermark.

At that point you're waving 4147 miles away.
As if by miracle I have seen you
on a computer screen in Basingstoke.

You're wearing a bunnyhug,
and your maple-leaf toque
is just showing.

Smiling in a thick Gore-Tex jacket,
a dark scarf, black goggles
and blurred woollen hands.

I'd like to take this instant from the shutter
and use it.

To be standing aside from the frame,
walk to you once it was taken,
and try to explain through my scarf

how awful it is without you today and, recently,
how much I have missed you
in the billowing plumes of Saskatchewan snow.

Djinn, a Pet Fish, Foresees
The Coming of the End of the World

I

Under the glass roof he quivers,
jostling the weave of his body. He glows
as if partly made from the deaththroes of a gas hob.

A prince of water-fields, he measures his days
rubbing his nose on the edge of the glass cave
either in bliss or wrongfully imprisoned – I cannot tell.

Among the onion plants we have put two plastic dinosaurs
into the gravel for him to swim around, from where
in some fish-like privacy, he can watch

the gigantic television of outside life;
the curious wide pink shapes that blur by, peek in
– pour ash into his silver sky.

II

The other day the brontosaurus came loose from the stones.
On a human scale it must have felt like Nelson's Column
unearthing, lions and all, and then

silent as an airship, simply drifting upwards.
In Charing Cross there would have been blind panic
as somewhere between overclouded London and deadly space

Nelson would have bobbed, bearing the mark 'Made in France',
in massive letters underneath. The brontosaurus rocked about,
casting a shadow like the dunking finger of God.

It would be nothing more than a cold, fast repair job;
but to our fish the event must have felt colossal, terrible even
like the end of the world.

HARRY MAN is currently working on an exploded sestina entitled 'The Wire Men', which concerns the curious properties of space, time and the social anxiety for the future preservation of the environment. Recently longlisted for the Bridport Poetry Prize, his work has been published internationally. He lives and occasionally sleeps at his desk in Bath.

Contact: harry.man@sparksanthology.co.uk

The Letter

Ruth Orson

a short story

You ordered a glass of milk and a pastry with white icing dusted on top, and took them to a table by the window. The centrepiece was a white flower in a china jug, made of plastic so it didn't need watering. You looked at the flower the way most people who come in here do, trying to figure out whether it was real or not. You tugged at the rubbery leaves, and decided it must be fake.

You ate the pastry with your hands, tearing off shreds and strips and buttery flakes. You drank by lifting the glass slightly, then bringing your mouth close to it. I watched you and your hands, and you and your arms, and you and your feet shuffling beneath the table. I watched as you sipped from the glass, I watched as you tore piece after buttery piece. I did not love you, not yet, not then. I was drying saucers. There was a large pile of them that I had just taken out of the dishwasher.

I thought about you as I did the saucers. I always had to be thinking of something, otherwise I might as well have been an automaton. A plate-drying, pastry-tonging, latte-pouring robot. Before you walked into the café, I had been thinking about letters. That morning I had received several bills with Cellophane windows; they were the usual kind of letters I received. There had also been an advert with my name printed on it, as though designed exclusively for me. I must have forgotten to tick the box that stops them from passing on your address, you should always tick the box. What else? I had got a leaflet from the local Chinese takeaway, which was useless, since they already had my custom. I went there so often, the girl behind the counter gave me free prawn crackers.

Then you had walked in and the bell above the café door had clanged, and I stopped thinking about letters for a moment as I poured you a glass of milk and used the tongs to pick up a pastry.

After you'd sat down, I thought about handwritten letters. The words in a handwritten letter are different from any other kind of words – their meaning isn't disguised by faces and bodies and eyes.

I looked over at you, I wanted to open you like a letter, with a letter knife, and read the words that you contained, one after another, in the order that your story was written. I wanted that as soon as I saw you; open and knowable. It wasn't enough for me to see you, sitting there with a pastry, I wanted to unpeel your pages, to read the words inside. I thought you looked about my age, or a little older. You must have known other places and things and people than this. But what?

I imagined how you must have once lived a day when you were alive in everything you saw. Alive in pavements and birdsong and sky. A day when just breathing in felt good. Maybe you were in love? Not just in love with a person; the person was a lens through which you looked and were in love with all things: light switches, radiators, the orange nets that clementines come in. You even loved letters with Cellophane windows, and when you heard the throaty gurgle of the guttering in the rain, you didn't mind the noise, even though that meant it needed fixing. It was a day when you heard a sea of strangers' voices roaring from the back seat of the bus, and the roll and sweep of their vowels and consonants was a fresh, salty wave all around you.

You must contain sadness too, I thought. Perhaps, inked inside you is the latent memory of a day when you were so sad, time stopped. Maybe you were grieving? It might have been one of those days when you go to the supermarket and walk along the shelves of goods and somehow forget why you went there at all and you're just standing there, in front of tinned sweetcorn and boxed soap powder and cartons of cranberry juice, not knowing.

How far you have come, I thought, to be here now, sitting in this café drinking milk and eating a pastry without a care in the world.

I had polished all the teaspoons by then. My tea-towel was drenched through, so I went out back and dropped it in the laundry bin. Then I started making coffee. I hooked the metal jug under the frother, positioned the spout and turned the dial until it made the sound of an aeroplane taking off. I let the sound continue until the red dial on the thermometer told me the temperature was hot enough. It was 4pm by then. I had made morning coffee and lunchtime coffee and now I was making afternoon coffee; my hands knew what they were doing.

You were still there, sipping milk. My hands were making five cappuccinos in a row and I was thinking about you, how you had probably been in love once, and now it was over. Maybe you were sad about the end when it came, or maybe the person you loved was the sad one. Or, maybe after paying the bill and leaving this café, you will go and meet someone who you love now. Today. You might take their hand. They might kiss you and taste pastry on your lips. You might leave here and go home to a house and a room and a bed that you share. They could know who you are, when sleep has shrunk you to mere contour and landscape. Lying beside you in the dark, breathing in and out in unison, taking possession of the part of you which sleep has rendered unknowable.

But then, why do you come here alone? Every day of the week.

By that point you were standing by the counter. You had put your hat back on because of the weather outside. There were raindrops on the fabric that hadn't dried off – they shone. You told me that you'd like to pay the bill for table four: a cherry pastry and a glass of hot milk, as if I didn't know.

I typed the numbers into the till and took your coins. Out came the receipt with the money you gave me and what I owed you in change printed on it. Nobody writes these days, I thought. All our text is printed. Nobody sends letters any more; there are no pleas, or vows, or declarations in the written word. And so I wrote a letter on paper with ink. And so I slipped a handwritten message between your change and your receipt.

As you opened the door to leave, the bell clanged and fresh air came in. I felt hot steam from the coffee machine on one side of my face and the freshness on the other.

When my shift was over I walked to my car. As I got close I saw a sheet of paper that had been folded in half and tucked under the left windscreen wiper. It had a sheen to it, the paper, so I assumed it was just an advert for insurance, but then I opened it up and found that the note had been written by hand. Handwritten. I felt my heart thump. I read the words. The words were written in capital letters and that meant they were important, urgent, and so I read them quickly and they said: MOVE YOUR FUCKING CAR SOMEWHERE ELSE THERE ARE LORRIES THAT NEED TO BACK OUT OF THIS GARAGE FOR FUCK'S SAKE. The author hadn't signed their name, of course. Those kind of people never do.

I got in my car and started the wipers going back and forth; they were squeaking like mice again. The incessant squeaking noise continued the whole way home. I had been meaning to get them fixed.

The traffic lights kept turning red when I got there. I sat in the queue and looked out the window. November 5th was coming up, so the streets were full of gloved kids holding sparklers. The kids spelled things in the sky. I couldn't read the silver and gold and turquoise words; they happened too quickly. The words got written on air, and then they were gone.

I got home and opened the door to a pile of letters. The other people who lived in my building hadn't bothered collecting their mail. It was obvious without opening what the letters were about; the pile was nothing but adverts and Cellophane windows. Two new notices had been pinned to the wall, computer-typed, to convey their authority. I read the words – 'Please remove rubbish sacks from top step and please switch off cellar lights after use' – and sighed.

I got in the lift and pressed number three for the floor to my flat. I looked in the kitchen cupboard and read the instructions printed on packets until I found an easy one, then opened it up and slid it in the oven. I put on a new CD that had just come out, then I gave up, and played one that was recorded in the 1960s and I could trust. I talked to friends on the phone about my day at the café and their day somewhere else, going through any funny and interesting incidents that had happened. All the while there was a simultaneous thinking about you going on. I thought about the one-way conversation of my letter and realised how I desperately wanted to take back the words I had written. I wanted to slip them beneath the flap of an envelope and lick it shut for ever.

The next day at work my heart was beating like a wing in a box. It was a day for dropping things, because, by the time I'd realised I was holding them, it was always too late. A lot of things met the floor: teacups, teaspoons, bags of sugar. For a while nothing smashed, and then something did. It was a glass ramekin. I took the ramekin out of the dishwasher and it was so, so soft. It had been softened by the heat and the washing powder and then its solid structure was gone altogether, crumbled into gritty crystals of glass. Sharp pieces, small as pennies in my hands.

I went to tables and wrote down orders with my biro on the white pad of paper. I pushed through swing doors into the kitchen to tell the chef what to cook, but when I looked down at my handwriting it was illegible. My hands had been shaking too much to spell. I had to go back to tables and say sheepishly to customers, who looked at me with their varying levels of disdain:

—I'm so sorry, but what was it you wanted put in your panini again?

It was while standing by the espresso machine with the usual puffs of hot steam coming off that I felt a blast of cool air from outside, and that meant an open door and coming through the door was you. I had a metal scoop full of freshly ground coffee beans in my hand, so there was the smell of that and the fresh cream in the cups and then there was you, and no time at all to become any more nervous than I already was because you walked straight up to the counter holding a white paper napkin in your hand. You were smiling and saying the words out loud, right there in the café in front of all those customers:

—Are you the girl that wrote this letter? I think you are.

I couldn't look you in the eye because of how beautiful you were. You were beautiful and that was the beginning.

RUTH ORSON was born in Southampton. She is twenty-three years old. Before she moved to Bath she did a degree in English Literature at Sussex University. Her MA manuscript was a collection called *Thirteen Stories*. She is currently working on some new stories.

Contact: ruth.orson@sparksanthology.co.uk

The Memory Stick

Nikita Lalwani

from a novel

Mahesh is sitting in his office, marking. He looks up at the arc of the window as a train rushes past, its urgency left behind in petrol scent and echoing clacks. The dank hush of autumn is settling into his room like a stale secret, a foregone conclusion. It is the tenth season of its kind in his experience in the UK. The fourth of its kind in this room. There are charts and pictures on the wall. The map of the world sits at an awkward angle, blue ocean disappearing behind the iron bookshelf. Books bulge in huge rows, pressing together files and papers, orange foolscap running in chunky alternation with black, white and grey. Up at the left corner of the room, by the whiteboard, the bumpy illustration of Gandhi peers out at him. In his mind there is an annoyance that delicately attacks his thoughts every few minutes.

Why did Rumi write that in her exercise book? This is the question that hooks into his conscience periodically: a tiny dental tool, piercing soft gum. Why did she write it?

I went to play with Sara Davies and Caroline Evans and Leanne Roper in the woods. They let me play handball which is like baseball but you use your hand. We only had 2 bases. Sarah said, 'Let's go and get the softball and rackets from my house.' When we got to her place we stood outside the gate and Sara said, 'I just have to check you can come in Rumi because my mum doesn't like coloured people.' Then she went in with the others and I waited outside. Thank goodness she came back and said it was OK. Then we went in and had pop ices and got the rackets. Mrs Davies was sun bathing in the garden and looked red. We took the rackets and played softball in the woods.

'Coloured'. The word made him think of a crayon spreading a thick grainy brown over a round face, like the awkward pictures Rumi used to draw under duress when she was younger; shuffling and embarrassed designs with no relationship to reality.

Again, he looks at Gandhi's picture, wizened and unflinching in the corner of his room. What would they make of this, back in Karaghar

College, he wonders, cocooned as they had been there, in the company of ideas? Trotskyites, Gandhian communists – they had plenty of names for themselves back then, chewing betel, relishing the bitter stain on their lips and debating whether class war was compatible with non-violence.

What would they think of this world that he had chosen to inhabit, placing a solitary, all-important offspring right at the centre? And what about his conversation with Rumi after he had read it?

'Do you like your school, Rumi?'

'I don't like the bullies.'

'What do you mean, bullies?'

'People who aren't nice to me.'

'Do not let these things affect you. You are ten years old now.'

'What?'

'You should be like a lion in the jungle. Like Shere Khan in *The Jungle Book*.'

'What do you mean, Daddy?'

'If someone hits you, then hit them back. If they hit you once, hit them twice.'

The words had come out of his mouth, as honest as a shotgun, and he had looked away when her eyes jumped. If you are shocked, so am I, he thought. But you are not going to be a victim. That I will not allow.

Another train goes past, carrying a heavy rattle inside it, dense as a migraine. The tremble of the room seems to jolt the Mahatma's picture imperceptibly. He can see a square of evening light obscuring part of Gandhi's face on the glass. Coloured? Why did she write it?

When Rumi was five years old, she came home one day and announced that Mrs Gold wanted to make an appointment to come round and meet her parents. Within a week, Mahesh and Shreene found themselves leaving their offices early and meeting back home at 3.30pm. Shreene nervously began to fry some bhajis, while Mahesh descended into a deep silence, waiting in his shirt and tie in the living room.

When Mrs Gold walked in, Rumi was holding her hand.

'What a lovely walk home we've had together, Mr and Mrs Vashey,' she said, letting Rumi go in ahead of her.

Mahesh stared at the teacher's peroxide coiffure – whipped and sprayed into rounded peaks and troughs, like a butterscotch dessert. He was confused. Mentally he fought against relaxing, a natural response to the lavish smile exuded by Mrs Gold.

'Is it possible to talk to you and your wife together?' she asked.

Shreene brought the snacks in and joined them, sitting with her hands in her lap, still formal in her workwear, tights and heels.

'What is it you wanted to talk about?' Mahesh asked Mrs Gold, feeling the accented curves of his voice as though for the first time. 'Is something wrong?'

'No... Far from it, Mr Vashey,' she said. 'I wanted to give you some news which I think will make you very proud parents.'

'And that is?' said Mahesh.

'Rumi is a gifted child!' Mrs Gold declared, unleashing the words triumphantly with a dazzling upward turn of the mouth.

Mahesh looked at Rumi, who was staring nervously at the floor, waiting for him to decipher the words. He watched Shreene, nervously biting the dry skin on her lower lip. And then he cast his gaze back towards Mrs Gold, and her radiant lines of teeth.

'You mean she is doing well at school?' he said.

'I mean more than that, Mr Vashey,' said Mrs Gold. 'I mean that she is special. Different. Gifted.'

Mahesh cleared his throat generously, making the noise stagger over several notes.

'Myself and my wife take Rumika's education very seriously,' he said. 'We are pleased that she is doing well in her studies and that her hard work has paid off. I am an academic myself...'

'With due respect Mr and Mrs Vashey, I'm talking about something else,' said Mrs Gold. 'I am talking about a gift. Something that only comes along now and then. Rumi is a gifted mathematician!'

'I am also a mathematician,' said Mahesh. 'I am glad that she is doing well in this subject, as you say – I have placed emphasis on it because it is my area of speciality.'

'We at Summerfield believe that Rumi deserves to have this gift nurtured,' Mrs Gold replied.

She leant in, pulling her skirt together, so that the pleat at the front disappeared neatly inside itself, pausing significantly, as though she was about to say something serious, possibly untoward. Rumi also leant in, automatically, to listen, her swaying legs forcing themselves to halt – pressing a temporary dent into the sofa front. Even Shreene moved her body forward, waiting expectantly.

'Have you heard of a place called Mensa?' said Mrs Gold.

Mahesh felt exasperated. He had seen all the same adverts as her. The toy-town ads for this place she named with such careful tedium, as though she was rolling a diamond round her mouth. 'Mensa'. He'd seen their childish IQ tests, fooled around with filling them out in the

Sunday papers. He knew what Mensa was, for goodness sake. And why was she so surprised that he and his daughter were able to string numbers together with reasonable panache? They were hardly shopkeepers.

He was 'peed off', as they said here. He tried to think of more slang, enjoying the taste of righteousness, dousing each word with it. He was 'hacked off' and 'cheesed off'. What did she think: that he was some third-rate charlatan, preening his fake feathers under the banner of academia? He felt a rumble in his stomach as the bhajis began to ferment, rising as though to validate his sense of pique. Oddly, the sensation cheered him up. He suddenly felt like making a grand statement to this woman, one that Rumi would witness, about how it was possible through strength and discipline to create your own destiny through the power of thought: through marks, percentages, papers, exams – numbers that all added up, in his case, to a big sum in small hands; a scholarship across the ocean.

He surveyed Mrs Gold's darting eyes. She was watching his wife as she sipped her tea. What preconceptions did she bring with her – this queer-spoken woman with her little smiles and polite contradictions? He was not going to make a grand statement. It would only confuse things. But if he could, he would tell her everything. He'd tell her he'd got into all their universities – all the bloody jewels they treasured so exclusively in this country; that he had been offered a place at their Cambridge and their LSE. He had ended up in Cardiff because they had offered the cash – all two thousand pounds of it, a sum that no one could deny for its totality. Full fees. They had wanted him here, a foreigner with no more than five pounds in his pocket and a slip of a wife, bare-toed and shivering. That is how he got off the plane with Shreene in 1972, newly wed and alert, dignified by the patronage of their red-brick institutions, sure as a compass, leading the way for them both.

He had not been part of the thirty thousand Indians haemorrhaging out of the ugly scar in Uganda's belly that same year, seeping into the dark spaces of Britain, afloat in the soiled bathwater of Amin's shake-up: the crawling masses who had fallen into the pockets of Leicester and Wembley. He was not going to be dissolved into the rivers of blood: part of Enoch Powell's armies of bacteria, defecating in people's nightmares on the landscape of their precious country.

He was Dr Mahesh Vashey, PhD, a man who began his maths career repeating times tables under a large tree in Bihar with fifteen schoolmates, embossed with dust and driven by the pure heat of numbers. Now he was here, speaking to a room of a hundred students each week, employed in name by the University of Cardiff. What about that, then?

Mahesh cleared his throat again, and considered how to proceed. He uncrossed, then re-crossed, his legs with an air of what he hoped was leisurely contemplation. He still had to learn how to relax, uncoil the ritual desire to please. It was shameful habit, nothing else, he told himself. Shreene leant over and offered Mrs Gold the plate of snacks. The vegetable fritters shone through the batter with a glistening heat: dark-purple aubergine skins and green courgettes pushing their thick curves through the fried covering.

'Please – have one,' said Shreene. 'Do you like spicy food?'

Mahesh took the opportunity to interject.

'I know Mensa very well, Mrs Gold,' he said. 'I'm happy to go there with Rumika and check it out.'

Over the next two weeks, running up to Rumi's entrance exam, Mahesh enforced a routine on his daughter that was not dissimilar to the one he had made Shreene follow in the first year of their marriage, during her pregnancy. They had lived in a student bedsit at that time, the kitchen breathing and squeaking its gaseous smells into the room where they slept. Mahesh came home late in the evenings, weary with the remote universe of his PhD, and would begin what Shreene (first jokingly, and later with a bitter regularity) called 'the police camp procedures'.

He had taken her out of the rich bustle of her world: interrupted the round stretchings of chapattis, the powdery rainbow of her spices, and punctured her pride at exactly 7.30pm each evening. He requested that Shreene make a single trip every lunchtime, to read the newspaper in the local library. She was free to read whichever paper she chose – all that he asked was that they have a one-hour conversation, dissecting it before dinner each day. When Shreene retaliated – steaming with humiliation, claiming that she had not bargained on being insulted like this by her own husband – he very clearly spelled out the positive outcomes that made this a logical course of action:

1. He would be able to converse with her on matters other than the drama and intrigue of their extended families. This could only be beneficial in the long run, for their interaction as life partners.

2. It would improve her English, thereby enabling her to work as soon as the baby was born. She was a Delhi University graduate. Her degree had covered literature, philosophy and fine art, albeit in Hindi. There was no reason why she should not be able to contribute to the

household's income. In fact, it was imperative that she did – considering that soon there would be three people in the family.

3. The trip to the library was both thrifty and empowering. It would thrust her into the world, thereby forcing her to interact with locals – again, beneficial for her assimilation into this society they were now living in, as opposed to nurturing the temptation to hanker for and idealise the society she inhabited back home.

4. The whole regime would prevent her from losing her physical and mental abilities through lack of usage, especially during this critical period in her life – pregnancy.

This last clause particularly angered Shreene. But she bit back her indignation and proceeded as he deemed worthy. For a while it almost seemed to work – she listed the plane crashes and hijackings, the earthquakes, the bombs and the shootouts in Ireland. If she wasn't able to pronounce the names of the places, then she always made sure to give an indication of the numbers involved in each case – gathering the digits in her memory to create a vast array of weaponry.

Sometimes she made events up, in unnamed places, a plane almost going down in the Indian Ocean due to a tiny error on the part of the pilot, small riots in a Muslim mosque on the border with Pakistan, a slow news day leading to a report on an esteemed guru rousing thousands of disciples in Gujarat like a latter-day prophet. These tales always invariably led back to the subcontinent. Mahesh forbade her to dwell on her past, but sometimes when she came up with these fabrications he found her unbearably cute. He battled with his heart, which was softening like a marshmallow on a fire, and tried to maintain perspective. 'Are you sure?' he would ask, curbing a smile. And so they continued, until Shreene began to crack, splintering into tantrums, ruefully losing control.

Eventually, one day – when, not satisfied with the figures, Mahesh asked her to give an opinion on Heath's plans for dealing with unemployment – she erupted. There were screams, plates were walloped on the worktops, teeth were gritted, and she trashed the ritual once and for all.

NIKITA LALWANI was born in Rajasthan and raised in Wales. After several years of writing and directing factual television, she has returned to writing fiction. Her poetry has been published in magazines, including *Poetry Wales*. She has also written for political magazine, *The Week*, and the UK's foremost advocacy website, *Pressureworks*. This piece is an extract from her novel, currently entitled *The Memory Stick*.

Contact: nikita.lalwani@sparksanthology.co.uk

Going Fishing

Ruth Deschamps

a monologue for radio

Set in Pretoria, South Africa. The main voice is that of Jannie du Toit, a white male Afrikaner aged thirty-two. He is driving his pickup.

<u>JANNIE'S CAR ON THE HIGHWAY – FADE UNDER.</u>

JANNIE   Hope I'm early enough to catch the meerkat – there was a whole colony last time I was at the dam. I like the sentry best – chest out, up on his hind legs, tail all bushy; calling the gang back into the burrow. There's no head honcho – they all look out for each other.
Hell, I might just adopt a new catch and release fishing policy today.

<u>FADE UP THE CAR RADIO.</u>

NEWS
READER   Here in the Cape on this *glorious* Sunday morning, the eleventh of February, 1990, the crowds are already begin ning to assemble to witness Mr Nelson Mandela's walk to freedom later this afternoon…

<u>FADE RADIO – RETAIN CAR UNDER JANNIE.</u>

JANNIE   Thank goodness the Cape is a thousand miles away. *My Magtig!* Don't you know it's illegal to cycle on the highway! Stupid boy! (TO HIMSELF) The sooner I get to the dam, the better – this highway feels too quiet this morning.

Why did Thomas do it? Behaving like a seven-year-old baby. Ruining the mattress like that. I couldn't take the twins fishing, not after that, and not after they dropped my electric razor in the bath on Friday.

<u>JANNIE LIGHTS UP A CIGARETTE.</u>

Hell, Monday tomorrow. *Ag man*, I've served my time
walking up and down those trains. *Alle kaartjies!*
Tickets please! Ten years of riding the Pretoria
– Jo'burg line; chucking off drunks, waving my flag,
blowing my whistle, screaming out station names in
English and Afrikaans... and what does the South
African Railways reward me with? A pay rise? No,
a *bliksemse* penknife. A flick blade between a bit of
wood and brass with the letters SAR in red. 'Your
brother tries to help,' says Esme. No use being
stationmaster if you can't promote your own brother.
Esme thinks it's my fault I'm not in charge of the
ticket office. I watched her at the boys' party on
Friday – nodding her head when Marius suggested
I cut down on the lager and go to church. Ma says
that's what comes of marrying a young English-
speaking wife.

JANNIE TAKES A DRAG ON HIS CIGARETTE.

I can't understand it. Esme's pestered me for the
past year to go to church. So I let her go with Marius
and now she says she dislikes the way the *dominee*
preaches – says she thought he'd be like her old
Anglican minister, but now *she* wants me to go – no
ways!
I remember all those wasted summer Sundays sitting
beside Ma and Pa, with my hot feet squashed into my
best shoes watching the men fiddle with their white
ties, and the women wearing shiny stockings and half
a garden in their hats, while the rich ones checked
their gold watches, desperate for the *dominee* to stop
his God-made-separate-races-hell-fire sermon so they
could escape to their air-con Mercs.

JANNIE TAKES A DRAG ON HIS CIGARETTE.

At collection time Pa made Marius or me put the ten-
rand note on the tray. (LAUGHS) Luckily Marius
taught me to how to slip it under all the twenties and
fifties.

Sometimes we'd sit behind Ma and Pa. Ma would fan
herself with her hands and peer over her shoulder to
make sure we were attending, but Pa didn't flinch, and
I'd watch the sweat trickle over the roll of fat on his
neck and I'd wonder how the hell he resisted wiping it
away.

Where did you get that bruise, Jannie?
My Pa, *dominee*.
Ja, I could've told Esme the church never helped
anyone.

A CAR PASSES.

I wonder if Marius is at the dam yet.
Lucky bastard, driving that new Audi.
But he looks like Pa now. Strutting around in those
short-pants safari suits with his tortoiseshell comb neatly
tucked into his long socks. (LAUGHS) That kills me,
man. Give me jeans and a T-shirt any day.

JANNIE BURNS HIMSELF ON THE CIGARETTE.

Einaar! Stupid Lucky Strikes! Always sticking to my
fingers.
Esme asked me once how I'd got the scars on my legs.
Dancing. I fell off my bicycle. I can't understand why
people have such a hard time lying. Words are just
words; think them and they're true.

A MOTORBIKE WHIZZES PAST.

'Go like lightning; crash like thunder', *pallie!*

Pa liked to bend the truth, especially to Ma. But she was
only too pleased to believe his lies. Fishing trips with
Boet. Hunting trips with Hennie. The veld called him, he
said. Ma said she didn't care who the hell called him, she
was just glad he loved nature so much. Not as glad as
Marius and me.
The duck-and-dive dance steps weren't needed when Pa

wasn't there. We stopped dancing. We were still.

(LAUGHS) Ma would bake us *koeksusters*. I liked to
eat mine slowly, biting carefully into the warm twists
of dough so the syrup stayed in my mouth, but Marius
would sit on the grass and untie the long sticky twists
and put them across his mouth like a pencil, and the
syrup would stick to his cheeks. *Heerlikheid* that made
me squirm! I couldn't stand to see anything on Marius'
left cheek, the one with the scar; the scar Esme thinks is
a dimple.

AN AMBULANCE PASSES – ITS SIREN FADES.

Ma still has the newspaper clipping.
Kids Play Cops and Robbers in Back Yard.
Pa was away. Ma was making a fruit salad. I remember
weaving in and out of the peach trees – waving our guns.
'Bang! Bang! You're dead, Jannie!' yelled Marius.
And I'd fall on the dusty ground under the trees or on the
thick *kikuyu* grass and play dead, then I'd jump up and
we'd change sides and begin all over again.
'Don't play under the mulberry tree,' Ma told us. But we
did. And our bare feet were stained a bluish purple from
the dropped ripe berries, but we played on until the light
faded and the damp night air made Ma call us in.
Then Marius fell – under the mulberry tree. He struggled
to get up – he'd weighed down the little canvas rucksack
with stones. (LAUGHS) Loot, he called them – we had
to be caught with something – otherwise we couldn't
shoot.
I stood over him. Bang! Bang!
He screamed – I thought giant mulberries were falling on
his face – I looked up at the tree and Marius asked if Pa
had come home. Next I remember rushing down a long
white corridor and when we stopped Ma put her hands
on Marius' face and he said he could smell mangoes.
They cut red bits out of his blond hair. And when they
stitched up his left cheek, I patted his warm leg and
whispered, 'Marius, you can have my marble collection.'

Pa should've had a gun safe like mine – I only did what any small kid would do with a pellet gun.

But that night Ma shouldn't have left me alone with Pa.

<u>FADE UP THE CAR RADIO.</u>

NEWS
READER   Outside the Victor–Verster Prison, as the sun rises in the blue Cape sky, the world's media are setting up their cameras in preparation for Mandela's release from…

<u>FADE OUT RADIO – FADE UP THE MOVING CAR.</u>

JANNIE   Marius hasn't held a gun since. He won't have one in the house and he makes me leave mine in the car when I visit. Don't know how he's going to protect his family when the time comes.

Hey lady, the speed limit is eighty, not sixty!
(CLOSE) *Ja*, well, suppose she can't drive fast – not with those AWB boys standing in the back of the *bakkie* like that. Brave lads waving that three-legged swastika today. (LAUGHS) Slowly, lady – the blond kid almost toppled over when you turned that last corner!
(CLOSE) Why must my kids always act like they're afraid of me? Didn't I let them have a birthday party on Friday? And they both got new shoes. *Ag man*, I know they preferred those stupid Ninja Turtles Marius gave them, but toys won't keep their feet warm in winter.
The day Ma bought me my black school shoes was one of my happiest. Grade Two – I must've been seven or eight. That night, after prayers, after Marius was asleep I put on my long grey school socks and slipped my feet into the new shoes. I slept on top of the bedclothes – like an Egyptian mummy – and when I opened my eyes the next morning, there they were, school regulation black lace-up shoes.
For the past three months Pa had made me wear Marius' old brown shoes. 'You'll grow into them,' he said.
Pa always was colour-blind.

<u>A JET PLANE FLIES OVERHEAD</u>.

If only I'd joined the Air Force instead of the
Railways...
Money.
Pa was always thinking up ways to save it. Once, while
waiting in the queue for the drive-in, Pa made Marius
and me climb into the car boot.
Pa lifted me in. The carpet smelled of his oily tools.
Then Marius lay down in front of me and held the boot
shut. The lights went out. The car moved so slowly in
the queue – the metal walls got hotter. I couldn't
breathe. I screamed for Ma!
'Shush,' said Marius, and he let in a gulp of hot air and
a sliver of light.

<u>FADE OUT THE CAR AND FADE UP THE RADIO</u>.

NEWS
READER   Mandela, the man who's served twenty-seven years in
prison, will be released today at...

<u>FADE OUT RADIO</u>.

JANNIE   Esme thinks I don't earn enough. Why else would she
want a job? Over my dead body, I told her. I blame
her mother – sending that typewriter round, putting
ideas into Esme's head. What else could I do but get
rid of it? But Esme should've known better than to dig
it out of the rubbish like some baglady.
But she gave me a fright yesterday – threatening to lose
the baby like that. I only meant to slap her.

This outing was supposed to be a treat for the twins – for
Esme. The doctor said she needed peace and quiet. But
when I pulled back the boys' bedcovers this morning and
saw the wet mark on Thomas's bed I felt that bang of
blood in my head. My mouth was dry and my hands...
well, I tried to breathe deeply... I tried to walk away...

<u>JANNIE OPENS THE PASSENGER WINDOW</u>.

Ah, that breeze feels good!

Jesus, look at that idiot tossing his cigarette *stompie* out the window. The veld is so dry, man – one spark and up it goes. (TUTS) People only think of themselves.

JANNIE TAKES A DEEP BREATH – CALMING HIMSELF.

No one is going to push my buttons. I'm going fishing. Finish and *klaar*.

Friday night, the boys pushed me too far. I admit it. They should know better than to touch my things. OK, I shouldn't have clenched my hand.
It was the first time.
But Esme's words hurt; she knows I can't live without her.

JANNIE SOUNDS THE CAR HOOTER.

Where'd you get your licence, man? A Lucky Packet?

Don't know why Esme had to scream, 'They're only seven!'
She thinks there's a right time to learn things. Danger doesn't announce itself. It pounces. Thud. Smack. Don't the boys know I hate doing it? It's their fault – Thomas peeing in the bed like that and Jason defending him…
Once Pa gave me ten lashes for wetting the bed. One, two, three… *Jesus*, he could count slowly. The bastard would stand so close to me I'd breathe in his foul breath as I pulled down my pants.
I didn't mean to take my belt to them this morning. I swore I'd never take anything other than my hand to my kids.

A CAR PASSES.

I remember Pa's belt.
Dark-brown polished leather with a large brass buckle.
Lena, the maid, cleaned it with Brasso every week – it

was so shiny it made *pragtige* light patterns on the white
walls when Pa snaked it across our backsides.
The patterns were never the same. I used to think the
lights would show me what I'd done wrong.

'Take it like a man,' said Ma.

We buried Pa with that belt.

JANNIE ACCELERATES.

(ANGRY) Now she speeds up. Goddamn women
drivers!

Marius acts all superior now he's the stationmaster, but I
won't forget how he'd wait for me in our bedroom
with toilet paper ready to wipe away what Pa...
(LAUGHS) 'Brothers who duck and dive, stay alive.'
That's what Marius used to say.

But Pa left him alone after he got that dimple.
I don't remember who helped Ma.

Hey! You're supposed to use your indicator when you
change lanes – *houtkop!*

Esme's face lights up when Marius visits. All pinks and
warmth. I saw it on Friday. It used to light up like that
for me – before Ma came to live with us. Before Marius
made me pay for that dimple.
But we used to make love – on the sofa, the floor...
Man, her legs were so thin her thighs didn't touch – the
Foyston Gap, they call it.
(LAUGHS) Sounds so *larney* – like a posh hotel, said
Esme.
Amazing what you learn in a rugby locker room. The
gap's disappearing now, she's put on so much weight
with the pregnancy – I noticed that on Friday. *Bliksem*, I
shouldn't have to blackmail my own wife.
Last time she wanted me right up until the twins were
born. But on Friday she held back – I felt it. But she's

so soft now; her flesh begs to be touched. My baby must
feel like a king inside there.
No wonder they come out screaming.

FADE UP THE CAR RADIO.

NEWS
READER   Mr Nelson Mandela, head of the recently unbanned
African National Congress, was convicted many years
ago of attempting to blow up an electric pylon...

FADE RADIO – FADE UP THE MOVING CAR.

JANNIE   Pa would *klap* us round the head if we screamed.
Especially on Sundays.
After church we'd head home. Three blocks. We'd set
off all the dogs in the neighbourhood barking.
(LAUGHS) One time this Dobermann jumps up –
rattling the padlock on the gate. Man, was I ducking and
diving inside.
The dogs never seemed to worry Ma and Pa. In the
summer they'd walk home hand in hand staying
under the cool of the jacaranda trees, and in winter Pa
would drape his arm around Ma, squeezing her fat
body closer to him. (LAUGHS) Marius would pretend to
stick his fingers down his throat.

Man, I hated Sundays. Ma always cooked the same
meal, roast beef with vegetables. And there was always
mashed pumpkin. Pa's favourite. The smell still makes
me feel *naar*.
'Jannie sits there until he's eaten everything on his plate,'
Pa ordered. Then they'd leave me sitting at the kitchen
table – staring at the cold sweetened pumpkin.
When Ma came in to clear away, I prayed she'd pick up
my plate and put it in the sink with the other dishes.
Once I pleaded with her, but she asked me why did I
have to be so difficult? Why couldn't I be more like
Marius?
After all, it was only a vegetable, she said. Three or four
mouthfuls. Swallow.

JANNIE OPENS A CAN AND DRINKS.

(LAUGHS) One Sunday, after they'd left the table, I
managed to throw the orange pulp through the burglar
bars into the garden. Pa smiled at me and patted me on
the head that day I produced my empty plate so quickly
for inspection.
Now he could relax.
Fetch me this, Jannie; fetch me that, Jannie.
Ja, Pa, three bags full Pa. *Voking* bastard. Always did
like to hit me on the back of the head as I walked away.
Sitting in his leather chair on the front *stoep*, fly swat
beside him, Lucky Strikes in one hand, Lion lager in
the other – Pa kept up a perfect rhythm for hours. Right
hand, inhale; left hand, swig. Then his arms would fall
limp on the chair; his head resting on his chest; air forcing its way through his closed lips, making them flap
loosely and his snore sound like a horse. The smoke
from his cigarette curled upwards and ash fell silently to
the floor.
Then I was free to play with Marius.
As I walked away I prayed he'd burn himself, but the
cigarette *stompie* always fell on to the tiled floor and
Lena would sweep it away the next day.

A CAR PASSES WITH PEOPLE SHOUTING MERRILY.

Once, Pa caught me eating *pap* and *sous* with Lena in
her smoke-stained room. I rolled the *pap* into neat balls
the way she showed me, and we'd take turns in dipping
them into her spicy, chicken liver sauce.
'Jannie, what the *bliksem* are you doing in here?' said Pa.
I moved quickly; I knocked over the aluminium pot with
the sauce and Lena said, 'Not to worry, Master Jannie,'
as I escaped out the door. (LAUGHS) Marius was proud
of my ducking and diving.
I didn't know Pa visited Lena's room.

A POLICE CAR WITH SIREN BLARING – FADE UNDER.

I can't understand why my boys hide under the bed
– it's not like I hit them every day. And I let them visit
Esme's mom yesterday. Well, not Thomas. I know she
hadn't seen them since they were babies but, man, what
else could I do? As Thomas got out of the car I realised I
couldn't let him stay, not with his face like… Anyways, I
didn't really believe Esme's mom had had a stroke.
(LAUGHS) Esme's face looked like thunder, or was it
panic?

I miss my boys. I wanted to spend the day with them.
Men together. Love the land; animals and fish aplenty
for the hunter, said Pa. Marius and me liked fishing with
him when his pals were around.
Up went the brightly coloured umbrellas. Then out came
the stripy fold-up chairs and blue gas bottles and *braais*
and packets of curled spicy *boerewors*, chops, mush-
rooms and Ma's still-warm bread rolls.
Pa's friends would let us prepare the bait. Marius would
open the tins of wriggling worms and I'd stick them on
the end of the shiny hooks. Pa had made special steel
poles – to balance his fishing rods on. And once he'd
cast his rod in the water, he'd let me stick the ball of *pap*
on to his line and there he'd sit – beer in hand waiting
for a nibble, waiting for the white blob to stir on the line.
Carp. That's what Pa and his friends caught at Rietvlei
Dam. And I'd clean them with Pa's pocket knife. The
one with the carved bone handle and stainless-steel
blade; sharp enough for slicing through scaly fish heads
or skinning a kudu. Pa was the only one who pulled the
blade from its cover.
It was the only thing I wanted from Pa when he died.

FADE CAR UNDER THE RADIO.

NEWS
READER   Later this afternoon Mandela will walk through
the prison gates, signalling…

FADE RADIO – FADE UP CAR INDICATORS.

JANNIE (READS) Rietvlei Dam and Nature Reserve – that's a
new sign. (LOUD) Turn, man. Can't you see the
robot is green?

FADE INDICATORS AS CAR TURNS.

I hope Marius brings his canoe – get a better casting
arc from the middle of the dam... *Ag man*, he shouldn't
have promoted that Black over me last week... Hell,
this holster is killing me.

There they are! Must be at least twenty meerkat! All
playing sentry... (LAUGHS) No... There they go, back
down the burrow! The boys should've seen that
– maybe I'll bring the family here next weekend. Just
the four of us (LAUGHS), or is that four and a half
now?
Ma can stay home; Esme can make a picnic – maybe
some of those cucumber sandwiches the boys like. Or
perhaps we'll make a *braai* – I'll let the boys decide.
(LAUGHS) No head honcho. Catch and release policy.
Ja, I think they'll like that. It'll be a real family outing.
Maybe I'll show them Pa's knife.

FADE UP JANNIE'S CAR ACCELERATING.

RUTH DESCHAMPS grew up in Kent, Andalucía and Cape Town.
While studying for her BA in English and Creative Studies, she had
a farce commissioned for a theatre in Bristol. She also won the BSU
Prose competition. For her MA she has written a play for radio.

Contact: ruth.deschamps@sparksanthology.co.uk

Charcoal and Chalk

Jason Bennett

from *Lumina*

Tomas has been summoned to the lake house he spent his childhood summers at to care for his dying father. There he is haunted by memories of his younger brother, Mikael. Tomas brings his wife, Lotta, and six-year-old son, Erik, with him. Located in the mythical heartland of Sweden, Sakkaman's Spit is a place where fact and fiction blur, past and present tangle and, as with all good fairy tales, there are things lurking in the woods.

Through the attic window I try to gauge the density of pine trees along the far edge of the lake. I want to catch the mischief of light and dark with just charcoal and chalk. Simple colours, true colours – no tricks, no lies, no blurring. It is a weary morning at Sakkaman's Spit. The cloud-cover sags under its own weight, and around the lake's edge paper-thin patches of ice have appeared. I will build the density of trees in layers, charcoal over charcoal, and, when the clouds have melted away, I will highlight where the sun slices between the branches, scores lines against the bark, and strikes at the water. If I concentrate hard enough on this, I can leave all worries behind. I can unhook those dead weights and float out of myself.

I open the attic window and let the cold air pass through me. Erik is outside. He is supposed to be sweeping the veranda, but he is parading up and down in his boots and running the end of the broom handle along the balusters. In the attic, the hollow knocking bumps through the wall and dislodges dust from the rafters.

In Johan's room below me, Lotta's voice is muffled. When I took Johan in his breakfast, he wanted to talk about Mikael, but talking won't change anything. It won't bring Mama back, or cure Johan, or give Lotta another child, or help me with my art, or pay for food or clothes or a new car. Talking about Mikael won't make any of us happy. The three days we've been here, I've only found solace in my art.

The picture is taking form – like a truth. Black and white are all you need; any other colour is just a complication. I stand back from the easel and wonder if I'll ever find that spark again, that something special I had once, when I was good, better than good, when – for a time – I was a real contender.

Talk to anyone and there's a fair chance that they'll still remember *Lumina*; and, if not the painting itself, then the reproduction postcard, greeting card or even poster that the card company in Malmö produced, riding on my fifteen minutes of fame. I can sometimes go into a house, perhaps one of Lotta's friends', and discover they still have a copy of the postcard, tacked on a corkboard in the kitchen, behind electricity bills and forgotten reminders and snapshots of long-deceased pets.

'I knew we still had it somewhere,' they might say when they've finally unearthed it. 'Did *you* paint that? How extraordinary. What else have you done?'

I was asked for more of the same: *Lumina 2*, *Lumina 2.2*, *Lumina* in charcoal and chalk, or alabaster, or bloody felt-tip. *Lumina* ad nauseam. At first I had shunned the requests. I thought the oil painting and its triumph was the beginning, not the end, and that there were other things to paint, bigger and bolder and better. For two years I tried, but nothing came close. The studio I was renting slowly filled with half-finished paintings, each abandoned at the moment I lost faith. I was left with landscapes with strange anaemic features, portraits with empty eyes and scratchy pencil mouths, paintings with starved patches of nothing encroaching upon the paper, each one left precariously in limbo. Just standing in the studio doorway and seeing the sheer volume of discarded projects propped against the walls often left me in a state of creative paralysis. After a while, I couldn't even face going and – instead – hours were dissolved in cafés and coffee cups or sitting on a bench in Humlegården, curling coins around my fingers.

When the art world finally lost interest in me and stopped asking for another *Lumina*, I took it upon myself to paint one. It was a desperate, defeatist decision. But versions two, three, four and five followed the path of every other painting I had started since Otto's Skåne collection. I couldn't recapture the magic; I no longer knew how to, or even where to, begin. After several months I stopped trying. I got a teaching post, evenings mainly, at the local institute, abandoning my own dreams in favour of those of the next generation.

Erik has crept in. He is sitting at the back of the attic, cross-legged, half in shadow, and with the hood of his top pulled over his head. Rabbit is bent double beside him. I pretend I haven't seen them and strike a pose, charcoal poised. I squint through the window, frame the view with fingers and thumbs, then return to the easel, and pretend to make flamboyant charcoal strokes. I don't know why I expect him to laugh, but I do, and he doesn't.

'Hello, Captain,' I say. 'How long have you been sitting there?'

'Not long,' he mumbles.

'Are you OK?'

'Uh-huh.'

I turn back to the easel. There are stark charcoal silhouettes, trunks and branches and shadows, the shaded stillness of water; as yet, no sign of light or life.

Erik sniffs.

With the eraser I erode a pale line, creating a smoky haze from behind a tree, and then change my mind, fill it back in, and soften and blend the readjustment. I wipe my hand on a cloth and look through the window across the lake at the fringe of Scots pine and Norwegian spruce.

After months of artistic rigor mortis, it comes as a surprise that here in the lake house I've not visited since I was eight – a house where memories lay in wait like trapdoors – the inspiration is returning. The easel is up, not oils but charcoal, and there are marks on the paper, images forming, and a sense of progress. Sakkaman's Spit – the memory of which had inspired the original *Lumina* – has bewitched me again. This charcoal and chalk creation is a new beginning, merely remodelled from the debris of the past.

Erik is gouging at the gaps in the wooden floorboards with something – slow, grinding strokes. He watches me like I used to watch my father, safe in shadows. I never ventured nearer, like Mikael used to.

'You don't have to sit back there,' I say. 'Come over here and keep me company.'

He trudges across the attic, bringing Rabbit with him, and climbs up on to Johan's chair, giggling nervously when he makes the leather fart. He dangles his feet off the end; little red socks more off than on. He produces a black feather from up his sleeve and punctures the embroidered cushion with its tip, again and again and again. Rabbit is wedged in by Erik's side, his ears mangled from sucking.

'Do you need your hood up inside?' I ask.

'It's an invisible hood.'

'Oh,' I say. 'Wow.'

'But I don't think it works any more.'

'Oh dear. Why not?'

'You saw me.'

'Erik, I think that was more to do with your sniffing.'

He pushes the hood off his head and sighs. His blond hair is damp and runs in his eyes like butter. He still has that baby plumpness: thick cheeks, a tubby belly. He jabs the feather into the cushion again, and turns it round and around, trying to stretch a hole.

'What do you think of my picture?' I ask.

He hangs over the arm of the chair and takes his time deciding.

'It's OK.'

'Wow, that good?'

He nods and I turn back to the easel. Erik settles himself in the chair but I'm too conscious of him watching to be able to draw with conviction. Eventually he slithers off it and goes to Johan's desk. He clambers on to the stool and scans the scientific equipment spread out before him, before reaching across for a pair of callipers and using them to pick up a pencil that shoots across the desk and clatters down the back. Erik gets up on to his knees and drags Johan's microscope nearer. He watches the platform move up and down as he turns the dial, and then puts a dead fly that has been dunked in dust on the tray and examines it through the lens.

'Euggh!'

'Come away from there, Erik, please. That microscope is very expensive. I don't think Johan will like you playing with it.'

'But—'

'No, come on.'

He pushes it back, accumulating clutter behind it and clambers down off the stool. He slumps back into the chair. I make inconsequential charcoal marks and Erik's stare tracks every stroke.

'If you had a little brother or sister, you'd have someone to play with,' I say. 'Would you like that?'

He shrugs.

'Like a new best friend.'

'I've got a friend.'

'I don't mean at school. I mean someone you could play with at home, or when we come to places like here.'

'He *is* here.'

'Oh? Who's that, then?'

We've had conversations like this before.

'I don't know his name,' mumbles Erik.

Last year it was a girl called Pella. Lotta used to have to lay an extra place for her at the dinner table. When Erik wouldn't do something, it was because Pella didn't want to. It was Pella who lost things, broke things, made a mess and never cleared it up. She stayed all summer and then Erik never spoke of her again, but things still got broken.

'Where does he live, then?'

'I don't know,' says Erik. 'But he gave me this.'

He holds the feather up, triumphantly.

'That's nice,' I say. 'You haven't been into the woods, have you?'

Erik shakes his head.

I go to the window, and unlock the latch. The air outside is chilling. Memories of Mikael are jostling. I try to push them aside, and take a deep breath.

'A raven came to see me yesterday,' I tell Erik.

'A raven?'

'Yes. Flew right in through this window. Perhaps he'll come again today.'

Erik has to stand on tiptoes to see over the ledge.

'He came in *here*?' he asks. 'Did you have to fight him?'

I laugh. 'He wasn't going to hurt me. He just came in to say hello.'

'Were you scared?'

'No. He flew away again in the end. I think he was just checking on me. Odin must have sent him to see what I was up to. Maybe that's one of his feathers,' I suggest. 'Maybe it's a magic feather.'

Erik holds it up to the light and scrutinises it. 'No, I don't think so.'

'It doesn't look like he's going to come, does it?' I say. 'Let's close this window again. It's getting cold; and I should get on with my work before it gets too dark to see.'

Erik climbs back on to the chair, tipping himself over the arm. He slumps against the cushion, one hand holding Rabbit to his chest, his thumb in his mouth. He is tired and quiet again, at his most agreeable. It is at times like this that the shouting, the tantrums, the strained conversations no longer matter. I can love him. I *do* love him. He is part of me, after all.

'When we get back to Stockholm,' I say, 'I'm going to start taking you to school and picking you up so that Mama can have some time to herself. We can go to the park after school if you like. That will be fun, won't it?'

Erik nods.

A second child will balance things out. That's what Lotta wants. Another Erik, because Erik is not enough. Four is always better. Four is better balanced. And in March, Erik will be seven. He will overtake Mikael. Erik will grow up and leave memories of my brother behind. And I will move on. Everything will be different.

Erik takes his thumb out of his mouth. 'When are we going home?'

'Not long now.'

'But when?'

'I don't know. Not long. We need to wait for Birgitta to come back out of hospital. We need to stay and look after Johan.'

'But when will that be?'

'I don't know. We will have to wait and see.'

He huffs.

'You don't mind being here for a few more days, do you?'

He is slouching down in the chair. His red socks hang from the end of his feet, like two lolling tongues licking dust from the floor.

'I want to go home,' he moans.

'Whatever for? I thought we were having fun.'

He buries his chin in his chest. 'Rabbit doesn't like it here.'

'Why not?'

'Bad things happen.'

'Come on, Erik. Don't talk like that. Nothing bad's going to happen.'

'Something happened to Mikael.'

'That was a long time ago. And it was an accident. I've already told you that.'

Erik looks up at me. He doesn't seem very sure.

'I know,' I say, 'let's *both* do some drawing. If I give you a big sheet of paper, perhaps you'd like to draw Birgitta a 'get well soon' picture, and then she will get well soon and we can all go home.'

He wriggles out of the chair and waits while I find him a piece of paper and Mama's coloured pencils, still in their cardboard tube. We lay the paper flat on the floor and Erik lies on his stomach, propped on elbows, feet in the air, red socks dangling. We both settle down to our work. I trace the light as it blends with shadows on the water, while by my feet Erik draws a red house, a matchstick family, and a big black bird flying over the top of them. We are quiet and content and industrious. There is just the scratch and scuff of charcoal and crayon, and the sound of raindrops breaking on the window.

JASON BENNETT was born near Oxford. In previous incarnations he has been a bookseller, publisher's sales representative, and a marketing manager living in London. If he had paid much attention to the advice, 'Write what you know', *Lumina* would have been a very different novel.

Contact: jason.bennett@sparksanthology.co.uk

Selected Poems

Caroline Heaton

Nuit Blanche – Norfolk

We are hunkered down,
three to the borrowed main room,
daughter beside us on a spare mattress
in case she wakes at three to the foreign dark:
instead we are all awake, all night long,
tossing in fits and starts, unsticking limbs
from the caramel counterpane,
one or other of us stertorous, sleep-groaning
or crying out in dreams twisted
by my brother's tales of broken windows,
scratched car, uprooted shrubs,
stone faun thrown in the pond.

The window is vented
to the ill-will of these neighbours
who know how to remark
a Russian wife, a man who reads
and doesn't wash his car on Sundays;
we sleep and stir, sleep and start
beneath the troubled histories
scrawling on parchment-coloured walls –
wake with relief to a rainy dawn.

Cley Beach, Norfolk

We walk a clear mile to the pebbled beach,
the path bordered by a hidden dyke
and the sedgy sweep of bird terrain,
where mallards and terns preen
beside inland seas.

It's raining and the sea's a dark blur
in the distance where oily green waves
heft seaweed, driftwood. We bend our heads
into the salt wind, search for sea treasure
to mark our daughter's day.

I peer through the afternoon drizzle,
but here's no prettiness, only flint
struck on flint, grey-black, ink,
a shingle bar, heaped up by tides
beneath a bruised sky.

We turn stones whittled into craters
or sheered smooth as a knife,
seize ebonies and viridians,
planetary landscapes,
that weigh our pockets down.

I stir old bladderwrack, plastic,
broken razor shells, nubbed sea-glass,
just as she clasps it, a star-fish
whose dry tentacles lightly rest
on her outstretched palm.

Tomorrow

I am five and it is my first long word
copied from the folded school card.
I print it out again at home,
sucking the sweet red lead,
pressing into the rough sugar-paper
the shape of a day;
now I have caught the future –
it lies quivering within its paper frame,
luminous with colour.

I tremble with pride, writing the world,
never dreaming of the cracks
it slips through, the spaces
between word and word.

Reading Mandelstam

The Russian poet made his poetry into a tacit tool of resistance. When, in 1934, he explicitly satirised Stalin as the 'Kremlin mountaineer', he was sentenced to the first in a series of increasingly punitive periods of 'internal exile' which led to his death.

With a handful of images,
bronze coin,
he strung his song:

black earth   black sun
cathedral   apples   salt
     wine   snow

– how to take their measure,
strike one coin
against another?

The bell note rings clear.

Half a pulse later,
an echo of iron hoof-beats
drawing near.

Amaryllis

It was a November gift,
sitting dull
upon the kitchen sill
with its fallow
of brown pot earth.

Then the green stem erupted
and it grew
at a rude pace,
inches a week,

stopped at a foot
and unfurled
the first
flamboyant petal.

Soon it was
Janus-headed,
lording it over
the kitchen,

with four flowers,
big as a fist,
each a slap,
a crimson shout
at midwinter.

Meditation on Mary Fedden's Painting,
Farmhouse Lane

It is the world at an angle – a white curve of lane bordered by two slate-roofed barns, the gentle bulk of the farmhouse jutting sideways, presenting its gable end-on. The stone frontage, with its porch and nine white-silled windows, is gently askew, pushed upwards by the gradient or distorted by the artist's viewpoint. A low wall sweeps across the foreground, just shaping the farmhouse garden with its gentle geometry, a wall which does not pen sheep in or keep men out. I lean over it into the late afternoon, the weather uncertain, rain clouds gathering over the near hills; breathe in the scent from soft mounds of shrubs, grey-green lavender, dark green rosemary. The fir bends towards the house. No smoke from the chimneys; the farmer's fieldwork detains him. I wait in the shelter of centuries.

CAROLINE HEATON works as a librarian and freelance writer. She co-edited (with Christine Park) two anthologies of short stories for adults, *Close Company: Stories of Mothers & Daughters* and *Caught in a Story: Contemporary Fairytales & Fables,* and published a children's picturebook, *Yi-Min and the Elephants*, in 2002. She has started to publish her poetry in literary magazines.

Contact: caroline.heaton@sparksanthology.co.uk

The Long Game

Parry Lee

from a novel

24th June 2003

*E*bony. Carrara. Verde. Rose. Quaker Grey. Jerusalem Gold. Ten-
nessee Blue. Zimbabwe Black. Each name, a stone. Each stone, a
memory. Strung together, your mantra. Repeated, your prayer. Words
that are holy. Words murmured in dreams. And now you have another.
Alabaster. Pure and innocent. A promise in your pocket.

*Walk through the iron gates of the cemetery. Ancient tombstones
huddle together like old crones. Generations of 'In loving memories'
line the path. Families buried together are now collapsed upon each
other. Plastic signs on their tombstones warn the graves are unsafe.
They have it wrong: life is unsafe.*

*Up the hill against the rain, towards her grave at the crest. A cop-
per angel cradles a dying child on a plinth of granite. Her name is
picked out in brass, Winifred Smythe. 1980–1990. Ten years. Her entire
lifetime.*

*Rest a moment at the feet of the angel. Count the other twelve stones,
one each year on this, the anniversary. Your fingertips limn their rough
and smooth. Your heart is formed of each. This stone is your last. Place
it there among the rest. This alabaster holds something new.*

Your promise of revenge.

The Royal Institution.

The auditorium darkened long enough for a collective intake of breath
before the slide lit the screen. It was copied from a fuzzy, poorly lit Polaroid which had the same iconic significance as Myra Hindley's prison
photograph. At its centre was a girl of ten, Winifred Smythe. She was
dressed in a school uniform and propped against a tree. Lighted candles
flickered just beyond her outstretched fingertips. Her eyes were half
open as if studying her Doc Martens.

She was dead.

Leaning over her, with the surprised look of a lover disturbed, was Daryl Stanley, his hand up the child's skirt. He was tucking her folded handkerchief into the top of her knickers.

Carpe Dailey shivered, remembering her seven-year-old self, the child whose bare legs were cold and scratched. The child whose legs had downy hair, prickly with goosebumps; legs which trembled in sympathy with the girl who had a man's hand up her skirt. She remembered the smell of death and decaying leaves and the hot breath of the candle at her first sight of that girl.

Looking at the Polaroid now through twenty-year-old eyes, she understood her mother's outrage at Uncle James. She had been there and Uncle James had taken her.

Carpe shook her head, as if to clear the memory, to bring her back to the Royal Institution, to the speaker in the wine-coloured dress, but she couldn't concentrate. She could only remember that night and how it had all started so innocently in the Wells Tavern.

This was the initial infraction cited by her mother whenever she catalogued Uncle James' failings as a godfather. 'Imagine,' she would say, 'taking a child to the Wells. He promised to take you directly home.'

Not that Carpe minded. She liked those excursions into the world of irresponsible boys. That night, Uncle James and Bill, an off-duty policeman, discussed the case of two murdered schoolgirls. Uncle James, a BBC researcher, was looking for inside information. They sat in a booth near the door, in consideration of Carpe, being a minor whose lungs might be adversely affected by cigarette smoke. Carpe had a pint of Coca-Cola and a bag of crisps in front of her, something her mother never allowed, and a new box of crayons from Uncle James.

At first the two men were more interested in comparing features of their new mobile phones, pressing the buttons, extending the antennae and calling each other from two feet apart. Carpe sorted her new crayons, confused by their colour names. Which was darker: brown, burnt sienna, mahogany, raw sienna or raw umber? Which was lighter: yellow, lemon yellow or goldenrod?

Talk of the murdered girls swirled around her, never requiring the same concentration as the colour-sorting. What order for the blues? – cornflower, turquoise blue, midnight blue, navy blue, cadet blue or plain blue? There was a pause in the conversation. The parish church bells chimed eight o'clock in the distance. When she had counted six of the bells, an out-of-breath man in a grey tracksuit charged into the pub and collapsed in the seat next her. His slippery suit rasped as he fanned the Polaroid.

It was the original of the slide on the screen.

'The Heath,' he gasped. 'Little girl. Dead. We couldn't catch him.'

He stopped fanning the Polaroid and placed it on the table. 'We were just walking through the trees and we found him. We found this.'

They crowded together and watched as the image emerged from the grey photosensitive square. When they saw what it was, James shouted at her, 'Pack up your things, now!' He punched numbers into his mobile phone.

Words swirled around her, shouting men's voices, multiple conversations at once.

'I'm an off-duty police constable,' Bill explained, as he called the station.

'Where was this picture taken?' James queried, as he called the newsroom.

The Polaroid man was still out of breath. James gave him Carpe's Coke. 'The main path to the ponds. My friend has a brown jacket – he'll show you where this is.'

James wasn't waiting for a police caution before investigating. Then the words around her stopped. Uncle James and Bill both glared at her. She smiled as appealingly as she could, not wanting to be left behind. Uncle James looked frantically around, to find someone, anyone, he could leave her with.

Bill shook his head. 'I'm not taking her.'

Uncle James narrowed his eyes. 'You'd better do just as I say.' As he lifted her out of the booth, she grabbed her school satchel. Still trying to catch his breath, the Polaroid man motioned towards the Heath.

This was the second infraction cited by her mother: taking a child 'at that time of night' on to the Heath. Carpe hadn't really liked it herself.

She remembered the shock of the cold as they emerged from the pub and that she hadn't listened for the last church bells. Uncle James put her down and strode ahead, shouting into his mobile. Carpe stopped to pull her sweater on. He shouted at her to 'hurry up, for God's sake,' then grabbed her hand roughly. The sweater trailed behind, half on, half off.

The path through Hampstead Heath ran through columns of ancient oak trees so close together that light rarely penetrated. The track sloped downhill; it was rutted, loose stones over hard-packed dirt. After dark, the Heath was silent but for strange scurryings in the undergrowth and the distant honking of Canada geese.

She whimpered, pathetic mewlings punctuated by her chattering teeth. Uncle James told her to be quiet or he'd leave her alone right there. He dropped her arm, then cupped his mouth with his free hand and shouted out, 'Hello? Hello?' as he continued to stride forward.

Terrified of being left behind, Carpe clutched on to his dark trouser leg as they ran downhill, stumbling and sliding on the rocks. Suddenly he stopped. She ran into the backs of his legs. His wool trousers scratched her cheek. She looked up – the man in the brown jacket.

He had a gruff voice. 'This way,' he said. They plunged into the even darker undergrowth.

Carpe slid down a bank, wet with rotting leaves. Nettles scratched her legs above her white socks, blackberry brambles clung to her hair as she climbed over fallen logs. Bare roots caught her school shoes. She couldn't see the man; she could only hear his voice.

'We chased after him,' said the man, 'but he was too fast. He ran off through the woods. We couldn't see him, couldn't hear him. He just disappeared. He may still be here.'

They stopped in a cleared path in the trees. Carpe struggled into her sweater. Twigs caught in the sleeves, scratching her arms. She tried to pick them out, while anchoring Uncle James' trouser legs in case he should run off again.

The man with the brown jacket had lost his direction. 'It's all so similar – all the trees, all the paths.'

Uncle James lit a cigarette, which cast a glow above her head like a firefly. She was about to suggest it was time to go home, she knew it was past her bedtime, when the man plunged off into the brush again.

'No, it's this way. I know it. Look, you can see the light from the candles over there.'

They strode off so suddenly, Carpe nearly lost them. She scrambled through, afraid of being left behind, frightened of the dark, the brambles and the terrifying events on the Heath.

Then they were there, at the scene made famous by the Polaroid.

It smelled of wax and earth. Uncle James told the man in the brown jacket to return to the path and wait for the police, to direct them here.

The man hesitated.

'Go – they may be looking for us now!' Uncle James dialled into his phone as the man disappeared through the trees. 'Don't look.' He stood before her, obscuring the view.

Then Uncle James was on his mobile phone again, speaking in his television voice. He described what they saw, an eyewitness account she would hear over and over again during the days to come.

But she did look.

First she saw the glow of the candle, thick and white. She grew bolder. She looked at the child's Doc Martens, just beyond James' trousers. Then she saw the child's socks and knees. Finally, stepping away from Uncle James, she saw the child. She was beautiful.

The child leaned against a fat tree coloured in mahogany and burnt sienna. Her head was tilted to one side and back. Her hair glowed lemon yellow and goldenrod in the candlelight. Her midnight-blue blazer had cornflower stripes at the edges, above her navy school skirt. Her hands, palms down, rested at her sides. Her shoes splayed in first ballet position. Her mouth was a little open.

In her own seven-year-old way, Carpe tried to puzzle it out. She knew the girl was dead and that this was another of those girls who died because she talked to strangers. Yet at the same time, the girl looked as if she was thinking, or that she wasn't a real girl at all, but a life-sized doll.

Then there was shouting and distant sirens. Light showed between the tree trunks, casting stripes on the doll-child. Uncle James had forgotten about Carpe and shouted towards the policemen. Carpe knew it was her last chance. She didn't know why she did it. Maybe she just wanted to find out if the doll-child had hard plastic skin like Barbie or soft rubbery flesh like Sindy.

In the moment left, she crept over to the girl and touched her little finger.

The doll-child was cold and damp, as if the spongy ground was seeping into her already. She looked down at the doll-child's finger – she had a bent baby finger – like a lazy 'c'. Before she could see whether the other hand had a similar finger, Uncle James snatched her away, hissing something about not destroying evidence. He picked her up, crushing her nose against the cigarette and beer smell of his wool jacket. Over his shoulder she watched the doll-child with a finger like a lazy 'c' fade into the Heath. Then there were people. Carpe was handed to a policewoman and taken away.

Uncle James hadn't even taken her home. It had been left to Carpe's mother to collect her from Hampstead Police Station. She could never figure out which was the greater transgression in her mother's eyes – that Uncle James had taken her to a murder scene, or that her mother had to travel all the way to Hampstead to collect her daughter.

The slide projector stuttered and whirred. As if emerging from a dream, Carpe became aware of the crowded auditorium, and the penetrating voice of the speaker, clinical psychologist Amalia Winston-Jones, PhD.

'Winifred Smythe was actually the third victim.' The voice was flat and over-articulated, with an accent which spoke of the best schools and a life of entitlement.

Two further schoolgirl photos clicked on to the screen, then a map showing where their bodies were found in various parts of west London. Dr Winston-Jones used a laser pointer to indicate the locations of the victims' homes in west and northwest London. She made it sound as clinical as filleting a chicken. 'In late 1987 and 1988, three girls between the ages of ten and fourteen disappeared from locations near their homes. Their bodies were later discovered, sitting up, neatly set out, like dolls.'

Carpe remembered it all, vividly. The next day she had run to school to tell her friends what she had seen. With them gathered around her, she told them about the dead girl and described how she was beautiful. Just as she reached the best part, Miss Pimm's bony fingers seized her shoulder.

'Nice girls don't talk of such things.' She sent Carpe to the headmistress' office. Her mother was called, and after what seemed a very, very long time, Carpe and her mother had a conversation with the headmistress and Miss Pimm. Carpe was sent to wait on a chair in the front office. Eventually, her mother came out, her neck flushed and angry. When they were outside, Carpe heard she was being sent home for the day, 'until she learned manners'. According to her mother, this meant until she learned to keep her mouth shut.

At the time, the story had the same prominence in the minds of the public as James Bulger. The reports had been in all the newspapers inciting safety concerns throughout London. For the next few weeks, Carpe's mother took time off work to walk her to and from school each day. For once, she was like the other children, whose mothers held their hands tightly and cared where they were. It was terribly thrilling, more exciting than the Grimms' fairy tales she was reading at the time. While the admonition kept her from talking with her classmates, it only made her more interested in the doll-child. She watched the television news, feeling a little angry that Uncle James was able to talk about 'their' story and she wasn't. Unable to get enough from the news, she sounded out words in the newspapers.

She learned that she and the doll-child were opposites, but the same. The doll-child had blonde hair and blue eyes; Carpe was dark, with dark eyes. They both wore glasses and were the top readers in their forms. Most crucially, she later discovered the doll-child had a father, but no mother, and she, Carpe, had a mother but no father.

Long after they arrested the murderer, the doll-child lived within her like an imaginary friend.

PARRY LEE's *The Long Game* is a crime novel, which asks what happens when a young medical student comes face to face with the paedophile who haunted her childhood. It charts the intersection of nice people with the real world, bringing the reader up close and uncomfortably personal.

Contact: parry.lee@sparksanthology.co.uk

Sushi Night

Kate Frost

from The Butterfly Storm

The bus stop was at the bottom of Hazel Road so I didn't have far to walk. It was early to be going home for a Friday night and it had only just got dark. I wasn't drunk but I could barely walk in my two-inch heels. I reached our house and fumbled with the key in the lock.

'Mum?' I called, shutting the door behind me. I kicked off my shoes and padded barefoot to the kitchen. The flagstones were refreshingly cool after the sticky floor and heat of the pub.

Mum hadn't left a note but there was a tray of Rice Krispie cakes, like the ones she made when I was little, and sushi and champagne in the fridge. It was 10.30; there was no reason for her to be out. She wouldn't be at yoga this late, or at a friend's house; in fact she'd made me promise to come home before 11.00 so we could celebrate. I hadn't even had time to get drunk.

I found a bottle of Baileys in the wine rack and poured myself a large glass. I lit the candles in the open fireplace in the sitting room and snuggled on to the beanbag next to the sofa. Baz Luhrmann's *Romeo + Juliet* was on the telly. It suited my mood.

I'd been stood up by my own mother. If a boyfriend had ever treated me like this, I'd have dumped him. I wanted to phone Candy and have a moan but realised she'd only say, 'It's Leila, what do you expect?' A bit of commitment, a bit of respect, a bit of mothering – that's what.

Claire Danes and Leonardo DiCaprio were gazing at each other through a fish tank. That was what Mum believed in: love at first sight. She found her Romeos in the strangest of places. They could be any-where: at the park, the Indian takeaway; she'd even seduced the guy be-hind the fish counter at Asda. There'd been plenty of them, too. I could count my boyfriends on one hand and still have a couple of fingers free. Some men lasted no longer than the first date with Mum. Her longest relationship was three years, the length of time I'd just spent at uni-versity. In my mind, three years was no time at all. I could have stayed a student, never having to face the world, never having to come back home. My bedroom was still the same with the navy paint I chose for the walls when I was ten. When I looked out of my bedroom window at our terraced garden, I felt trapped within perpetual childhood. My view at university had been the side wall of a house in my first year, the concrete wall of our weed-filled courtyard garden in the second and the tops of houses framing a triangular patch of sea from my attic room in the third year. The difference was, they were my views, my room and it was my life. Despite removing posters of Green Day and The Beastie Boys from the walls and replacing them with my artwork, it felt as if I'd come full circle back to who, and where, I was three years before.

A key clicked in the front door. Romeo and Juliet were in the swimming pool trying to hide from Juliet's nurse. I wanted to stay hidden. I wriggled further into the beanbag and sloshed my watery Baileys around the glass. The front door slammed.

'Sophie?' Mum appeared in the sitting-room doorway clutching her red sequinned handbag. She frowned. 'You're home early.'

'Actually, I thought I was late.' I turned my attention back to the TV and flicked channels. Eddie Izzard was on. 'Where have you been?' I asked without looking at her.

'I completely forgot I'd said yes to drinks with Stu from work.'

'You couldn't cancel?'

'I've turned him down too many times before.'

'I was out with friends I wanted to be with and managed to get home early.'

'Come on, don't be cross with me,' she said, squatting down next to me and kissing my forehead. 'I thought I'd be waiting for you.' She blew out the candles, switched off the TV, took my hand and pulled me from the beanbag. 'I hope you haven't eaten?'

'I had one slice of pizza.'

'Stu wanted to go to some fancy French restaurant but I plied him with cocktails instead. He told me sushi was an aphrodisiac,' she rolled her eyes. 'I told him he wasn't getting any.'

'Getting any what?'

'Sushi, of course.'

She was dressed provocatively enough to have got something else. She was slim, in black trousers and a top that showed her tanned cleavage. Mum dressed my age and got away with it. I felt like a child around her.

'Bloody gorgeous night out.' She threw me a box of matches. 'Light the lanterns, would you.'

It was a still night and clear, although the stars were blurred by the orange glow from the streetlights. Frogs splashed in the pond; it wasn't peaceful, not even this late. Mum opened the kitchen window and passed me a handful of tealights. I dotted them along the middle of the picnic table and lit them. Mum slapped across the patio in her flip-flops and put a plate of sushi on the table. 'They get more action than I do,' she said, waving her hand towards the pond.

'I'm not so sure about that.' I lit the tall lantern that was stuck in the flowerbed. I liked the way our garden was so atmospheric with very little effort. 'Are you going to see him again?'

'Who, Stu? I work with him.'

'But romantically?'

'No. He's good-looking and a top bloke, but so bloody boring.'

'He didn't invite you back to his?'

'Yes – but I told him I was going home to celebrate my daughter getting a First.'

'Was he shocked you've got a twenty-one-year-old daughter?'

'I couldn't give a fuck. Champagne!' She threw her arm around my shoulders and we headed for the door, bumping into the sides as we tried to get through it together.

Mum took one of the bottles from the fridge. 'Outside,' she said.

I grabbed two tall wineglasses and followed her. The drone of the TV from next door now accompanied the frog orgy.

'How many cocktails have you had?' I asked.

Mum turned away from me and pointed the bottle towards the sky. The cork punched the air with a bang like a rocket and smoke trailed from the neck. 'Enough to make me merry,' she said.

She filled our glasses to the top with bubbling champagne. 'Well done.' She tapped her glass against mine. 'You deserve it.'

We sat down on either side of the table and dipped a piece of sushi in the bowl of soy sauce. Mum pursed her lips and blew air out. 'Bloody hell, that's hot.'

'You made them.'

I sipped my champagne and let the bubbles burst on my tongue. There were shouts from the other side of the rooftops; it must have been kick-out time at the pubs.

I was glad I'd come home early now and had forgiven her. It was hard not to. I liked spending time with her. When she was happy, her mood rubbed off on me and I could feel contentment building as we laughed together. I had missed her in Falmouth and looked forward to her weekly phone calls, filling me in on the gossip.

'Are you going to miss being a student?' she asked.

'I'm going to miss living by the sea.'

'You're OK about moving back in with me?'

'Mum, my life was like a student's even before I went to uni. Living with you is like having a housemate.'

'Thank you,' she said. Only she could take that as a compliment. She filled our glasses up.

'How's work?' I asked. 'Do you still hate it?'

'Hate is a little strong. I'm bored. The people are boring.'

'You said Stu's boring.'

'Times him by ten and you've got the idea. I want to get my teeth into something. Be passionate, like you are with your art.'

'Then go for it.'

Mum knocked back her champagne. 'It's not that easy.'

I knew how frustrated she was at work. Talking about it wound her up even more. I moved away from the subject and, between mouthfuls of sushi, we talked about everything else: my childhood, parties, university, her friends, my friends, sex... This was the woman, after all, who got more action than I did. Mum talked to me about sex the way friends discuss last night's *EastEnders*.

By the time Mum headed inside to get the strawberries, she could barely walk in a straight line and giggled as she staggered into the open doorway.

'You're a disgrace!' I called after her. I had a warm fuzzy feeling from too much champagne and laughter. Mum and alcohol were a lethal combination, and she was a bad influence on me.

She reappeared in the doorway a minute later with a bowl of strawberries in one hand and a bottle of squirty cream in the other.

'Is your head spinning?' she asked as she wavered towards me.

'No. Is yours?'

'A little,' she giggled.

'Lightweight.'

'Hey, I had Sex on the Beach twice and god knows how many Screaming Orgasms.'

She shook the cream violently and squirted a pyramid on to a plate. She sat down opposite me. I took a strawberry and dipped it into the cream. We ate in silence. The frogs were still splashing in the pond, on their own now Ella and Ken next door had turned their TV off. Mum groped for her champagne.

'You should slow down on the champers,' I said, glancing at the empty bottle.

She shrugged and took another sip. I felt her watching me over the rim of her glass. I took another strawberry and looked up. Her eyes were searching my face. She reached across the table, brushed a loose hair from my forehead and tucked it behind my ear.

She gave me a weak smile. 'Elliott would be so proud.'

'Who?'

'Your dad.'

Elliott. The name tumbled around my head. Dad. The word, un-familiar, unused. I held her gaze, but didn't say anything because she wasn't making sense. I didn't know my father, had never known him. I'd never had the chance, because Mum said she couldn't remember his name, said she wasn't sure if they'd even exchanged names before exchanging bodily fluids. She remembered he had green eyes like mine.

'So proud,' she slurred.

'You know his name? You said you had no idea who he was.'

She looked at me through half-closed eyelids and shook her head slowly. She reached her hand across the table and found my arm.

'That's not strictly true.'

'What?'

'He didn't want you to know about him. I couldn't tell,' she said in a drunken whisper. 'I know he'd be proud of you.'

Her eyes filled with tears. My head pounded, not from too much champagne but sheer incomprehension.

'You actually knew him?'

'It's no big deal.'

She said it in such a serious voice I wanted to smack her. 'I hope to God that's the alcohol talking.' I pulled my arm from beneath her hand.

'He didn't want me to tell you. He was afraid...'

'Of what? Me?'

I stood up. I couldn't stay still, I couldn't think straight. Mum was a drunken mess, words spilling from her that I knew she was going to regret.

'Who was he? Why the hell didn't you tell me?'

'I promised I wouldn't. It was complicated.'

'So you decided to lie about it all this time?'

She looked small and weepy where she was sitting, hunched over the table.

'It was easier for you not to know,' she said quietly.

'Then why the fuck tell me now?'

'I don't know. I kept thinking about him today. You remind me of him.'

I wanted to walk away from her, but couldn't. 'But it's no big deal, huh?'

'Soph, calm down...'

'You tell me my father's name and you didn't think I'd have some thing to say about it?'

'You know me, Soph. I don't fucking censor my words.'

'So he wasn't a one-night stand?'

She shook her head. I hoped she regretted opening her mouth in the first place. I wasn't going to let it go.

'Who is he, then? Why the hell couldn't you tell me?'

'He's married,' she said. She looked away and stared at the empty wineglass. Her fingers pinched the stem tight and she started to turn the glass rhythmically. 'We were lovers.'

'For how long?'

'Ten months. I was eighteen.' She stopped twirling the glass and breathed deeply.

'How old was he?'

'Thirty-two.'

I paused. 'Does he have kids?'

She didn't answer straight away, and in that moment, her words, her emotion and the briefest of pauses sank in. I had a father with a name, a face, an age, a history.

'Three children.'

And a whole other family somewhere: brothers or sisters, or both. I shook my head in disbelief. 'How could you keep this from me? I'm twenty-one.'

'He chose his family over us.'

'No. He chose them over you. He doesn't know me.'

'It hurt, but I respected his wishes. Do you know how hard that's been?' Tears slid freely down her face.

'Don't you think I deserved some respect, too?' My voice tightened. 'You lied to me.'

She put her head in her hands and wiped away her tears. I stood my ground.

'Do they know about me?'

She looked up with red eyes and a frown. 'His kids?' She shrugged. 'I doubt it.'

'Did they know about you?'

'His wife never knew. He ended it and I promised I wouldn't contact him again. I hope he's been looking back over his shoulder ever since.' She stood up and came over. Without her heels on, she was an inch or two shorter than me. She took hold of my hands but I shrugged her off.

'Your timing sucks,' I said. I left her alone with a moth flitting round the candles and shut myself in my bedroom. I cried. Not for the father

I'd never known but because Mum had lied. We'd lost something special. That's what made me cry.

KATE FROST was born in 1977 and wrote her first novel aged seven. After studying Drama at university, she started writing again and had stories published in *QWF*, *Bullet* and *The London Magazine*. Kate also works as a supporting artist and can be spotted in *Vanity Fair*, *King Arthur* and occasionally wandering the corridors of *Casualty*.

Contact: kate.frost@sparksanthology.co.uk
        www.kate-frost.co.uk

Corpus Christi

Joan Wiles

a short story

'Come on now, Bridie, the taxi will be here in an hour.' My mother's voice filters through the veils of sleep. 'Don't worry about your prayers… Our Lady knows we're pushed for time.'

My communion dress, hanging from the wardrobe in a halo of light, gradually comes into focus. The glass of warm water on the bedside table is a reminder that I must keep my fast. I take a sip. Without the usual slice of lemon it tastes metallic and unpalatable.

Never forget, children, that the devil lies in wait. You might find a sweet in your pocket and, unable to resist temptation, pop it into your mouth, and there would be your undoing.

For weeks we have prepared for this day. Father Daley has given us instruction every afternoon.

'And what does "Corpus Christi" mean, children?'

'The body of Christ, Father.'

'And what happens at that part of the mass we call the consecration?'

'The bread and wine are changed into the body and blood of Our Blessed Lord.'

'Correct. And this miracle is called?'

'The miracle of tran-sub-stan-tiation, Father.'

Whenever he speaks of such matters, he lowers his eyelids; rocks back and forward on his heels; and extends his hands like a mystic in ecstasy. The slightest cough or whisper breaks his communion with the Divine. The culprit is hauled out, ticked off and made to kneel on the splintery floor.

When he considers us to be sufficiently composed, we practise receiving the sacrament. A reading book, passed from child to child, serves as a communion plate. We listen moon-eyed, to stories of saints who survived without food: Saint Francis of Assisi, Padre Pio, Blessed Theresa Newman. Their only sustenance was the sacrament of the Eucharist. Some were visited by the stigmata. Every Friday, the wounds on their hands bled copiously. The pain was excruciating.

The most important thing is to be in a state of grace. The week before my first communion, I receive the sacrament of penance.

Within the confines of the musty box, I pour forth the accumulation of sins: disobedience, dishonesty, neglect and omission.

'Get on with it, child; I haven't all day,' the priest hisses through the grille. The votary flame, illuminating the crucified body of Christ, flickers blood red in the darkness.

'And for your penance, say three Our Fathers. Now tell Almighty God that you are truly sorry for your sins.'

'O My God, I am very sorry that I have sinned against Thee, because Thou art so good and by the help of Thy grace, I will never sin again.'

The priest makes the sign of the cross and says the words of absolution.

My penance said, I quietly leave the church and float above the soot-encrusted buildings. I am oblivious to the traffic's roar and the wind snatching litter from the gutters. My soul knows the purity of baptismal day and sings:

White as the lily O.

Everything I put on that Corpus Christi morning is white and new. No one will ever know of my mother's care and dedication, of the endless fittings in draughty changing rooms.

'Much too fancy,' she said, as the assistant selected yet another garment from the rail. Calyx upon calyx of tulle was removed from the glass cases to be inspected by her critical eye. Every haberdasher's drawer was ransacked and subjected to the same scrutiny.

'Nothing but white,' she exclaimed at the sight of a pink rosebud, or an offending blue ribbon. 'Mother of God, give me strength. Will these non-Catholics never understand?' A jingle that the Protestant children chant started up in my head:

Trinity, Trinity, ring the bell
Send every Catholic straight to hell.

Shelves were scaled like medieval battlements as dozens of shoe boxes were brought down from the heights.

'Perhaps something like this without the bows... Or this pair with a lower heel... Now, do you have these in white?'

The shopkeeper sighed; removed his spectacles and pulled a rag from his sleeve. He wiped the lenses and mopped his brow. His eyes narrowed with an expression that said, 'Micks... left-footers... po-faced papists.' And on we trudged in search of a pair of white buckskin bar shoes, which no one wanted to stock.

I step into the lawn petticoat and slip into the voile dress. My mother battles with a multitude of buttons. She says she is getting arthritis in her fingers but 'such things are sent to try us'. She arranges the veil; secures it with a crown of lily-of-the-valley – 'Our Lady's Tears'. They say that where Our Lady's tears fell, the white, scented bells appeared. The headdress in place, she stands back and surveys her work like a painter contemplating her canvas. Then she reaches for her coat, adjusts her best feathered hat and says she's not having that Josie Walsh thinking she's a cut above, just because their Theresa has her name down for the convent school. She's sick of hearing about their new three-piece suite, their pilgrimage to Lourdes. Her words dissolve like mist.

Should the wafer stick to the roof of your mouth, children, ease it off with your tongue and swallow it reverently. It should not graze your teeth and on no account must it be chewed. And remember that you must never, ever, touch the body of Christ with your fingers. Only a priest ordained by God, Himself, enjoys this special privilege.

'For the love of God, will you stop dreaming, Bridie?' She fishes in her bag for her compact and powders her face.

'What if something goes wrong?' I say.

'Goes wrong... What could go wrong?'

'If I can't swallow communion.'

'You'll swallow it like everybody else swallows it.' She takes out a lipstick and traces the outline of her mouth. 'Such notions... I've never known a child like you for getting funny ideas into her head.'

Doesn't she realise you can easily lose all the grace of the sacrament... Even fall into mortal sin?

What happens to those who die in mortal sin?
Those who die in mortal sin go to hell for all
eternity.

The first communicants assemble in the church porch. Miss Riordon checks off the register with her usual efficiency.

'Mary Boland, Jimmy Breen, Kathleen Byrnes...' She is wearing a navy blue suit and a hat like Ali Baba's.

The boys are in white shirts with bow ties. Their faces are scrubbed and shiny. Their hair glistens with Brylcreem. They discuss the special breakfast the Mother's Guild are laying on after mass. The girls giggle and exchange confidences.

'I'm having my picture taken by a professional photographer,' says Theresa Walsh. She toys with her dark ringlets and smoothes down her dress. But the promise of presents and photographs no longer holds me in its thrall. I know only the fear of the wafer sticking to my teeth… refusing to dissolve… remaining in my mouth long after I leave the church. My tongue feels dry and stale. A net of butterflies flutters beneath my heart.

Mass is about to begin. We are ushered into the church. The altar is draped in white and gold. There are flowers everywhere. I turn to the statue of the Madonna, her face gentled by candlelight.

> *Mary, most pure, pray for us.*
> *Star of the Sea, pray for us.*
> *Mother Inviolate, pray for us.*
> *Refuge of Sinners, pray for us.*

'Queen of Heaven,' I pray, 'help me in my hour of need. Let me be worthy to receive the body of your blessed son. Help me to swallow the host.' A large tear rolls down my cheek and splashes the tiled floor.

'Bridie Nolan's crying, Miss Riordon,' announces Theresa Walsh. All necks are craned. Miss Riordon peers over the rim of her half-moon spectacles.

'You mustn't cry today, dear. Your first communion day should be the happiest day of your life. None of the others are crying. Dry your eyes now, there's a good girl.'

She pats my head and gives me her lace-edged handkerchief.

Silently we file down the centre aisle and take our places in the pews reserved for the first communicants. The organist strikes a chord. The congregation rises. The vestry door swings open and the celebrant in gold vestments, followed by a procession of servers, makes his way to the altar.

> *I will go unto the altar of God*
> *To God who rejoices my youth.*

I try to fix my attention on the altar and follow the prayers with devotion, but the smell of Theresa's newly washed hair above the scent of lilies and incense makes me feel sick and lightheaded. Around the walls hang the stations of the cross: gloomy oil paintings depicting scenes from the Crucifixion. I read the captions below some of the pictures.

Jesus falls for the third time
Jesus is stripped and drenched with gall
Jesus is nailed to the cross

Someone fiddles with her veil. Miss Riordon clicks her tongue disapprovingly. A server rings the offertory bell. The Brothers of Saint Vincent de Paul stride to the front and pick up the collection baskets. Coins jangle as men search their pockets for loose change. Women fumble in their handbags. Everyone sings softly:

Soul of My Saviour sanctify my breast
Body of Christ be Thou my saving guest.

Soon, it will be the consecration, when the bread and wine are changed into the actual body and blood of Our Lord, Jesus. This will be followed by the priest's communion, and then the people's communion. The thought of the terrible sin I am about to commit obliterates all else. I stifle a sob. Theresa puts her arm round me and whispers words of comfort. Miss Riordon runs her eye along the pew; wants to know the reason for the commotion.

'Bridie Nolan's crying again,' pipes Theresa.

Miss Riordon places a finger to her lips and beckons me to her side. Material rustles and kneelers clatter as the others allow me to pass.

'What's the matter, Bridie? Are you ill, dear?' she whispers.

But the words are stuck fast. My breath comes in gasps.

'Shh… It's all right, there's nothing to worry about. I'll stay with you while you make your communion.' She holds me back until the last child leaves the pew and, placing her hands on my shoulders, guides me to the end of the line.

Sweet sacrament divine…
Sweet sacrament of rest…
Sweet sacrament of peace.

Everything is in pieces like a dream. The sun through the stained glass splashes the aisle with jewel colours. The painted statues swim in the candlelight as the procession of pale, veiled ghosts glides silently towards the altar rail.

'Corpus Christi.' The first recipient receives the sacrament. With every utterance the priest draws closer.

Lord, I am not worthy to enter under Thy roof.
Say only the word and my soul shall be healed.

I shut out everything with the constant repetition of the prayer.

The priest places the host on the tongue of the girl on my right. She makes sucking noises with her tongue. My dress is cold and clammy against my skin. My palms drip with perspiration. The moment is upon me.

'Lift your head, dear,' says the priest, but I bury my face in my hands, afraid I will be blinded by the incandescence of the beatific vision. He repeats the words with greater urgency, and I go through the practised motions: take the plate and stick out my tongue. The host melts with the sweetness of an ice-cream wafer. Flowers and candles fuse together in blobs of tears.

My mother and Aunt Monica are waiting in the presbytery garden. They pet and cajole me and fuss about my hair. They have brought presents: a tiny missal, engraved with a cross; a pair of glass rosary beads, a statue of Our Lady of Fatima. Miss Riordon gives me some holy pictures with bits of gold in them and says, 'You're a brave little girl. Your daddy, God rest his soul, would've been proud of you.'

The French windows of the presbytery rooms are flung open. Trestle tables draped with white cloths are laden with plates of sausage rolls, iced buns and slabs of Woolworth's fruit cake. Trays are piled high with sandwiches, filled with ham and fish paste. Their crusts are beginning to curl. The smell of strong tea wafts from steaming enamel jugs. The knot in my stomach tightens.

'Won't you join the others, Bridie?' my mother asks. I shake my head and clutch her coat.

'If you don't want the breakfast, we should say a prayer of thanksgiving and be on our way.' Her voice is laced with disappointment.

In the shadow of the ivy-clad wall, Our Lady of Perpetual Succour smiles serenely from her moss-covered grotto. The scent of roses mingles with that of damp earth. Silently I make my devotion.

'Dear Mother Mary, I thank you with all my heart for taking care of me this blessed day.'

JOAN WILES' theatre credits include two London productions and a national tour. Her one-woman show *The Scent of Frangipani* was sponsored by Southern Arts to tour regional art centres. She is a winner of the Bridport Poetry Prize and has an MA in Irish Studies, also from Bath Spa Universtiy.

Contact: joan.wiles@sparksanthology.co.uk

Selected Poems

Helen Pizzey

A Terrible Hardness

'We sail out of season into oyster-grey wind,
over a terrible hardness.'

Anne Sexton, *Crossing the Atlantic*

Your voice wavers like your unsteady legs;
grey and translucent, you are thinning.
Taking your pulpy arm to steer you
is like putting my hand into running water;
we walk to a bench and I sit you beside me.

The unseasonable northerly wind
chills our conversation,
turning it to memories
of newspaper sailboats
and the death of your best friend.

We get up and stroll round the paddling pool,
once my 'little sea'; silted, it has dried
like a beach at low tide.

The sunlight weakens and we lock arms,
tighter, as if with sudden cold.
We brace ourselves, not speaking,
facing that terrible hardness,
your imminent crossing.

Bells and Lemons

Daddy was a Peter Rabbit crouched in the vegetable
patch, hiding from Mother McGregor: just the top
of a cap visible and a rising swirl of tobacco smoke.
Later, after draining bottles stashed behind the hay
bales, he was boisterous with feigned bonhomie,
crowding the kitchen with confusion. At the mental
hospital, the barbiturates left him slumped in his
chair, a moist roll-up stuck flattened to his lower lip.
Or, when less sedated, he hovered between latrines,
fondling women who exposed mottled thighs. Our
Sunday visits ended in a café, Dad giving me
sixpence for the one-armed bandit while he and Mum
stared into filmy cups of tea. Bells and lemons rolled
around – but never a line of three, never the same thing
at once.

Healer

The blind man lives alone in a loft on
the seafront. There he hangs villagers' nets
to dry and mend, aware of their lattice
shadows falling on his spent retinas. With
each new net he spreads his arms wide,
measuring the extent of his work; embracing
the waters that cover the earth. His fingers
slowly feel their way across its surface,
looking for bony knots or slipping through
ruptures. He unpicks the tangles and fixes
the tears, making good the damage; easing
off the tension.

Iceberg

On the pulsing rim of oceans,
frozen water snaps,
breaks booming into pieces.

Calving with a roar,
the berg is born independent
and heavily set afloat.

A slowly drifting icescape,
noisily eroding:
sculpted by wind,
hewn by waves and
notched by whittling currents.

Nothing lives here,
on this piece of frozen sky;
it is the blue of airless space –
or white: the bubbled breath
of ages trapped within.

Like cubed sugar
this past dissolves,
bitter to the taste
of present generations.

La Vuelta

Because in Spain we were free;
because on holiday it was never 'too early'
or 'too late';

because the terracotta tiles were warm
and bared skin was sweat-beaded,
responding to touch;

because of the slow-moving cattle –
the sound of their tugging at parched grass
outside our boundary wall –

perhaps we will leave
the disciplined hedgerows,
the lime-lined cricket squares
of this temperate English summer,

and return to brazen heat
of reckless arroyos
where, free of pretence,
we live barefaced
and without constraint.

The First Cut

In the womb we sucked each other's thumb. As toddlers we
curled together like kittens and rubbed each other's earlobes.
Thirteen years later, she sits in front of me dressed in a hospital
gown. Her body is still that of a child, and her hair, which has
never been cut, is braided into one long plait and draped over
her shoulder. Her emaciated arms are discoloured by lesions.
'You brought the scissors?' She extends her palm with a cold
solemnity. I hand over the scissors and hold taut the tail of
her plait while she cuts, cuts, cuts thickly at its base, close
beside her neck. I am stunned by its weight when it falls into my
lap. There it lies, measuring the distance that has always been
between us.

HELEN PIZZEY, an irrepressible humorist, exhibits a discernible flair
for the weathering and surviving of life-threatening illness. Hand-
reared in Somerset and subjected to the smog of a vocational training in
Birmingham before working in publishing in Bedford Square, she currently mostly writes and broadcasts poetry and short fiction for adoring
fans online in America.

Contact: helen.pizzey@sparksanthology.co.uk

The Big Things Are Maybe

Emma Hooper

from a novel

The Big Things Are Maybe *is set on Canada's trans-continental rail-way and is an exploration of the coming of age of both a character and a country.*

Roger and I board a night train to Moncton, pushing past rows of already-sleeping bodies sprawled like drying laundry across the seats. We slip into the only spaces remaining with no one's head or leg or fingers dripping into them, two seats near the front of a car, on the right. These seats seem smaller, more cramped than any we've had before, claustrophobia brought on by enclosing dark and sleep. Roger takes the aisle seat, settling into a nest of a pillow and a jacket worn backwards. Even though he is able to stretch his legs out into the aisle in a way that seems satisfying, I am happy to have the window seat. Quebec glides by in shapes made fuzzy with night. Hills and cows and cars are all softened and undefined, like children hiding under dark, dark green sheets. I think about soldiers and their sweethearts drift-ing and dispersed and constant as oceans. People were so patient then. Waiting, just waiting, for years, for someone or something that might not come home at all.

Roger has managed to balance his pillow behind his head nicely, and his eyes are closed. He looks like a babied executive in a comfort-airline commercial. Mind you, Roger always looks like an executive. He could be wearing a polka-dot bikini, and he still would. A white-collared professional, always. Maybe this is part of why I know he will always succeed. A wave of faith for Roger's shining future washes over me. A rock. That's what he is. A rock who insists on carrying his own pillow with him at all times.

I try sleeping with my head against the window, but the vibrations keep me awake. I try sleeping with my head leant back, but I'm too short to reach the headrest in the way it was designed to be reached. Leaning away from the window towards Roger won't work, either, be-cause his sleeping arms are lolling right where my head would other-wise be super-comfortable. It is almost possible to sleep if I pretend that I am John the Baptist and lay my head on the serving tray folded down from the seat in front of me. I can rest with one cheek pressed to the cool plastic of the tray for about fifteen minutes before I have to switch my body and head so that I'm resting on the opposite cheek. At one point I sleep without switching on my left side for about forty minutes. When I wake up, everything is locked. My neck, my back, my legs, all locked in one left-leaning position. I try stretching out, but this is difficult to do without disturbing Roger, who has – with enviable ease – been asleep for ages.

Trying to sleep is futile. I put up the serving tray and fumble around in the swampy darkness under my seat until I find my wallet, water bottle and book. Roger doesn't even twitch as I step over him and make my way in depressingly crumpled jeans and my PandaMania! T-shirt towards the twenty-four-hour smoking car.

It takes my eyes about thirty seconds to adjust to the sudden jump in light and activity level. Blue-white fluorescent lights buzz above a dozen or so individuals. I am one of the more presentable. I settle with my book (I've just started *Harry Potter 4* and I'm quite eager) into a seat at a table for six. At the far end of my table two men play cards, gambling for pennies. The younger man is about twenty-nine, with a schoolboy's cut to his dusty auburn hair. He's in a tired grey suit, with a pale blue shirt and no tie. He keeps his pennies in careful piles of ten, counting and arranging so they're all face up, like hoodoos. I watch his hands, almost transparent under the blue lights, counting and piling, tiny auburn hairs beneath his knuckles shining like water. I'm struck with the need to get closer to this man. To help him make his piles, to iron his suit, to have his children. I move over by one seat and open my mouth, with no real plan as to what's going to come out of it. The older man, in a tangle of grey beard and a woollen fisherman's sweater, says, 'Well, Hello Betty Page. Do you know how to play the spoons?'

Once I realise this is not some sick metaphor, that he is asking a serious question, I tell him no, I don't really know how to play the spoons. I mean, I have fooled around and pretended, but no, I am not an actual spoonist (spooner?). I look to my hero of the penny-hoodoos. He shrugs an I've-never-met-this-guy-before-tonight shrug and smiles. I melt towards him. 'OK,' says the elder, 'it's time for you to learn. The both of you.'

The older man, whose name I learn is Dale, gets the twenty-four-hour snack shop to find six metal spoons for our cause, although it takes some time, and William (the beautiful man) and I overhear some stern reproaching from across the car: 'What is this? Plastic! You think I can work with plastic?! Why not just give me forks...'

Dale has William and me practise our spoon-holds twenty-five times before we are allowed to make a sound. The utensils stick gawky and unnatural from our fingers, one held just above the middle finger, one just below, in a sort of fist with the thumb on top for support, their rounded backs to one another. Dale drops his top spoon and smiles sheepishly. His hand grazes my right calf as he reaches to pick it up.

We start with very simple rhythms, playing along to the beat of the train, taka-taka taka-taka taka-taka. The goal is to keep perfectly steady. You've got to keep the angle and distance between the spoons exactly right; you can't let the top one slip off the bottom. If there is too much space between them, you'll lose your control, fall out of the proper angle, and lose the tempo. However, if your spoons are too close together, there won't be enough momentum for either the connection or the bounce-back and you'll miss beats. It's stressful work, this, and William drops his spoons three more times before we hit an established stride, taka-taka taka-taka taka-taka, constant with the train. 'Keep it up!' orders Dale, preparing his own spoons. By now, many of the others in the car have turned to watch the spectacle; a couple in the corner with matching spiky hair work away with their own plastic canteen spoons and a pretty Japanese girl taps along with the pencil she was using to do crosswords. As we continue to taka-taka with schoolchild glee, Dale begins his concerto.

All at once his spoons are dancing and jumping and running across his fingers, his legs, his head. The rhythms syncopate and double and triple against ours, impossibly melodic through cadence alone, ti-kum-ti-kum-tripalet-ta-tikka-tikka-tikka-tikka-tripalet-ta. The fluorescent lights bounce off the convex backs of his instruments in a lightshow as Dale plays on and on.

After maybe two minutes, maybe twenty, Dale stops abruptly. No grand finishing flourish or melodramatic denouement – he just stops. 'I'm tired now,' he says, and walks his spoons back over to the refreshment booth. William and I dribble out of our steady beat and put our spoons down on the table. My fingers are surprisingly sore and there is a little red welt between the pointer and middle finger on my right hand. William must be sore, as well, because he's rubbing down the reddest of his fingers. Watching his lovely hands massage one another, I notice a worn band of skin round his ring finger, on the left hand. The kind of mark that comes from wearing a ring, always the same ring, for years and years. I look at this, and then up to his adorable face, highlighted by a faint blond stubble.

'We haven't properly met,' he says, shifting into the seat next to mine. 'Can I get you a drink?'

Dale has disappeared, and we are alone in our corner. After fifteen minutes of discussing our respective lives and habitual lack of musical spoons therein, there has been no mention of wives or girlfriends or boyfriends. William's shoulder is leant into mine and I can feel his chest expand and contract. His breath is sweet and grainy, like wild honey or expensive beer. The grain of his suit touches my bare skin at the small gap that has emerged between the bottom of my shirt and the waist of my jeans; it's cool and smooth. He is telling a funny story. I laugh. He pulls at the collar of his shirt, and says, 'Have you ever seen the inside of a private Silver and Blue Class cabin, then?'

As we stand, William lets his left arm fall around my shoulders. His hand opens and closes gently, caressing my bare arm. I watch his ring finger, sliding up and down with its band of wear. The fire in my stomach is suddenly replaced by a deep liquid sick. I notice I've stopped moving. 'Coming, yeah?' says William, his robin's-egg eyes gleaming.

'I don't think… I mean…'

And then I am walking down dark, wobbling cars to my seat, alone. I climb over Roger and pull my jacket out from under my seat and over me. I'm shivering like crazy. Roger has not moved. I lean over and kiss his dark forehead before putting my head down on my serving tray, closing my eyes, and pretending to sleep.

EMMA HOOPER is a freelance violist and writer from Canada. She is lucky enough to do what she loves most of the time, including performing as a core member of the popular modern string quartet The Stringbeans and composing written work of all genres.

Contact: emma.hooper@sparksanthology.co.uk
              www.stringbeansquartet.com

Robbin' Hoodlums

David Catzman

from a screenplay

*Guy's previously humdrum existence has been enlivened only by his klep-
tomania. His life takes an adventurous turn, however, when he unwittingly
becomes the getaway driver for Mac, a seasoned bank robber.*

INT. MAC'S DUPLEX – FRONT HALL – CONTINUOUS

MAC stands against the door, waiting, gun in hand. GUY knocks.
Mac opens the door, pulls Guy in, then closes the door quickly and
locks it. Mac pushes Guy up against the door and puts the gun to his
head.

A television can be heard in the background.

>   MAC
> What the hell are you thinking, bringing your heat up
> in here? You have five seconds to give me a reason
> not to kill your sorry white ass.

>   GUY
> Uh... uh... I'm a bleeder.

>   MAC
> What?

>   GUY
> I bleed a lot. I'd make a big mess in your front hall.

>   MAC
> That's it? That's your great reason?

>   GUY
> I don't do well under pressure.

>   TV REPORTER
> In other news today, a man was arrested after a failed

bank robbery at Key Bank.

Mac looks over to the television. He lets go of Guy and runs over. He turns up the volume.

                    TV REPORTER
The man, later identified as Tim Piper, opened fire on the crowded bank, killing a teller who activated the silent alarm. Piper's accomplice ran from the scene and escaped the police after a high-speed chase. The police are currently looking to question Guy Peterson, the owner of the red Volkswagen Golf in which Piper's unidentified partner fled.

Guy's eyes widen and he begins to scream uncontrollably.

                    MAC
Shut up. Man, shut up. Shut it.

Mac stands up and grabs Guy from behind, covering his mouth. They both fall back on to the couch, Mac's hand still covering Guy's mouth.

                    MAC (calmly)
Now, I'm gonna take my hand off your mouth, but any more screaming and I'll need a good team of carpet cleaners. Get it?

Guy nods slowly. Mac slowly removes his hand.

                    GUY
The cops are after me... I'm a fugitive!

                    MAC
Listen. You leave here, ditch the car and report it stolen. Then, call the cops and tell them I threw you out of the car after we lost them. You don't know anything else. Got it?

                    GUY
There's one problem. The cops are at my house right now.

MAC

So?

GUY (embarrassed)

I have a small... um... kleptomania problem.

MAC

What?

GUY

I've been stealing stuff lately. A lot of stuff.

MAC

Why?

GUY

Boredom. What's your excuse?

Mac glares at him.

GUY

Sorry.

Guy thinks to himself.

GUY

I have nowhere to go. Maybe I should just turn myself in.

MAC

No can do, bro. You know what I look like and you know where I live. (He thinks) Tell you what, stay here tonight. Sleep on it. I could use a lift somewhere tomorrow any way.

GUY

Really? You'd do that for me?

MAC

Yeah. Let's get your car off the street, though.

INT. POLICE STATION – BRADLEY'S OFFICE – LATER

BRADLEY paces in front of DOYLE and HUNT, smoking.

                    DOYLE
I've never seen so much crap. I mean, it looks like he's
been stealing stuff for years. Stuff that no one would ever
notice went missing. The guy has about twenty sets of
stolen salt and pepper shakers.

                    HUNT
Who would ever need that much salt and pepper?

                    BRADLEY
I think it's pretty clear what's going on. (To himself) The
guy started out small. He liked the rush he'd get from
stealing things. But, as time wore on, the feeling wore
off. He wanted to steal more things, bigger things. He
found Piper and his partner and figured he'd give bank
robbing a try. Now, he's in over his head. He's scared.
He's gonna run. (To Hunt and Doyle) I want you two to
get over to his office right away. We've got to find this
guy before he skips town. Find out if anyone has any idea
where he might go. Friends, family, neighbours, anything.
I don't want this one to slip through our fingers. We've
got to get him while the trail is hot.

                    DOYLE AND HUNT (Together)
Right, chief.

They exit.

INT. GUY'S CAR – OUTSIDE UNION BANK – THE NEXT DAY

Guy drives.
                    MAC
Right here. This is perfect.

Guy pulls up at the side of the road. Mac puts on a ski mask and grabs
his Youth Development Centre bag.

                        GUY
                 Whoa! What are you doing?

                        MAC
                 Sorry, kid. I need some cash.

Mac pulls out a gun. Guy looks out the window and sees that Mac has
had him pull the car over in front of a bank.

                        GUY
                 You're robbing another bank?

                        MAC
                 Yeah, and you're my getaway driver.

                        GUY
                 No way! I'm not a criminal.

Mac rolls up his ski mask.

                        MAC
                 Then why did you have to sleep at my place last
                 night?

Guy thinks about this.

                        MAC
                 Face it, Guy. You're running from the law and no-
                 thing's gonna change that. You have nowhere else to go.

Guy realises that Mac is right. Mac exits the car. He leans into the car
through the window.

                        MAC
                 And if you leave me stranded...

                        GUY
                 You'll go to the police?

Mac rolls down his ski mask.

> MAC
>
> I'll hunt you down and kill you.

> GUY
>
> Pleasant. Don't worry, I'll be here. I have to collect my cut.

> MAC
>
> What?

> GUY
>
> I get half of what you take. That's only fair.

> MAC
>
> Fair would be me killing you for showing up at my place last night.

Guy takes out a cell phone.

> GUY
>
> Fair would be me calling the cops and giving them their bank robber.

> MAC
>
> You drive a hard bargain. Gimme your number in case I need to get a hold of you.

Mac takes out his cell phone.

EXT. UNION BANK – CONTINUOUS

Mac begins walking up the steps to the entrance.

Guy watches him from the car.

Mac gets to the bank doors and enters.

INT. UNION BANK – CONTINUOUS

GUARD #1, an elderly feeble-looking guard, stands by the entrance.
Mac grabs him.

                         MAC (quietly)
              Don't say a word. Gimme your piece.

Guard #1 is wheezing. He takes his gun and gives it to Mac.

                            MAC
              Afternoon, everyone! If I could please have your
              attention for a minute!

Everyone stops what they're doing. Some scream. Others drop to the
floor.

Mac takes the handcuffs off Guard #1's belt and hands them to Guard
#1.

                      MAC (to Guard #1)
              Cuff your hands together behind your back.

                          GUARD #1
              You pansy.

                            MAC
              What?

                          GUARD #1
              You heard me. Can't even take out an eighty-year-old
              guard without a gun.

                            MAC
              What'd you say, grandpa?

                          GUARD #1
              Your hearing worse than mine, boy?

Guard #1 starts to sweat.

                          GUARD #1
              Someone oughtta beat the wax right outta your ears.

                    MAC
        You're writing cheques your ass can't cash, old man.

                  GUARD #1
        Try me, bitch.

Guard #1 raises his fists.

                    MAC
        Alright, let's make this quick, though. I've got a
        transaction to make.

Mac holsters his gun in his pants, puts the bag on the floor and
raises his fists.

Guard #1 begins panting.

                  GUARD #1
        I'm gonna beat you so bad... you'll be eating through
        a straw... for the rest of your life.

Mac winds up, preparing to punch Guard #1. Guard #1 goes wide-
eyed, grabs his chest and falls back before Mac throws a punch.
Mac looks around curiously, realising what has happened and is
embarrassed.

INT. GUY'S CAR – OUTSIDE UNION BANK – CONTINUOUS

Guy nervously checks the car's mirrors for any sign of the police.
He is jolted when his cell phone rings. He picks it up.

                    GUY
        Hello.

                MAC (off screen.)
        We have a situation that requires some assistance in
        here, now.

Guy timidly gets out of the car. He looks on the front seat and sees
another ski mask. He reaches over, picks it up and puts it on. He

enters the bank.

INT. UNION BANK – CONTINUOUS

Guard #1 lies on the floor in obvious pain.

> GUY
>
> You shot the guard?

> MAC
>
> No.

> GUY
>
> Well, he doesn't look too comfortable.

> MAC
>
> I imagine he's not.

> GUY
>
> What did you do to him?

> MAC
>
> Nothing.

> GUY
>
> You expect me to believe that he's writhing in agony
> on the floor and you had nothing to do with it?

> MAC
>
> Yes.

> GUY
>
> Well, I'm not that dumb. So why don't you cut the shit?

> MAC
>
> He's having a heart attack.

Guy begins to freak out.

                           GUY
              We have to call an ambulance.

                           MAC
              That's not an option.

                           GUY
              So we let him die? That's murder.

                           MAC
              If an ambulance is dispatched, a squad car comes with
              it. That can't happen.

Guy undoes Guard #1's shirt and listens for a heartbeat.

DAVID CATZMAN, born in Toronto, Canada, has been writing since before he could crawl. He has had two of his plays produced – *Four Padded Walls* and *Murder Most Foul* – and has recently finished his first full-length screenplay, *Robbin' Hoodlums*.

Contact: david.catzman@sparksanthology.co.uk

A Place of Safety

Tamsin Reeves

from a novel

March 2001. Martha's husband, Colin, has left her. Here she meets her potential lodger, an Afghan asylum seeker.

I opened the door to a clean-shaven, softly spoken man.
'You are Mrs Anderson?'

It was a frosty evening and he had the collar of his leather jacket turned up. I could see remnants of Genghis Khan's genes in the slightly oriental features but he was taller than I expected and had green eyes. It was difficult to guess his age. Somewhere between thirty and forty.

'You must be Ismail. Come in.'

He took his shoes off at the door, which I liked. But he wouldn't sit down in the living room. He kept looking round as if he expected someone more interesting to walk in. I smiled, but he didn't. I wasn't sure if he was nervous or arrogant. He seemed pretty surly. We discussed rent, terms and conditions. He kept nodding and I searched for a polite way of saying I didn't want him. I'd have to show him the room first. Then I'd tell him there was someone else to interview and promise to let him know. He followed me up to the attic and smiled at Jessica. So he could smile.

'I am Ismail.' He shook her hand. She liked that. He was taking her seriously, treating her as a grown-up.

'My daughter, Jessica. She's been helping me clean the room.'

'Thank you. Is very lovely,' he said and drew out a tape measure. I began to warm to him. It would be difficult to say no, anyway, after he'd gone to the trouble of measuring it up. And no one else would ever call the attic lovely.

'You help Ismail. Hold the tape measure while I make some tea,' I said.

I heard them all clattering downstairs a little later. Curiosity must have dragged Josh away from his computer game.

'Joshua's my brother,' Jessica said. 'He can be very noisy.'

'Is OK. I like noise.'

'And anyway, I'm not noisy,' Josh shouted.

I prepared some cheese and biscuits to give them time together. I'd leave it to the kids to decide. If they liked him, he could have the room.

When I took the tea through, Ismail was sitting cross-legged on the floor showing Josh how to fold a paper aeroplane. That sort of thing would really piss Colin off. I offered Ismail the room.

Needling Colin had become a hobby. I told him about my lodger on a Friday night in late February. It was bitterly cold and he was hiding his new haircut under a woolly hat. He was there to pick up the kids but Jessica was still helping Josh pack his bag. Colin had to come in and wait.

He tried to be reasonable but his mouth twitched with the effort. 'I see. Well, it's good of you to take in a refugee.' There was a pause. He sipped his tea at the kitchen table and struggled with the knowledge he'd no right to interfere. 'It'll boost your finances, won't it?' But he couldn't help himself. 'Do you know much about him? Has he got references?'

'No, but I didn't drag him in off the street. A friend of Carly's sent him.' I crunched a nicotine tab and he winced.

'You're not supposed to chew those things. Or take them for longer than a few months. They're not supposed to become an addiction in themselves.'

'Tell me something I don't know, Colin. At least I'm not smoking. And if I want to crunch instead of suck, you should be grateful it won't be your problem.'

Jesus, I slept with the man for thirteen years and he was looking surprised, as if nothing so vulgar as sex had ever been mentioned between us.

He was an expert at sidestepping. 'Yeah, you've done well with the smoking. Now you can become the founder member of Tabs Anonymous.'

'Actually I joined the PTA thinking it was Patches and Tabs.'

He laughed and I glimpsed what it could be like if I suspended hostilities. There was a moment of weakness when I longed to take his hand and hold it to my cheek. Then I looked at his new hairstyle. He'd been recreated in another's image. Hair still flopped over his forehead but the untidy-yellow-mop look had gone. She must have decided to smarten him up, and it was sleeker, more layered. It didn't go with his old personality.

His mind was still running on the strange man in the attic. 'This woman knows your tenant well, does she? I mean, you have to be careful with kids in the house.'

'I don't think Carly's friend would send me a paedophile.'

'No, not deliberately, of course. I'm sorry. It's just, you know... I can't help worrying about you all.'

'So far he's a perfect lodger,' I told him. 'He's been here a week and he's very courteous when we pass on the stairs. No trouble really, except for a bit of banging and sawing while he works on the conversion. He has his shower at five in the morning so the bathroom's free for us and he always carries his shoes upstairs to protect the carpets. It's nice to have a man in the house again, especially such a considerate one.'

'Fine. Well, I hope it works out. Do you think the kids have finished packing?'

Colin now knew as much as I did about Ismail, who kept to his room. I barely saw him. He didn't bother me and I didn't bother him. I couldn't leave it like that, so I invited him for dinner. His English was much better than I expected but he was so formal and polite, avoiding all eye contact. He was very vague about how he came to Britain. When he left his chicken untouched because it wasn't *halal*, I began to wish I'd kept my curiosity in check. Perfect tenant he might be, but he was a boring guest. Jessica and Josh were rapidly losing interest, too, but after dinner Ismail picked up Josh's fire engine and the other half of its ladder.

'You want I fix this?' he asked.

Josh shrugged. 'Mum stuck it but the glue didn't work.'

Ismail disappeared upstairs and came down with a tube of super-glue.

'You are using this?'

'No,' I said. 'We don't have superglue any more because Josh got hold of it and I had to cut off some of Jessica's hair.' I demonstrated the problem using my fingers as scissors.

He laughed for the first time. 'Same like me. In London my friend was saying be careful but my fingers are like this.' He held two fingers together. 'I must cut my skin with a knife.'

'How long were you in London?'

'More than one year.'

'So why did you come to this place?' I couldn't imagine wanting to leave London for a small, very English, market town.

'My friends tell me Swindon is good place for jobs and cheap for living, so I was asking agencies. They found for me this job in Malliston.'

While he spoke, Ismail worked on the fire engine, holding the two ends together to give the glue time to work.

'So you couldn't find a job in London?'

'For six months is not allowed for asylum seekers to work. After this time, I got my papers. But I must have reference to get jobs. And CV. In my English class they are teaching me these things, but was too difficult in London. Many refugees. People are giving us jobs but they want pay cash, small money. I don't like this kind of work. It will take long time before the Home Office is asking me to come for interview. After, they will tell me if I can have asylum or I must go back. If I pay tax, have proper job, is better for this interview.' He released the ladder and it slowly bent at the joint. Ismail shook his head. 'Is for fingers, not fire engine,' he said.

When he laughed, his face became younger, softer. It was his clothes that gave him his slightly dishevelled appearance. They were clean and ironed but hopelessly unfashionable – a grey diamond-patterned sweater over a grey shirt and shapeless brown trousers. He must have bought everything in a size too big, but he gave the impression of having shrunk inside them.

The next day he rang the doorbell. I thought he must have lost his keys but he held out a plastic bag.

'I want give this for Josh and Jessica.'

When I called them he presented Josh with a new fire engine. For Jessica he had a white linen handkerchief, heavily embroidered across one corner.

'My sister made this,' he said, shaking it out. 'How old you are?'

'Eleven, nearly twelve.'

'My sister was making this when she is twelve. She will be happy if I give it to you.' He turned to me. 'Thank you for the dinner, Mrs Anderson. I'm sorry for my English. I want take English class but I can't find in Malliston.'

'I'm afraid you'll have to try Swindon.' I was thinking: I'm an English teacher... but don't offer. I've got enough to do. I'm a single parent with a full-time job. My mouth was already in motion, though, and I heard myself say, 'I could teach you if you want.'

'How much you want for lessons?'

'Nothing.'

It was the fire engine's fault. If he hadn't come bearing gifts, at most I would have offered to find him a teacher.

'So I will cook for you and family when we are having lessons.'

'Great. That would be lovely.'

I was immediately furious with myself for creating a situation we couldn't get out of. He seemed to want to repay every kindness and I was doing the same. I was sure we'd both end up regretting our loss of privacy.

It worked out better than I thought. The kids had grown tired of my uninspired weekly menu and loved his kebabs. He wouldn't cook pork, of course, and always used *halal* meat he bought in Pakistani shops in Swindon. Not that I cared how my lamb became a kebab, so long as I didn't have to witness the actual throat-slitting. On the nights he cooked, I taught him English for an hour afterwards and then he disappeared upstairs. I was on to past participles before I persuaded him not to call me Mrs Anderson. And became Mrs Martha.

About that time we also established eye contact. It was the night I asked about his job in Afghanistan. I was used to looking at him full on while he addressed the side of my head or my mouth.

'I was medical technician.' This time he looked directly at me.

The intimacy was disconcerting and I dropped my gaze. '*A*,' I corrected him. 'I was *a* medical technician. But can't you find the same work in a hospital here?'

'Ismail shook his head. 'I was working for leprosy and TB patients.'

'Oh I see. Yes, leprosy's not really a problem round here.'

'Is big problem in Afghanistan. My father was farmer – *a* farmer. We live in small village. Also my two brothers bigger than me, my small sister, my mother. One day my father put his foot near to fire like this. We can see his foot is too hot but he can't feel burning. When my mother was touching his arm with a needle, nothing. He can't feel it. Then we understood is leprosy. My uncle was also having this disease. When people saw it, they made him go away from his village. He was sick, can't work, but they sent him out. Leprosy is just a disease, but in my country they think is because you did something bad in your life. But also they are thinking they can catch it. If it is punishment, how you can catch it? But they are very afraid of this disease.'

I remembered beggars with leprosy in India. Often they'd lost fingers and toes and it had disfigured their faces. 'But I thought there were drugs now to cure it,' I said.

Ismail nodded. 'Yes, but you must take different medicines every day for long time. My father went to Bamiyan, a special clinic, so no one in our village will know he is sick. My brothers must take care of the farm and my mother. I went with my father.'

'Bamiyan? That's just been in the news. Isn't that where the Taliban blew up the giant buddhas?'

He looked at me steadily. 'Is terrible thing, Taliban destroy our statues. Everyone in the world is very sad for the buddhas but what is in English newspapers when Taliban killed all Hazara people in Bamiyan?'

I didn't know what to say. I couldn't remember reading about a massacre there. Seeing my embarrassment, he smiled and changed the subject.

'Was good time for me. Was one English doctor in the clinic. His wife was teaching me English. She found for me a school. My father was working in this clinic and taking medicine. After one year he went home. He said was better for me I stay in school. In the night I was working in a hotel to get money. After, they gave me job in the clinic, sent me to Pakistan for training. In Afghanistan, people see me like a doctor.' He shrugged. 'Here, I am nothing.'

I opened my mouth to say something reassuring but his watchful eyes defied me to pity or patronise him. He was stating his current position but he wasn't defining himself. 'Let's look at the future tense on page thirty,' I said.

Jessica chose the cinema and pizzas for her birthday. Colin, Josh and I sat at one table while the girls giggled at another. Her aunts gave her a selection of boy bands for her new CD player. Mum sent her another bible, a grown-up version this time, with all the begettings and begottings and no pictures. Colin stayed until she went to bed and we both went up to say goodnight.

'I wish I could wake up and find you here in the morning,' she told him.

He stroked her forehead. 'I'm not far away, Jess.'

We all knew that was a lie, however true it might be in miles.

'If you want to stay over, you can have Josh's room tonight,' I offered. 'I'll even cook you egg and bacon.' I was trying. For Jessica's sake? For mine? To put Colin on the spot? I wasn't sure why. But I wanted him to say yes.

'Please, Dad.'

There was a long pause. In the mirror we resembled a tableau from the manger scene, except our baby was twelve and wrapped in a dressing gown.

'I'd like to. Really I would. But you see... er, I promised...' And the tableau fell apart.

TAMSIN REEVES left Britain as soon as she could, to teach in Nigeria, Kuwait, Sri Lanka and Ghana. Along the way, she picked up a husband and produced four children. She also worked in Pakistan, on a leprosy programme with Hazara Afghan colleagues, an experience which spawned this novel.

Contact: tamsin.reeves@sparksanthology.co.uk

Selected Poems

Yasmine Haldeman

My Mother the Horse

My mother once embodied a horse named Shadow,
She was the biggest horse in the yard.

Beneath me I could feel her strength
And I was faced with the ever-so-appropriate

Who will take control?
I rode her in the English countryside, the Mendips.

The entire time I felt sorry for putting my weight
On her back so I tried to lift my buttocks,

Relieving her bladder while she peed
And you know how she thanked me?

She took off, took off in a gallop
And she knew I couldn't handle the pace

So I screamed, I screamed bloody murder!
I must have scared her as much as she scared me.

She threw me off the saddle
Kind enough to halt in soft bunches of grass.

I tried not to cry, to show her she had gotten the best of me
I took her reins and struggled to lead her by foot

But she was too strong and drug me through the mud.

Brown

She be flashin them shades,
That chocolate,
That caramel,
That butterscotch,
Brown

That golden,
That honey-kissed,
That sun-blessed
Brown

Skin in white cotton,
Hand-picked by
Great-grandmother
Brown

Brown skin don't be,
Wearin' tights,
Don't be,
Glarin' ghost-like,
Don't be
Brown in a bottle
Brown…

White beds with blue lights,
Your skin sizzles,
Wrinkled-white,
Bone-white,
Always-white, you will never be
Brown

African Brown,
Brazilian Brown,
South American Brown,
Indian Brown,
Beautiful skin,
Beautiful Brown

Birdland

Haven't you noticed
Chirping has ceased,
Branches are empty,
Formation is square?

I guess the swallows
Never left Capistrano,
They still soar above
Santa Catalina Island.

The vacant limbs of
Douglas fir
Are left silent to hover
In cool Pacific breezes.

Feeders are full of seed,
Gaping to the brown
Squirrel, the black crow;
Those curiously vicious.

When's the last time
You saw the egg of a
Blue jay; baby blue
And speckled grey?

I might have spotted
A great blue heron,
Sipping from a lake
In the Sandia Mountains.

The Deception of a White Flag
A *Maria* poem

On the phone,
Words are wired
From New Mexico.

Say she's got a dog,
And a new house,
Say she's happy without

Me and off to meet
The Girlfriend's parents,
Anxiety pervades.

I'm doomed cause
I never met a love
Who didn't love me

That I didn't love,
And now she's saying
I can stay at her place.

Yasmine Haldeman

Scenes from a Hospital Room Window

After the first August rain,
I look down to a cement garden,
Watching dinosaurs form and saturate in shapes.

I look out to the skyline,
Notice the variegated colour;
Forest-green-aqua-blue-endless-sky.

Inside the room behind the glass,
I can barely breathe,
Mother is taking up the room's oxygen.

Plastic tubes snake through her nose,
And in her neck a central line
Connects four possible ports to Narcotic Island.

Again, I look to the cement garden
And, as the sun battles Pacific fog,
Precipitation begins to vaporise.

Midnight Blue

I stare out my window;
To the left there is bird shit,
To the right there is a church tower,
And in the middle,
Rising through slate grey clouds streaked
With midnight blue,
Is you.

Tonight you are nearly full.
In sync with my cycle,
You have me disturbed,
Stirring in my bed,
Watching as your butter-yellow light
Hits my eyes through fluttering branches,
And sluggishly moves out of sight.

YASMINE HALDEMAN was raised in the northwest United States.
She received a BA in Visual Arts from the College of Santa Fe in New
Mexico. She chose the MA programme at Bath Spa University to
explore sexuality and relationships through confessional poetry. She is
now living in the States, where she continues to write and perform her
poetry.

Contact: yasmine.haldeman@sparksanthology.co.uk

A Glitch in the Frame

Joachim Noreiko

from *Drowning in Air*

Billy, with seventy-two years and five husbands behind her, has decided it's time to come and live nearer to her family. Daughter Maddy, son-in-law Greg and grandchildren Zo and Barney, now in their early twenties, are all helping with the move. Sally, the youngest grandchild, is absent, for reasons not yet explained.

The dismantled table, the chairs, the sections of the wardrobe and several stacks of boxes were all in Billy's drive by the time Barney and Zo got back from taking the unwanted things to the charity shop in town.

As Zo carefully reversed the van, Barney looked in the wing mirror and saw Maddy coming out of the house carrying a stack of boxes. He saw her head straight for Greg's back, but didn't have time to cry a pointless warning.

Maddy crashed into Greg, and the top box toppled. Barney didn't see the rest, but imagined it: Maddy sidestepping, trying to rebalance herself and catch the box at the same time. Doomed to failure.

Billy had come out to see what the noise was. She was opening the boxes with Maddy to check for damage by the time Barney got round from his side of the van.

Maddy looked into a box.

'Oh,' she said.

She took out one of her father's sketches of Billy. Something had punched through the cardboard backing; the paper was ripped.

'I'm so sorry, Mama,' she said.

'Accidents happen,' said Billy. She took out the other one, in a similar condition.

'They're ruined, both of them,' said Maddy, her voice despondent and flat.

'Nonsense,' said Billy.

Greg hunkered down beside Maddy and took the creased one from her hands.

'We can iron them flat and get new frames. You won't notice a thing.'

Zo and Barney were standing, unsure what to say.

Maddy shook her head slowly. Billy reached out her hands to take her daughter's shoulders, and brought them near to her, but Maddy didn't respond as she let herself be tilted. Her face had an expression of profound despair.

'They're only drawings, and quite plain ones at that,' said Billy.

'They were Dad's,' said Maddy, her voice beginning to break. 'My dad's drawings,' she said.

Barney suddenly felt very uncomfortable. He glanced towards Zo.

'Your real dad, but not your proper dad,' said Billy quietly, meaning the man who'd fathered her rather than raised her. 'Not the dad that counts.'

'He still matters,' said Maddy. 'There's not much else we have of him.'

Billy made shushing noises. Barney instinctively reached for his sister's hand. It was sweaty. He thought of ice cream on sunny days like this one, dribbling down the side of cones and on to palms.

'Shall we go in?' asked Billy. 'Maybe sit down and have a glass of water?'

'I keep losing pieces of my family,' said Maddy. Her lower lip was white where her teeth had pressed into it.

Billy looked meaningfully at Greg. He put a hand on Maddy's shoulder, awkwardly, as though making a contact that could easily result in something being broken.

Zo turned to Barney and said, 'We should go inside.' She tugged on his hand but he resisted. Billy glanced at them but said nothing.

Maddy moved in towards Greg, her entire body shifting on the spot where she knelt, though her face didn't respond to him at all. Contact was made between them for a moment, then Greg moved back, rocking on his heels, almost an involuntary movement of recoil.

'It's always going to be like this,' said Maddy. She stood up, steadying herself with her hands on her thighs rather than on Billy or Greg either side of her. 'I'm so sorry about the drawings, Mama. I wish we could... I don't know.' Billy and Greg stood up, too.

'It doesn't matter, it doesn't matter at all,' said Billy.

'Will you be all right to start loading the van without me?' said Maddy. 'I'd like some time by myself.'

'Of course, Mum,' said Barney. Maddy nodded and raised a hand to rub across her eyes, then went into the house. It was only then that Barney realised what he'd called her: she was always 'Maddy', never 'Mum'. No one else appeared to have noticed.

They resumed work without talking, and broke off for dinner a couple of hours later, when Greg declared that there wasn't really much left to deal with other than what they needed to eat with and sleep on.

Maddy wasn't in the living room or the kitchen. Billy supposed she might be in the garden, maybe sitting on the mildewed bench that was being left. She stood aimlessly outside for a few moments.

'Is Maddy upstairs?' she asked back in the kitchen.

Zo was trying not to laugh at Barney messing about with the frozen pizza he was unwrapping, pretending to be a stereotype Italian chef, whizzing it around his head, then twirling his moustache while sprinkling toppings onto it.

'I thought you went to get her from the garden,' he said. He stopped the act, mid-twirl.

'No sign of her out there.'

Zo went upstairs to look. They heard her tread on the floorboards, moving around the different rooms. Barney and Greg got back to setting places at the kitchen table and checking the oven was warm enough. Billy had a bad feeling. Something tugged at her memory but refused to show itself in clear light.

Zo's voice came from the top of the stairs. 'She's not anywhere up here. Billy. Where is she?'

And Billy remembered her husband, David, the teacher. The awkward decay of their marriage as her fortieth birthday approached. The point at which she realised she didn't want the comfortable routine that life with him offered: the proofreading, the odd research trip to some minor historical site, the cosy evenings. Maddy had been difficult and irritable for months, beyond the usual teenage strop, and Billy had a hunch her daughter sensed the change in the air. So when Billy decided the time was right to make her feelings known, she did so to both husband and daughter, thinking that at sixteen Maddy was old enough to be included. It hadn't gone well: Maddy shouted, then cried, then seemed to calm down and said she wanted to be alone. 'She needs time, Belinda,' David had said to Billy. Then he'd added, 'As do I.' And then Billy knew it was really over. He wouldn't protest, he wouldn't be angry. He just wanted to talk, in a dispassionate way that made Billy feel the matter of their marriage was being analysed like some historical decline. It had meant they didn't realise Maddy had gone until it was dark.

Zo must have caught something from Billy's face as she came back into the kitchen.

'She's gone, hasn't she?' she said.

'Yes, I think so,' said Billy.

The family was divided. Barney thought she'd come back soon;

she'd only gone for a walk in the cooling summer evening. Greg was rather more worried. 'Where can she have gone?' he kept repeating. Billy suggested a few old friends still living nearby she could have gone to see. She spoke slowly, as if after some thought.

For a few minutes, they talked round in circles (what to do, where to start looking), until Zo broke a link by asking Billy for the addresses of Maddy's friends. That done, she went to put on her shoes. Barney followed.

'You're just going to knock on the doors of people who won't know you?' he asked her.

'Why the hell not? Look, the sooner I find her, the sooner this is all over. She comes back, we have dinner, get to bed, and tomorrow we go home, end of story.'

'It's really not that big a deal. She'll have just gone for a wander and forgotten the time,' said Barney. 'This is her home, too, that she's leaving behind. That matters to some people.'

Zo looked up from tying her laces.

'You're not coming along with me?' she asked Barney.

'I will, on second thoughts,' said Billy, arriving from the kitchen. 'It'll be quicker if one of us knows where we're going.' She slipped on her shoes.

'I'll stay here,' said Barney. 'In case she comes back.'

Zo flipped out her mobile and checked the display. 'Well, call me if she does.'

Billy opened the door and stepped out. She huffed at the evening. 'I could do with a cardigan, but they're all in the van now.'

Zo followed.

'Louise will remember you,' said Billy as they turned on to the street. 'Maddy took you and Barney along a few times when you were little.'

'Right,' said Zo.

Neither of them said anything for a while. Billy walked with her arms crossed, Zo with her hands in the pockets of her pale cotton trousers.

Some children were gathered around a lamppost, throwing something up at it that looked like an item of clothing. At first Zo thought they were taunting one of the group, but then she saw the boy who was without a T-shirt was just as keen on flinging it as high as he could. One caught Zo's eye and said, 'Yeah?' accusingly. Another stated openly, 'If we cover the top, the light comes on.' Why they might want to switch on a streetlight in the first place needed no explanation, obviously.

Zo shook her head to herself as she and Billy walked on and, not for the first time, thought of what the kids in her classes turned into after hours.

'I did think Maddy might have wanted to see her friends up here anyway,' said Billy, once they had left the kids behind. 'Even though she hasn't seen them in a few years. It's been different since Sally died.'

Zo reacted as if stung.

She dropped her pace a little, falling behind so Billy couldn't see her face.

'Everything changed, didn't it?' Billy continued, walking on without missing a beat. 'Your mother and father, you, Barney. Everything changed.' She spoke like she was reciting a sad poem.

'We're managing,' said Zo.

'Yes, you are,' said Billy. 'Here's the street.'

Louise and Guy lived in a house similar to Billy's, semi-detached and set back from the road. It was only as they walked up to the door that Zo really thought how silly it would feel to ring the doorbell and say she was looking for her mother. Her earlier resolve had gone.

But when a man Zo assumed to be Guy answered the door, Billy greeted him, and without hesitation explained that Maddy was on an errand, but had left her purse behind and, since she'd said she might drop in on Louise and Guy, might she be there?

Zo watched Billy gloss over the exact nature of the errand and how Guy bought it completely. He beamed at Billy, then looked at Zo.

'Of course, you must be Zoë! Do come in, both of you. Louise would love to see you.'

'Well, we really should find her, but just for a little while,' said Billy.

Guy called into the house, 'Lou! Billy and Maddy's daughter, Zoë, are here!'

'Zo,' muttered Zo, but to herself. Nobody had called her Zoë since she was about four, when Barney shortened her name.

Guy went ahead of them in the hall, and Zo had a chance to whisper, 'What are we doing?' to Billy.

'She might turn up here,' Billy said back to her.

'What about the other people you mentioned?'

'We can't leave; we only just got here,' said Billy.

They turned into a room whose dominant hue was pink. A sofa glared from beneath a tall lamp with a tasselled shade. Matching pelmets and tie-backs faced each other from opposite ends. For a second, Zo thought the armchair by the window had a large cushion on it with a needlepoint picture of a cat, but it moved and greeted them and re-vealed itself to be Louise, a small woman in a loose jumper. She came forward towards them.

'Zoë! Zoë!' she said, as if not quite believing it.

Zo couldn't keep her eyes off the huge cat on the front of the jump-er. It was the most tastelessly vile thing she could imagine. She wanted to say to Billy, *Hang on, we're in the wrong house. No way can these Murgatroyds be Maddy's friends.* Murgatroyds were dorks, those with a penchant for the naff – an old Barney word. It applied perfectly.

She couldn't believe how different this place was to their own house, or that of any of Maddy's gang. It wasn't just the style of the place; there was no mess or clutter, no indication that the space was ac-tually being used for *living in.* At Julia's, for instance, you could prob-ably find socks drying on the hall radiator; at Other Ann's there'd be children's toys strategically placed where most likely to cause injury to the soles of the feet.

Billy and Louise chatted politely about the vagaries of moving house. Guy occasionally looked at Zo in a way she found uncomfort-able, leery. Listening to the conversation, she learned that they'd never had children. It made sense: this wasn't the sort of environment that kids could live in and not ruin, in her experience.

She also thought she understood why Maddy hadn't been to see these people in three years. How could they understand what she had lost? How could Maddy take their heartfelt platitudes and thank them with sincerity?

Her mind drifted to Sally, and the sketches of Billy, and the draw-ings on the stairs at home.

The day Sally died, a panicked Barney on the phone said: *Zo, Sally's not answering.*

Oh, she's deaf. Count it as a blessing. (Zo was drunk, back from a Sunday-afternoon pub crawl with the other trainee teachers.)

No, she's in the bathroom; she's been there over an hour.

Tell her she still smells.

I can't get her to answer. I keep knocking, but there's the radio, but surely she must hear me, and Maddy and Greg aren't back till late to-night. Fuck, Zo, what should I do? Break the door down?

(Something *clicked* in Zo, like a switch. The effects of the alcohol dissipated, but it was like clarity rushing into her mind.)

When did you last hear her?

I don't listen at the bathroom door while my sister's in there! Nathan rang, so I knocked on the door to tell her. Fuck it, I'm breaking it down.

(A bang. A grunt of pain from Barney: knocking down a door is harder in reality than on television. A string of bangs, Barney kicking as hard as he could.)

Zo, Zo – she's under the water, I've got to hang up, I've got to call—

(Nothing.)

JOACHIM NOREIKO is thirty-one, and lives in a village on the York-shire coast that applied for middle-of-nowhere status but wasn't central enough. He is a classically trained pianist and is learning to juggle. He is working on his second novel while the first languishes.

Contact: joachim.noreiko@sparksanthology.co.uk
        www.joachim.org.uk

The Tale of the Frozen Potato

Anthea Nicholson

from *The Region of Roses*

The Region of Roses is set in Georgia. The narrator recalls the events that led her into the confused and corrupt world of the post-perestroika interim period. Her story is constantly interrupted by the overlapping 'tales' of her lover, a Georgian writer.

When Jafa suggests the potato expedition, the friends instantly agree. They take practically nothing. They start off straight away. Night. There's supposed to be a curfew but they pass others slinking through the dark streets. If you don't stop, don't make an alarm, it's safe. There are no snipers. Unless, of course, you count the stars being shot at.

Maybe that accounts for the UFO that many citizens confirm, without a doubt, they see hovering over Tbilisi. The craft can only be recognised as an absence of stars, oval or circular or even square, many variables, because it's impossible to distinguish between starless space and the true outline of the spaceship. On overcast nights it hovers below the clouds and throws its smudged, ever-changing shadow up on to the water vapour.

Some claim its real form is similar to a multi-tiered wedding cake, but revolving. Others say it reminds them of a pillow. One is convinced it's a copy of his left shoe. All agree that its lights, which come close enough to illuminate the sides of buildings, are day-coloured. It makes no noise.

Children insist they can see it at noon, but its day-coloured light is invisible without the contrast of night, and its impressionistic form easily confused with the distant mountain peaks or the flash of sun on a tower block window. So that can't be proved.

Maybe the star-aimed bullets reached their destination far beyond the atmosphere, maybe they went whizzing past the windows of a space-craft and the adventurers inside couldn't resist coming down for a close look at what's going on.

Not just market traders see the lights of the vehicle but intellectuals and politicians too. Anyway, that night when the three friends make their way out of the city, the UFO must've flown away. Tbilisi is in darkness.

'I saw it,' Petre tells his friends as they walk. 'It was a sign but I didn't take notice. If I had, she'd still be alive. I saw it twice. Sunday night and Wednesday night, seven and three, ten, that's one. See? The One, and I missed it. I could have saved her. If I'd looked more carefully into their lights, I'd have known what was going to happen. They came to warn me and I didn't see.'

'Here, have a swig.' Jafa passes the bottle to Petre, hoping it'll calm him down. He hopes the mission will take Petre's mind off his sister. Really the outing is mainly for Petre. Ramazy's good for taking care of any trouble they might meet on the way.

'Three musketeers,' they joke as they set off towards the countryside in search of potatoes.

Although Jafa suggested it for Petre, the potato mission's also a reason to keep going when everyone else is stuck in one place. Even intellectuals take up a position and don't move from it. They've worked out complicated maps showing where everyone's supposed to stand, but their brains don't save them from being killed too. Jafa and his company of friends pull their hats down over their ears and try to muffle out the sound of fighting.

The only car that passes them stops. The driver opens the door without a word, the musketeers get in and they drive in silence through the deeper darkness of the outlying towns. Nothing to see. Power cuts have abolished everything except pure night. Invisible remains of industry pass by. Invisible tower-block settlements pass by where workers sit with nothing to do. One beam from the car headlight cuts a path for the car to swerve slowly round holes in the road. Deep enough to fall and break your leg. It doesn't take long for roads to give up being roads.

Petre counts wordless things off on his fingers. Ramazy hunches next to him in the back, half asleep. Jafa takes the front seat for a chat but the driver isn't responding. His only comment is to prod his silent car radio to prove the communication tower's still out. Whenever they pass a roadside petrol-seller the driver stops and Jafa gives a few coins for a wine bottle full of fuel. The engine clatters and shudders as it grinds along sucking out its last dirt-clogged reserves. Jafa opens his window to release the fumes. The car's cold anyway, so no one complains.

Their fuel and alcohol are multi-purpose, the space adventurers conclude from the windows of the UFO (lights switched off, since they've noticed the inhabitants of the earth looking up at them).

* * *

When he stops to let them out, the driver reaches down to the floor under his seat and comes up with a newspaper-wrapped parcel. A little blood stains the paper.

'Here, take it. I'm going to my village now. I can get more there.'

Then he drives off taking the narrow beam of light with him. Then they walk under the star-filled sky and the road becomes more and more countrified, smells of mud and grass, until morning, and the sun comes up.

'Keep a look out,' Jafa says. 'There'll be fields now. Watch out for the potatoes.'

They find fields. They use one to sleep in while the sun's high and gives a bit of warmth. Another they piss in, and in another they make a fire and sit around it eating salami and dried figs. There are no potatoes to be seen.

'You know why?' Ramazy says. 'The leaves have gone by now.'

He takes up a clod of frozen mud, drops it and gives it a professional kick. Too long since he's had a practice; most of the old team have taken up arms for one side or the other.

They come to an abandoned chicken factory. Plenty of straw mouldering in the corners, bitter as hell, but it makes a good fire. Jafa cuts the top off a tin of sausages.

'Give it a rest,' Ramazy says as Petre starts counting out the divided bits of sausage.

Petre's all bent over his share of the sausage, his trousers pulling up over his ankles, grey nylon socks slipping down into his shoes, leg showing white and spotty. Since the death of his sister (aged twenty-three, two years younger than him, she'd taken an overdose of out-dated but still effective Soviet pills), he's plagued by numerous versions of accountability. Petre ought to have prevented it. He should have killed the man who raped her. It's that simple. He selects the reasons for his guilt. One bit of sausage, I should have been there and killed him on the spot. Two bits, I didn't kill him when she told me. Three bits, he's still walking around. Four, I'll kill him. Five, it's too late. No more sausage, but the anguish is endless. He arranges sticks of straw into numbers, laying them out carefully on the concrete floor.

'What's that?' Ramazy looks around the shadowy shed.

'What? Can't hear anything,' Jafa whispers, but he sits up straight and peers away from the pool of firelight.

Petre's staring at the straw numbers, his arms wrapped around his knees, concentrating.

'Maybe rats,' Jafa says.

'Shut up a minute,' Ramazy hushes him. 'Listen.'

Is it a knife-point being drawn across a wall, or a nail scratching along the floor? A big shed, this – concrete, with asbestos roof. Pitch black out of the firelight.

'What is it?' Jafa whispers.

'Shh.'

'Gone.'

'Listen, though.'

'It's nothing.'

'Can't see anything.'

'Yes, there. Look.'

'What?'

'Saw something in that corner.'

'Shadow, that's all, from the fire.'

'Hushh, listen.'

Ramazy's first to stand. With his back to the flames he tries to see what's scratching in the corner. But he doesn't take a step away from the fire. Neither do the others, though they stand, too. A ragtag three-some they are, in their worn-out overcoats and tatty trousers, heads made small with their tight, woolly hats.

Trouble is, it's cold outside the shed and they've made this little haven by the fire. Jafa accidentally scuffs away Petre's straw numbers as he nervously shifts from foot to foot. The musketeers listen to the night, holding their breath. Nothing. They light up cigarettes and settle back down by the fire. Jafa builds it up bright as he can and they finally fall asleep.

While they sleep, the space adventurers (they've been there all the time) switch on their accumulation lights and have a good look at every-thing that's been. They see beneath the sleeping friends where husks of chicken's claws fall free from the straw on to the concrete. Transparent toe-shreds, left behind by the chickens who lived all their lives in the shed.

Step-step, step-step – the chickens lift one foot, then the other. Tuck an aching leg into their breast feathers. The feathers don't give comfort, so the chickens pull them out in despair and shift from foot to foot.

The space adventurers' accumulator shows before the chicken fac-tory era, when an ox listens to its master singing and, before that, when moss covers a forest of oaks, and before, when whiskered fish swim through lightless water, and before, when there's nothing but pure white snow, and then before, when a glacier forces its way over the chicken-shed site scouring the earth with its passing, and a faraway period with no shadows, and farthest of all a great flood, when Noah, who lives just here on this exact spot beneath the chicken factory, sets off to sail his ark all the way to Mount Ararat.

Ah yes, the space adventurers conclude, *Noah was a true keeper of their earth.*

In the morning the discarded chicken toes get crushed to nothing beneath the friends' feet. All day they jolt and doze in the back of an open truck. Sometimes the driver stops to get out to furiously beat the engine with the end of a spanner. It works. The road divides and he says goodbye to his passengers. They've reached the entrance to a wide, uninhabited valley where the River Mtkvari flows through sandstone mountains on its way from Turkey towards Tbilisi.

'How many kilometres have we come? How far away is Tbilisi? How near are we to the border?' Petre needs to know, but the others can't say.

They make camp in a homely cave overlooking the river. In another age the mountains here were carved into perfect underground cities with drainage pipes, baths, refectories, bazaars, dwellings and frescoed chapels. But that's for the tourists, if they ever come.

The musketeers get busy gathering firewood. Jafa unwraps the bulging parcel given them by that silent driver. Fresh meat's a luxury these days; plenty in the countryside, but it can't get to the cities – no transport. Ramazy gets his knife out and peels green sticks, cuts the meat into chunks, spears them on the sticks.

'Where's the salt; got any garlic?' he jokes.

The fire's died down to embers and the meat's slowly cooking, sending out delicious smells that take all thought except food from the three friends' minds.

The space adventurers look on enviously. *One more circuit round this galaxy, then let's head for home,* they agree.

A sharpened crescent moon rises in a star-packed sky.

'C'mon,' Jafa says when they've finished eating.

'Bare feet! Follow me! Run!' he yells, and the others pull off their shoes and socks and yell back, 'Yeeeaaahhh!'

They charge down the steep slope to the river, the lamb in their bellies making them nimble. The ground becomes soft, spongy, warm and wet. They splash through tepid, muddy pools covered in green slime, smelling of farts and blood.

'Take your clothes off!' Jafa calls, as he pulls off his coat and everything else till he's naked and shivering in the cold night wind. He wades into the river shallows towards a standing pipe gushing out a long jet of water.

'Ayiiii! Fuck, it's hot!'

The friends, pale as roots, with their feet in the cold river and their bodies in the hot mineral-rich stream, raise their arms to the sky as they let the water pulverise their skin. They scatter the jet stream into millions and millions of vaporised droplets, each one catching a tiny, individual sparkle of moonlight.

'Stars!' Petre yells. 'Look, stars.'

And for once he isn't trying to count. He just turns and turns in the fierce outpouring, sending more and more liquid stars into the sky.

They wake in the early morning, cold and hungry, by the ashes of their fire.

'Come on, let's get going,' Petre says. 'Exactly how many hours will it take to get back?'

On the way home the musketeers find a field. They don't know it, but the field's illuminated by invisible beams of daylight streaming down from the UFO's undercarriage. Maybe that's why our recalcitrants choose to dig there.

From the spacemen's point of view their woolly hatted heads look like round, black berries. *Olives? Are they olive growers?* The space adventurers look down on the three humans stooped over the earth. *Yes,* they agree. *This is what they do after war. Yes, the olive branch is their emblem of peace and their crown of victory.*

'Get a stone. You start here and I'll go up the slope.' Jafa organises his friends.

Ramazy goes at it hard, finds a good, flat stone and hits the earth till it's loosened into frozen lumps. He drop-kicks a clod over an imaginary crossbar and trots exultantly up and down the field. Get the blood going. He's panting heavily as he bends to his work again.

'Permafrost,' he shouts. 'Fuckin' permafrost. Maybe find a mammoth!'

Jafa's on his fourth hole already, digging like a dog, two stones attacking the hard ground.

'Don't go deep,' he shouts. 'Keep trying different places.'

He stoops over, sending sprays of earth and small stones between his legs. His knuckles scrape on the icy ridges of the field. Sometime, someone has ploughed it.

Petre gets busy walking up and down the furrows, counting as he goes. First one at the edge of the field, then the second, the third, fourth, fifth, till he's reached the middle. He picks up a bone. Not human, he thinks. Maybe panther, boar, wolf. He flings it. Where it falls will be the place. He uses the bone to dig. Carefully, so not to damage what lies beneath.

Her skin shows first. A pink blush flushing her cold cheek. A curve, smooth and firm, the muscle filling out as she smiles. A tiny dimple. The small mound of her nose, shadow of nostrils. Petre's hand eases her out, carefully curls under her, cupping her, releasing her from the earth's fierce grip. He lifts her up. Brushes away the dry flecks of soil on her eyelids. Petre touches his lips to hers. She's frozen. He warms her. He wraps his hands round her and breathes on to her. Tucks her inside his coat, nestles her safe at last under his armpit.

ANTHEA NICHOLSON was born in London in 1948. She now lives between Bristol and Tbilisi, Georgia, eastern Europe. Her work, in a wide variety of media including live arts events, writing and short film, has been supported by Arts Council awards. She is currently working on her first novel.

Contact: anthea.nicholson@sparksanthology.co.uk

Fade to Black

Peter Mallett

from *Phosphene*

The narrator, a university lecturer in Japan, has been writing a screen-play inspired by the student he has fallen in love with. In this final chapter of the novel, the fantasy he has created collides with reality.

I jumped into my car and drove off fast through the city, not knowing what I was going to do. I took the loop round the city centre to give me time. At this time of night everyone was driving as if on a race track. The lights of the skyscrapers of Namba and the neon of the pleasure quarters flashed by. As I glanced down to turn on the CD player, I noticed the petrol gauge was on empty. Damn, I was going to have to stop.

The attendants greeted my arrival noisily, indicating with dramatic gestures where I was to stop as though I were driving an aeroplane into its parking bay. They filled my tank, cleaned the windscreen and emptied my ashtray. I paid them and drove off. I knew what I was going to do now. I had to see Akiko and enact the final scene of this drama.

I also knew what was going to happen. It was in my script.

Scene 145 – TAKAYO'S ONE-ROOM APARTMENT – INSIDE/NIGHT

Takayo, looking worried, is sitting very still on a chair in front of her electric piano.

I stopped the car in front of Akiko's apartment building. Light was coming from the window of her room. As if in a shadow play, her form was silhouetted against the blind. I think she was playing the piano.

I got out of the car and dialled her number. There was no reply. As I stood waiting, a change in the intensity of light falling on the pavement caused me to look up. She was staring down at me, frozen to the spot. When she saw me look up, she stepped backwards. A few seconds passed and I caught her face once more at the window before the blind was dropped suddenly, separating us again.

The door to the entrance was locked. I tapped in Akiko's room number, 311, though I knew there was no point. She didn't answer. But I had to be inside; this was where it all finished.

Luckily for me, at this moment a couple appeared and let themselves into the building. They were too engrossed in themselves to notice me follow them in before the door locked shut again. I was now in position for the finale.

Scene 146 – TAKAYO'S APARTMENT – INSIDE/NIGHT
Takayo, stunned, stands beside the telephone, which she has just hung up. After a few seconds, it rings, making her tremble. She does not answer at once but eventually picks up the receiver.
(Conversation in Japanese)

                    POLICE OFFICER
                    Takaba police box.

                    TAKAYO
                    Yes?

                    POLICE OFFICER
                    You tried to call us?
Takayo does not answer.

                    POLICE OFFICER
          We've just recorded a call from your telephone.

                    TAKAYO
                    (hesitating)
                    Yes…

I didn't bother with the lift but climbed the two flights of concrete stairs to the third floor. Akiko's apartment was halfway down the corridor. I approached the door and was about to knock, but no, the scene shouldn't end with a confrontation. Nor was it to be a happy ending – rather, beautiful and tragic. I sat down on the floor, my back against the wall, facing the door to Akiko's apartment.

Scene 147 – TAKAYO'S APARTMENT – INSIDE/NIGHT
Takayo hangs up, looking off into space, and mechanically moves towards her electric piano. The piano is not switched on, so all we hear is the hesitant tuneless rhythm of her fingers tapping the keys. She is now playing with her eyes closed. Then, all of a sudden, she opens her eyes, freezes, then goes towards the window.

She cautiously pushes aside the edge of the blind to look out.

Outside Takayo's – I mean Akiko's – apartment, I maintained my silent vigil. The noises of the city filtered through the windows. In the distance, I thought I could hear a police car approaching

Scene 148 – TAKAYO'S APARTMENT – INSIDE/NIGHT
Seeing nothing, Takayo takes her hand away from the blind. She sits down again in front of the keyboard of her electric piano and switches it on. She puts on headphones. She plays.

The camera approaches her. We recognise Chopin's 4th Ballade. She plays with her eyes closed; after a while, a few teardrops seep from beneath her eyelids and fall down her cheeks.

Fade to black.

Chopin's 4th Ballade played in my head and I closed my eyes, seeing now the final credits appear on the screen. But there were other noises that shouldn't have been there. Shouts outside and then heavy footsteps running up the stairs and down the corridor towards me. I looked up and saw, uncomprehending at first, three men in uniform. Two of them grabbed my arms roughly and jerked me to my feet. This wasn't supposed to happen: it wasn't in the script. This wasn't the way the story ended. The policemen manhandled me towards the lift, led me out of the building and into their car.
 We drove away.

The camera follows the tail-lights of the police car until they become two red spots in the distance.

Fade to black.

PETER MALLETT has lived in Japan for twenty years. A university position provides him with an income; work for a film festival and arts events takes it. After many years of freelance journalism and editing, he has now turned to fiction. *Phosphene* is his first novel.

Contact: peter.mallett@sparksanthology.co.uk

Selected Poems

Susan Taylor

The Valentine Ring

I was the one Joan chose to give the ring
that had belonged to Great Aunt Marion.
Two amethyst hearts escort three opals;
surrendered gems that set me thinking –
should I be warming up her purple stones,
valentines set long ago, still hopeful?

I'd find romance, they seemed to testify,
these transfixed hearts so comfortable to wear.
The ring reshaped like a hoop of skin
made of gold leaf, worn faint as ancestry,
but then its golden shank snapped like a snare,
dug in my finger, like bone, worn too thin.

Aunt Joan, who'd passed it willingly to me,
lies in a home now with no memory.

After Breakfast, Nothing of it's Left

She wakes and sees the sky is moving. It snows and she looks upwards where snow's coming from – hypnotic dimensions in a bounty, bound over, out of childhood. No more is made of morning than a slow determination to wonder, as all her memories of colour fall into a green lake. Sky descends in veils, on and on. More remarkable than falling stars in flight, these are spars snapped off from some high haven. Here in Newton Park, they make soft cradles in crooks of branches – rare nests of whispers. Air becomes a whisking bowl.

The open window breathes out words and breathes in snow – small, wet pockmarks on a page. Before breakfast, she's tasting clouds by sticking her tongue into the air.

Below the Ultraviolet

We make scant reference to animals or birds, though there is a suggestion of ducks in a flight of feathers from a pillow fight. Laughter's scarce, except at the ecstasy of the pillow down. The stone house is a sequence of lights turned on and off. There's no food on the table, apart from metaphors for honey. The patois of what we share is stuff not on sale in shopfronts, showrooms, shows. We stopper all we can in see-through phials marked fragile, organic, caution. These drink up the light as we turn and examine them for streaks of humour, trajectory, repetition. The wasps above fly towards the ultraviolet, to be zapped in the high-voltage grill.

Refuelling at Bridgwater Junction

He leans, throwing his burly frame into prevailing rain
as proof of Somerset reed's potency;
willow man morphing his form South West.

He's a demigod whipped up in wind;
dark force with no hands to connect him back to Devon
as I drive to the North East edge of his region.

He has speed spun into his wrists,
water and live willow lapping his ankles.
Those arms like strikes of lightning carry a charge.

I look at my hands clamped to the wheel of this jeep
and wonder why, in my insulated world, I chase
that heavy diesel tanker out in front.

Fabrics

Nottingham Lace

In the factories here, they make lace for covering windows. Each little red house is veiled by nets with roses on. The blooms are always white, smell of nothing and hold together like cobwebs. Petticoat drapes conceal intimacies, or lack of them, like the nothing flowers spun in this city.

Chinese Silk

I discovered an apron made of silk in my mother's dressing-table drawer. I asked her where it came from, but she never told me. It was woven in heliotrope and red gold, unlike the mundane clothes we wore. I was small and sneaked in, when she wasn't looking, to perch in front of the mirror and tie myself in her sumptuous apron.

Ashburton Pennants

You always pull the same fluted ribbon of longing out of me. I brush your arm in a doorway and become a line of bunting threaded over East Street. Passers-by ignore the triangles of sailcloth beating in the wind above like multicoloured birds. Once more, I choose to overlook the bright flags in your eyes.

From Homebase

The days of our Christmases
are represented in the front window
by these odd things hung
on a moulting fir tree:

a sunburst of straw
with a ring neatly plaited
to anchor its eight rays
representing a fraying star,

a smooth grey plastic dove,
wings outstretched,
bearing a synthetic olive twig
on delivery to nowhere,

a string of bells with no clappers,
a Santa with a mutton-faced grin,
found at a motorway service till
while heading south,

the paper angel Tom drew before
he got ill; it still sings
and floats as an angel well might
in a sea of backlit clouds,

a flat wooden bauble
hand cut by Imma
for Matt and Tom,
with lots of love written on it,

satin baubles off the first tree
when we four were together,
scarlet apples with silk leaves
from back then,

a new bauble, chosen by Amy,
with a blue net of pearls
set on to a bubble of frosted air
and the latest angel from Homebase:

doll-faced, gold-crowned,
gauze-skirted, two-centimetre
trumpet optimistically poised
in case she needs it to herald.

SUSAN TAYLOR, originally a farmer in Lincolnshire, now lives and writes on Dartmoor. She performs with MythRythM, which specialises in folk tales, poetry and music from the Moor. Her successes in 2005 included three poems, commissioned by VOICE Poetry Festival at Dartington, and a collection of poetry, forthcoming from Oversteps Press.

Contact: susan.taylor@sparksanthology.co.uk

Distractions from Borges

Andrew Warburton

narrative nonfiction

What follows are pages from Andrew Warburton's private notebook, centred on his obsessions with the writer Jorge Luis Borges. Make of it what you will.

Prologue

I 'm supposed to be writing about Borges, but, as ever, I'm scared of failure – of showing myself up. I've led people to believe that I'm some kind of genius, and I know that's bullshit, although part of me would like to believe it.

I've decided to write about the way his ideas are more important than his people. His characters certainly aren't real. They're symbols. Half the time he's a show-off. A cerebral narcissist like myself. The only character I actually remember is Funes. There's a strong image somewhere, of his body at dawn, sprawled on a cushion, I think, with smoke trailing from his hand; the feeling that he'd used opium to dull his enormous brain. It got me to thinking – God, so many things – about writing and opium and which is which and what they do differently. I thought I used to drink to dull myself. Now I've replaced one addiction with another. Writing and reading – it's all a distraction. One is said to numb, and one to elevate and move. Is it not the same when push comes to shove? It all goes back to Apollo and Dionysus. Both are aimed towards the same thing, but in opposite directions.

The only thing stopping me from plunging in is the process involved in getting inside his head (it was Stephen King, I think, who said writing was telepathy) and writing even if I don't believe what I'm putting down, and trusting that it will come. It will come. I have to tell myself that. I'll feel better when I'm 'in' it. In fact, I'll probably feel high. But it's the getting 'in' that drains you. You have to shed yourself, the world, and become immersed in a purely cerebral world.

And then, what for? To convince you that my point of view is correct! Surely it would be better for me (and for your enjoyment) to give my subjective impression. There's so much external stuff going on; you just have to open your eyes.

Valancourt

I was walking in the park, watching the ducks form a queue to dive into the lake, when a man jumped up from under the willow tree and called me by my name. I'd noticed him on my first round of the park – he'd been lying with one leg thrown lackadaisically over the other, the pages of a book concealing his face – and, as ever with someone reading in my presence, I'd wanted to know who the book was by. When I bent over to look at the title and the author's name, the sun shone brightly on the glossy cover and hid the words from my eyes. It was as if I was being deliberately tantalised. Standing in front of me now, I could hardly make out the man's intent, or even if I knew him at all, because the sun, shining on his back, threw his face into shadow. It was only when I heard the light, musical tone of his voice that I realised it was Valancourt! I threw my arms around him and cupped his full, round buttocks; his hand, as if in response, encircled the back of my neck.

Valancourt was a member of a secret fellowship I happened to be a part of, which I won't go into now for obvious reasons. He'd taken his name from the handsome Chevalier in the Gothic novel *The Mysteries of Udolpho* and it was a name that perfectly suited him, I thought. It gave him an air of mystery and courtliness, which, to some extent, he already possessed. As it turned out, he was in a mad dash. He could only stay long enough to dazzle me with his pale blue eyes before rushing off along the park's main thoroughfare, dodging briefcases, Zimmer frames and skateboards. It was only after he'd disappeared in the melée that I noticed, on the ground by my feet, something sparkling in the sun, and on closer inspection I realised it was the book he'd been reading. I picked it up and flipped it over. On the cover I read the words, 'Jorge Luis Borges, *Labyrinths*'.

Magenta

On the cover was a black-and-white photo of rows of men, each one turned away from the camera, each one a doppelgänger of the original man (although who that was, I didn't know). For a while I stared, as if it was a puzzle to be figured out – and then I left it where I'd placed it on the windowsill. Later, whilst standing at the mirror fishing for an eyelash that floated on the surface of my eye, I noticed the light shining through the glass, reflected in the book's glossy cover. Again I was gripped by that feeling of strangeness that had come over me when Valancourt first approached me in the park. The feeling remained for the length of time it took me to extract the hair and dab a tissue in the corner of my eye. I could see the black and white photo on the cover – the rows of identical men – and just for a second I thought I saw a splash of magenta. I can't remember where it was on the book. It was just a splash. But I remember the startling colour. When I picked it up and brought it close to my face, there wasn't a speck of magenta on it! It was definitely black and white.

Over the next few days, the feeling of lightness in my blood, which had accompanied my odd brush with Valancourt, gradually subsided. Life returned to normal. I went to work; came home in the evening; cooked dinner; kicked my feet up in front of the box; everything was going fine. And then, a week later, I walked across the hall, on my way to bed, when something glared at me from the floor. It looked like a pool of blood, half-hidden under the coat-tails on the stand. The hallway was dark. I crouched down. First I noticed the rows of identical men. Then the words: 'Borges, *Labyrinths*'. It wasn't a pool of blood at all; it was the book. Now there was nothing unusual about it – the same black-and-white photo decorated the cover. Black specks hovered in front of my eyes. I fainted.

Tessa Hadley

By one of those 'paralysing' coincidences – a synchronicity, if you like – I joined a short-story class run by novelist and James scholar, Dr Tessa Hadley, which required me to read the book in question. I'd had no intention of reading it; I merely liked to take it to bed with me and finger the corners and wonder how the gloss managed to retain its coolness through the night. When I saw it among the books on the reading list, I was overcome once more with that lightness of blood, and I had to sit down.

By no means was that the only coincidence. In Waterstone's, where I worked on quiet Sunday afternoons to pay for my travels to and from university, I'd seen Tessa Hadley's books stacked in perfect columns. It doesn't take much for a book's cover to seduce me, and one of hers, in particular, drew me: the picture on the front showed a succulent melon with a gouge in its side. When I saw it lying innocuously among the others, I picked it up and pressed the pages together; I released my grip, let the book exhale and fill the air with a fresh, inky smell. I had to have it.

First I had to read *Labyrinths*. I read it very sleepily in bed, loving the snaking sentences. The discussion in class was elaborately philosophical, but ultimately of not much use. The calibre of my fellow students wasn't the problem. No, I was the problem. I had issues to work through – defensiveness, speaking over people, witty put-downs, childish displays of jealousy, etc. etc. – all staggeringly boring stuff that surfaces in the presence of talented people and comes from a deep sense of inferiority, I'm sure. It's part of my grandiosity – I cultivate an image of myself that's so inflated and unreal, it shuts me off from other people. Thank God we were talking about Borges, not me.

The Essay

The central idea of my essay was that Borges is akin to those devils in *Paradise Lost* who sit 'on a hill retired and reasoned high… and found no end, in wand'ring mazes lost'. I thought this was a bit obvious, perhaps – the parallel between the demons' 'mazes' and the title of Borges' book – the quote from Borges, in 'A New Refutation of Time', describing his work as 'the feeble artifice of an Argentine lost in the maze of metaphysics'.

(This can be drawn quite easily from a cursory reading of his work. Why write an essay that would only bore you? Why launch more words on the mulchy sea of language already in existence?)

The thing is, Borges nearly always writes ironically. His admissions of defeat are never what they seem. When he says his work is 'feeble artifice', we know he doesn't mean it. In fact, in our postmodern age, it is his refusal to declare anything *true*, or even trustworthy, that makes him so important. He can be linked with the recent reappraisal of the sophists when he writes, 'I do not exaggerate the importance of these verbal games.' But even then we're not sure if he means it.

I was going to summarise in overblown terms that, in the end, it is their relentlessly ironic, internal awareness of their limits that saves these stories from the yawning chasm of futility. By pointing out how language works, revelling in the tangled mazes language creates, making us take part in a process of questioning while we read, Borges points to what *lies outside language*; the most powerful, breathtaking thing that language can do. We get the feeling that he's hit on something crucially important, almost mystical, because in a way he has. By sensing the place that language doesn't reach, we glimpse (if only from the corner of our eye) the infinite.

* * *

The Chasm

My skin tingles. I begin to hyperventilate. *Infinity lies behind the shapes of things.* It has nothing to do with Borges, though when I think about it the two are intimately linked. It's inextricably bound to language, the spaces between words, the bodily sensations injected into speech, the blank page. I'm having trouble expressing it... Do we only put down words to experience their finiteness? Is that where their beauty lies – in the knowledge that we're experiencing an imitation of the real, and in this knowledge at least sensing the real, which is always out of reach? At times it comes close to mystic ecstasy.

We all have an idea of the sun, but if we look straight at it, it blinds us. So we look at the sky to the left or the right and, indirectly, we see it. That's what language is, and Borges shows this well. He hovers around the sun, pointing.

We might well think that Funes is a god. That his all-encompassing language gives him the ability to *know* everything. But rather than transcending, he grows weary. Starved of the beauty of the moment, he'll never know what it's like to know fleetingly. His world is the perfect mirrored imitation – the antithesis of art. He'll only ever know an intricate sprawling illusion; an infinity filled with words. The writer who doesn't have Funes's resources, on the other hand, totters on the brink of the chasm (though winds rage and threaten to suck him down), drawing the edge before it gives way. Literature rests upon this chasm. The pull is felt beneath the words. By privileging ideas, Borges approaches this in a rather obvious way, and perhaps his standing suffers as a result. A writer whose images spark from the void, on the other hand, shows the same, but more movingly and beautifully because his or her writing is not merely cerebral but rooted in the body and the emotions.

Finale

I'm writing this on the plane. I'll soon be at my brother's in Geneva. I need to write about what happened last night when I woke in the dark. From across the room, magenta-coloured eyes stared at me. I won't attempt to describe my fear. Let it stand that the words 'icy dread' come close. The eyes made the room appear darker. They contrasted with the blackness and burned. Was it a cat? Impossible. How could a cat have got in my room? Was it a burglar? If so, why the magenta eyes? My thoughts went to Borges and his infernal book. I switched on the bedside lamp but nobody was there. I rolled over in my warm bed and pulled the sheets around me, up to my chin. On the other side of the bed, someone stood very still looking down at me. A white face and bright-red eyes – not red, but magenta – yes, magenta. I gasped. My body went rigid. My eyes hurt, presumably bulging from their sockets. In an instant, the figure vanished. I had to get out of bed. I couldn't lie there any longer. I went downstairs to the kitchen and made myself a coffee. I stood beneath the strip-lighting and sipped. I'll ring Valancourt, I thought. This stuff has only been happening since he dropped that book in the park.

The phone rang and rang, then clicked. 'Hello?'

'Valancourt, I need to talk to you. It's about that book you were reading in the park. I've got it – now some really weird stuff is happening.'

There was a long pause and then someone spoke. It certainly *wasn't* Valancourt: 'I'm sorry Andrew, but Valancourt's finished. You're next on my list. You must understand—'

I dropped the coffee. It splashed everywhere. I felt the blood drain from my face. I understood, of course. But that didn't make it any easier to stomach.

Immediately, I thought of flight.

Appendix

These fragments, considered relevant to the work in question, were collected by Shaun Champion, who found them scrawled in the back of Andrew's notebook:

I

Can't I have the daffodils *and* the poem? Can't I have the wheelbarrow? The nightingale? The rain at the end of 'Whitsun Weddings'? Can't I have the carriage as well as the movement? The glass window and what it reveals?

Can't I have the words?

And the breath that pours into them?

II

I climb the stairs, shut the door and draw the curtains, come to a dark hallway lined with books, at the end of which is a door. I knock. A mole in an apron and a shawl leads me to a darker, colder place, where a tall, silhouetted man hands me a box with no colour or taste and watches as it slips inside me.

III

Writing is a dungeon. A dungeon I write. A writer in a dungeon whose words are abortions. I envy those who breathe.

IV

Spring comes over me slowly, though I spend my days stuffed in this room. I go outside and don't want to come back in again! The air is warm. The magnolia sheds its petals on the lawn. The neighbours potter in their gardens. *This is life – it's more than words.*

ANDREW WARBURTON is twenty-four. His poetry has appeared in issues two and three of *Chroma*, the Arts Council-funded 'queer' literary journal, and his erotic short story 'Hustler' will feature in a forthcoming anthology. Andrew is working on his first novel.

Contact: andrew.warburton@sparksanthology.co.uk

The Stone House

Rosalind Cook

from *The Stone House*

The Stone House is set in 1900 on a transatlantic liner.

I arrived in the *Lucretia*'s lounge quarter of an hour before our agreed time the following morning. This time I was the keen one, anxious not to miss a moment of what my cousin Edgar had to tell me. I had barely touched the breakfast that was brought to my suite, and had managed to drink only half a cup of tea.

Edgar sauntered into the lounge a few minutes late and even paused to pass the time of day with a moustachioed gentleman in the middle of the room, who had been noisily shaking the three-day-old newspaper he was reading. I was a little annoyed at the delay, but too impatient to begin complaining. Edgar threw himself into the armchair opposite me, crossed his legs with a sigh, and rested his hands lightly on the arms of the chair before looking at me directly.

'So tell me,' he said, 'where do you want me to start?'

I took a deep breath and leant forward a little.

'Well,' I said, clasping and unclasping my hands, 'why did you want to go to Borneo in the first place? You and I both know the story of my father's wild dreams of wealth and opportunity in the East after his humble beginnings. Your background is rather different, though, Edgar. What drove you to ask my father to send you out to work for our family business?'

Edgar's eyes narrowed a little. Light splashes of rain speckled the window to his left.

'That's not *exactly* how it came about, Polly,' he said. 'I sought your father's advice on the direction I might take next. I quite fancied going out on my own for something, like he did. He wasn't altogether encouraging, though.' Edgar shifted in his seat. 'He, too, made the point that he'd had nothing when he first went out to Borneo, and this was strong motivation indeed to succeed. He obviously thought, that without such desperation behind me, I was unlikely to prosper as he had. I thought I knew better.

'He lectured me on the current state of trade in the world: "Trade is all about China these days, and of course India," he told me. "Borneo was only ever, at best, a stop between the two. Even Singapore is becoming barely more than a convenient resting place en route to Australia and New Zealand these days. When I went out there, the Straits were alive with commerce and development. I fear it is no longer so."

'I was surprised to hear him so defeated,' Edgar said. 'If the situation was really that dire, I asked him, how had his business continued to thrive? He looked gloomy and confided that it wasn't thriving at all at that time, that some major changes had to be made, and soon "The time has come," he told me, "when I must face the fact there's no longer a commercial reason to keep the business going in Borneo. There is only sentiment." He looked old to me then, for the first time.

'During this conversation we came to an agreement: that I would go out to Borneo and be the one to initiate these changes. It turned out that he had been considering setting up office in Singapore for some time, with the purpose of removing himself from some old and dying agreements made in Kuching decades ago. But, as it turned out, the Singapore move wasn't the real reason he sent me to Borneo.'

I was surprised. What other reason might my father have had for sending his nephew out to the East? I knew very little about the family business that provided so comfortable a life for me and my family, but I assumed Edgar would explain it to me while telling me what I was really interested in – what that wonderful far-off land of jungle and river was truly like.

'Your father always thought he would one day return to Borneo, for one last short visit: to complete one final, twenty-year-old transaction. He still believed he would go, right up until that day I went to him for advice. That afternoon he decided I would go in his place, as his emissary. And he had to accept he would never see Borneo again.'

'One final transaction?' I prompted. I felt as if he was teasing me. He had dropped this crucial piece of information, and now he was moving away from it again and again. Even out here, hundreds of miles out to sea, away from England, from Colmouth, from my family, he still made me feel like the young, silly cousin.

'After my mother burst into your house, screaming for your father and accusing him of sending her only son to a diseased tropical hell for his own profit, your father took me up to London for what I assumed would be a business briefing. We settled in at your father's club, and for two days he related long reminiscences from his time out in Borneo all those years ago.

'I thought this was pure self-indulgence on your father's part,' Edgar said, 'and doubted much of it was directly relevant to my own imminent journey. I dismissed most of his stories as folklore, actually.'

He shook his head. 'It was only thousands of miles and several months later, while I was on my first trip up-river to a Dyak long-house community, that I began to understand what he was trying to tell me as we'd sat in those cracked leather armchairs back in London.

'What has your father told you about Jake Sullivan?' Edgar asked suddenly.

'Oh,' I said. 'Well, the two of them were good friends. He helped my father out a great deal, especially when he first arrived in Kuching. I think Sullivan worked for the Borneo Company, didn't he?'

Edgar nodded thoughtfully. 'He has quite a reputation in Kuching,' he said.

'What sort of reputation?'

'It's said he knew everyone, from the lowliest Chinese coolie to numerous Dyak chiefs up-river, as well as being personally acquainted with the Rajah and his administration. The further I travelled away from Kuching, the more often I heard him referred vaguely to as James Mulligan, or Jack O'Sullivan. He took on a kind of mythical status out there. He seemed to know more than any other white man did about trade and war between the tribes.'

'Did you ever meet him?' I asked.

'No. In fact, as time went on I began to have severe doubts about the man...'

'Doubts? What do you mean?'

Edgar shook his head, and gave a half-shrug.

'When I first arrived in Kuching,' he said, and a tingle of excitement raced through me, as it always did at the mention of that exotic-sounding place, 'I saw before me a town barely bigger than a fishing village. I couldn't believe I'd just left spectacular Singapore behind for this. In direct contrast with your father's first impressions of the two places, I was dazzled by Singapore and thoroughly disappointed with Kuching.'

I glanced out the window of the first-class lounge of the *Lucretia* at the endless grey-blue of the Atlantic Ocean as Edgar drifted away from the real issue once more.

'After the alternating dust and then mud of the tropical ports I had visited en route from England, the lush soft expanse of lawn that formed the colonial heart of Singapore amazed me,' he said. 'With an impressive clubhouse at each end and the stark white spire of St Andrew's Cathedral forming a dramatic backdrop, its wide field of green played host to any and all occasions that polite Singapore society required a public arena for. I loved to walk south from there, between an imposing collection of buildings – Parliament House, the law courts, the town hall – to the Singapore River. I would stand on the spot where Stamford Raffles had first stepped on to this tiger-infested, jungle-covered island and seen such potential, and gaze across the narrow stretch of river at the brightly painted shop-houses fringing the opposite bank which signalled the beginning of the Chinese settlement. It was another world over there.'

I shifted in my chair and stifled a cough under my breath as my gaze wandered once more to the window. Edgar's time in Singapore didn't interest me. I wanted him to get on to Kuching and, more importantly, this issue of Jake Sullivan and the mysterious 'true' reason my father sent Edgar there. I was silent for now, and my gaze kept being drawn to the rain-lashed window and the horizon, which disappeared periodically in the gloom.

'I was in Singapore for a week waiting for my onward connection, and in that time the diamond-shaped island port became the essence, in my mind, of the East. When the time came for me to leave, I had to remind myself that Borneo was the true destination of this journey, and not a chore to be borne.' He sighed as though reliving the wrench all over again.

'As the steamer approached the mighty, fabled Sarawak River,' Edgar said, causing a thrill of anticipation to run through me again, 'we dropped speed to drift into the river-mouth. The velvet-green cliff of Mount Santubong was left behind as the ship steadied in the channel and the water around us turned from glinting pale sea-blue to river-silt brown.

'I leant on the railing of the upper deck and remembered your father's tale of awe at his first arrival in Kuching. He told me there was a sweetness in the air of the jungle as it closed in and shut out the ocean, the outside world. Trees soared up and across and met overhead, as vines strangled their trunks and encircled saplings before drooping their tentacles into the water. Above the low rumble of the ship's engine, I could hear the screech of hundreds of insects as though they were all in competition to be loudest, but I didn't see any of this with your father's lyricism. Rounding a final bend, the town of Kuching quietly appeared before us, clinging to the banks of the Sarawak River.'

I could almost feel the light coat of moisture the humidity would form on the skin approaching that tropical city.

'It was such an anticlimax,' Edgar said, interrupting my daydream. 'The first thing that came into view were ugly sago factories. We passed the Borneo Company building and Fort Margherita before the impressive trio of buildings that make up the Astana finally appeared, gleaming bright-white amidst carefully tended lawns. Opposite the Rajah's palace stood the town of Kuching, an untidy tangle of godowns, whitewashed public buildings and rickety loading piers.

'I was in Kuching more than a week before the almost permanent mist finally dispersed at dusk to reveal a sketch-outline of a mountain on the north west horizon,' he said, his tone softening now. 'The sky was painted deep orange by the setting sun, and lay, a stripe of pure copper, on the still surface of the Sarawak River. It was breathtaking.

'For the first week I didn't even know there was a mountain there, and on that eighth night I stood transfixed – I'm not exaggerating. The perfect square of colour on the river was so intense it looked almost like fire. I finally, finally understood,' he said, grinning broadly. 'I think I spoke aloud, as if your father was standing there beside me, to tell him that, after everything I had seen and done in the past month, only now did I truly realise what he tried to tell me about Kuching.

'Just like each of my previous nights in Kuching, I walked away from the river and up to the Victoria Hotel, but that night I was an hour later than usual. One of the mahogany-skinned, gin-and-tonic-swigging expats I had struck up conversation with one of the first evenings asked what had kept me. I accepted my own dose of quinine from the bar and he followed me on to the verandah as I searched in vain for any last trace of that glorious colour still in the darkening sky. I asked the name of the mountain I'd seen, and he gave a knowing chuckle before replying: "You could see the mountain this evening, could you? Well that explains it. This was your first *real* Kuching sunset, Milner. That calls for celebration."

'That night, eating in the open-raftered dining room with a few of the expats, fans squealing above us, I heard the first echo of Jake Sullivan's reputation.'

ROSALIND COOK grew up wanting only to write novels, but got distracted travelling around six continents and working in travel. Although she was in Western Australia when inspiration struck for *The Stone House,* she never thought travel was a major part of her writing, but somehow Borneo and New York crept in…

Contact: rosalind.cook@sparksanthology.co.uk

The Prize

Richard Redman

a short story

L ate-winter sunlight filters through unwashed windows into Lliswerry
school hall. It falls on the squinting faces of a hundred children
sitting cross-legged on dusty hardwood. Aged eleven and twelve, they
are divided boys from girls. They sit in silence, hushed by their teachers and oppressed by heat throbbing from huge, muddy-brown radiators. The boys cast despairing looks toward a playground, their football
dreams forlorn. A fart, followed by giggles, voices their dissent.

Matthew's eyes are turned to heaven, observing tiny dust-flakes cir-
cling, descending and rising again in the hazy stillness of afternoon.
Dancing in light-shafts the particles burn gold and bright, their movements attuned to music from a violin. Suspended in this small yet sacred moment, Matthew opens his ears to the 'Meditation' from *Thais*.

'Too slow, girl,' barks the music teacher, accompanying on piano.

Matthew winces.

Coughing on a cigarette the teacher instructs his child prodigy from
the corner of his mouth. 'Come now, like we practised, A sharp…'

With a rictus smile, the headmaster, Mr Davies, nods at the violinist, trying to instil her with confidence and the correct beat.

Matthew tugs at a strand of grey wool, loose at the end of his pull-
over sleeve, and begins to silently mouth mysterious words. His eyes
close suddenly at the summoning of a fierce concentration. Are his lines
there? Fear certainly is, but he will not surrender to it; he must attack,
attack, attack.

Mr Davies applauds the violinist too loudly as she is led away. 'Marvellous, marvellous!' he bellows, confident he can rescue his school
from its funding crisis through a constant flow of exhortations and su-
perlatives. 'What a tremendous conclusion to the musical section of our
eisteddfod. Yes? Wonderful stuff! And now, without much further ado
– in theatrical monologue – our sole entrant…'

Anticipating the call, Matthew springs to his feet. He strides to the
stage sensing opportunity. Today they will listen. Who *they* are exactly,
he cannot determine, but he hopes they will be listening nonetheless.
He lays a tentative foot against the edge of the stage, comprising of
wooden block sections, and pushes down on it to be sure it will safely
support him. With reluctant alacrity he takes the centre of a performance

space, which then opens out around him, a wide and lonely expanse.

'What are you going to do for us, Matthew?'

'Hamlet, Prince of Denmark.'

There is an audible sigh from the children.

'Hamlet? Mrs Price has placed some faith in your precocity.'

'Sir, I chose and prepared it myself.'

'Marvellous, marvellous!' Davies exclaims, leaving the stage.

Ay so, God bye to you! Now I am alone.

And so he is.

Panic threatens momentarily as a mountain of blank verse looms over him. The rows of children, rendered catatonic by heat and boredom, stare at him with vague resentment. This makes him aware of his shabby black trousers, inches too long, breaking in folds over his scuffed brown shoes, and the grimy sweatmarks on the cuffs of his only white shirt, which has to last him the week. He knows, although he has not been told, that there is another life for him, and now stands ready to meet it and refuse his parents' fate. An intake of breath, he begins.

> *... this player here*
> *But in a fiction, in a dream of passion*
> *Could force his soul to his own conceit*

Matthew shouts Shakespeare's words at first, as though they are there only to fulfil *his* desperate need to be heard. Yet he gives special emphasis to 'force his soul'. He feels Hamlet's envy for tears and a broken voice; he needs them to express the anger and ambition inside.

> *For Hecuba!*
> *What's Hecuba to him, or he to Hecuba*
> *That he should weep for her?*

What's Hamlet to Matthew, or he to Hamlet? He has no intellectual understanding of the Prince, but the singing quality of the language affects a striking transformation.

> *And can say nothing; no, not for a King*

'To say nothing...' How he feels the self-scorn of those words. He remembers his grandfather, dead from cancer the year before, singing on his deathbed though he had never joined a choir. The silence of men with small hopes that prove too large will never close over Matthew.

Now, at the heart of the speech, his pace becomes slower, more measured, his nerves have surrendered to the magic of words. While the precise meaning of what he is saying still eludes him, he delights in the alchemy of these purple words, whose new sounds create new feelings. His mouth opens wide.

... am I a coward?

'Coward' is given a hard kick at its beginning and a crushing thud at its end. Each phrase of self-loathing Matthew chews with relish. There is undoubted authenticity in this element of his performance. And, though his vocal tone has little light and shade, there is fire. Enough for the lash of 'pate' and ''swounds' and 'malefactions' to please his ear. It is not the language of his home – of his family – yet he feels it is his.

... Bloody, bawdy villain!
Remorseless, treacherous, lecherous, kindless villain!
O, vengeance!

His lips quiver. With both arms at his sides, his hands flex open, then close in fists. Several teachers now stir from marking homework and lower their mugs of tea. They are bemused at how this shabby little boy has acquired a regal arrogance, spouting the Englishman's lines in full voice, daring to consider himself as something other than he is. The children have been paying attention for longer, surprised by Matthew's intensity. Several of them laugh uneasily as, thrilling to a climax, he throws off his containment and, arms flailing, races through the last ten lines.

... the play's the thing
Wherein I'll catch the conscience of the king!

Matthew rolls off the last line with a rapid, metallic shout, raising a hand with pointed finger high above his head, just as he had seen Olivier do in the film version. Yet no applause follows. He stands still, hearing only the sound of his breathing. The lack of reaction disconcerts him; he would rather receive boos and hisses than silence. He bows with a flourish before the school. Laughter from girls in the front row makes him straighten up quickly, his face flushed.

Then, prompted by a teacher at the back of the hall, the children begin to clap, slowly building their applause until some feel able to cheer. Davies leaps on to the stage and throws an arm around Matthew's shoulders.

'Spectacular, my boy!' he booms.

Matthew enjoys 'my boy': not that he is particularly fond of his headmaster, but the expression of ownership confers value on him. This is something his father, a steelworker, seems unable to do.

'I haven't seen passion like that since I saw Richard Burton play Prince Hal!'

Later the eisteddfod winners are announced, each one receiving a certificate and five pounds in book tokens.

Davies clears his throat. 'Our winner for theatrical monologue… and a truly heroic Hamlet, is…'

Matthew is oddly less confident this time as he walks to the stage, venturing as himself and not the Prince of Denmark. The quiet of the hall throws him off balance and he breaks into a jog to shorten the distance. Davies hands him his certificate crested with a Welsh dragon. There, in beautiful calligraphy, Matthew reads:

Lliswerry School Eisteddfod, 1985

Winner – Theatrical Monologue Competition
Matthew Evans

Matthew has never before seen his name written by another's hand. Its shape was a secret he thought he kept alone. Previously his name was only spoken, very often under breath or unfeelingly yelled out. It seemed as ephemeral as a moment. Now he sees that his name might register, that it could be an indelible mark to be made somewhere. This is just a beginning, he tells himself.

RICHARD REDMAN is the pen/stage name of Phillip Morris, who trained and worked as a classical actor before becoming a playwright. His plays have been staged in London and Cardiff and he has lectured in acting at the University of Dubuque in the US, the Academy of Musical Theatre Wales and lectured in playwriting at LAMDA. He has recently completed a screen adaptation of *Bel-Ami* by Guy de Maupassant.

Contact: richard.redman@sparksanthology.co.uk

Selected Poems

Beth Kendall

At Meltimi's on Yailos Beach

During the night in the beachfront room,
the air is thick as if under water.
Across the harbour a ferry heaves into the port
and smashes its anchor into the black skin of sea.
You open the door and windows
and lie outside on the roof,
while I try to sleep in the small bedroom,
feeling your stillness penetrating the air,
listening to crickets in the heat.
In minutes you draw me out with a sigh,
and I stumble into your lap, drowsy fingers
tracing the white of your skin.
The sky is cloudless and unmoving.
Your breaths in my ear come as slowly as
morning takes to wash over the ocean.

The Beach

From our hotel balcony I watch you
run to the sea and back upstairs to the room,
your body studded with droplets.
Dripping wet on the marble,
you say the salt burns your face.
Long after you are dry it still sticks like powder,
snaking white patterns
on your arms; across your chest
the shapes of waves.

Later, as you shower, I watch
from our perch on the third floor
the boy who clears the beach.
He collapses the umbrellas, stacks the sunbeds,
and hoes the sand, until the light diminishes
and he becomes a small, white thing, flitting about,
his quick movements forming shadows across the bay.

In the dark, the beach looks the colour of smoke.
My eyes have to adjust to the night sky, as I walk
out of our room and down the stone steps to the road, away
from the spill of electric light, until the hotel is a small dot
of orange on the curve of the bay.
The sound of the ocean drains into the hills and across the bay.
Here on the beach road, it's as close as the sound
of my own breath, and the pressed dry earth beneath my feet.

The Rub

Our bodies sprawl on the beach
like pieces of a shipwreck. The sky is brown
with rain, and like washed-up fish
we open our mouths to taste the storm.

Rain taps and splatters, the drops
small and countable,
and then it is everywhere.
We lie on the wet sand until dark,
the waves rolling over our feet.

The water pounds and spumes
and sweeps out flat;
you slither your body further in
and take my feet in your hands.
They are numb in your grip,
glowing white and bloodless.

I can't feel your touch,
like stones in your grip, my feet
could belong to someone else,
until I feel the warmth rise
from your damp palms as you rub,
rub, until my bone-stiff toes
slowly begin to uncurl,
hauling in blood.

Beth

A white boat,
my name painted
in red nail varnish,

lies on the sand,
rigid and heavy
like a wax seal,

while your green eyes
watch me through
your thicket of hair,

as I walk slowly
across the beach
in the lunchtime sun.

While He Sleeps Below Deck

As the sun rises on the left side of the ship,
the sea illuminates the sky with a bruise
of violet, purple and mauve.
The ocean is thick in my hair,
wrapping my body in vapour
I don't notice until I'm wet through.
Over the railings of the ship
my arms hang like plumb lines
towards the white water
breaking in peaks like cream.
In the distance the sea is as smooth as paper,
as empty as the heat and this morning alone.

Archaeology

A week after we return home I feel
like a tourist in a Greek souvenir shop,
when I find myself kneeling by the bath,
fishing out grains of sand
you've left around the plughole.

BETH KENDALL is twenty-four, and after living in Bath for five years
she has returned to live in Herefordshire. Her poetry addresses issues to
do with close, personal, often sexual, relationships and happenings that
are sometimes overlooked and underestimated. Her time spent working
and travelling around Greece has inspired her most recent work.

Contact: beth.kendall@sparksanthology.co.uk

Jeanette

Rebecca Saalbach

from a novel

This is the point at which I stop caring. Here, in the fiction section of the city library. All the reasons I never should have come back here are crystal clear. Toby's got a gun jammed against my temple. A 9mm Glock. Both my arms behind my back, with one of his looped through them.

We were supposed to be checking the internet for some website with satellite photos. Photos that might show us an alien ship approaching, some crap like that. I didn't even think about not walking in. Of course, that was before the click, fifteen whole minutes ago, when life was actually moving away from guns and bodies. Fifteen minutes ago, the thought of running away from a library because it gave me nightmares seemed pretty dumb. Seemed like something I'd do before I skipped town and broke things and beat people up and burned down buildings.

I should stop trying to learn things.

Now it's a waiting game – how long until the gunshots; how long until there's blood on the pages and all over the computer terminals? One minute? Ten? The circle of the gun barrel is cold against my temple. Sometimes Toby moves it, to wave at the two librarians and three patrons sitting terrified in front of the reception desk. But then it comes back, the circle, like something dependable I can lean against when I get too tired to stand here any more.

'You,' he shouts to the receptionist. 'I told you to call the news! Pick up the telephone!'

She reaches, slowly, and wraps her fingers around the handset. 'Pick it up!' Toby shouts. 'And put it on speakerphone.'

The dial tone starts broadcasting, low and constant, like a heart monitor and a dead heart. 'I, uh...' the receptionist says. She's looking down at the desk, her right hand hooking her hair behind her ear again and again.

'What?'

'I don't know the number.'

'We're in a library!' Toby explodes. 'We're in a library! Look it up!'

The thing with the hair is becoming a tick. She's starting to break it each time she tucks it back. If she starts to hyperventilate now, we'd better hope someone here's got a brown paper bag. Finally, her eyes come up, 'The... ' she starts. 'Telephone books,' she points right, to a metal shelf bolted to the wall. It's full of ring binders and a couple of those big, fat telephone directories. It's next to a row of framed certificates, things proving the two scared men huddled in front of the desk are qualified to catalogue books. One of them is kind of young. He has dark hair and his eyes are closed. The other I know. It's Bob, or Fred, or Jack, or, I squint at the picture frames, Thomas. The guy who runs the children's reading corner.

Thomas has one hand resting on the young librarian's shoulder, and the other on the shoulder of a middle-aged woman. His eyes are open, but not exactly seeing.

The gun's gone from my head.

Toby's using it to wave the receptionist over to the shelf. She's shaky on her legs. I keep thinking she's going to drop the Yellow Pages.

Through this, the dial tone is constant. There are only two other things in this room so certain as that tone. The gun in Toby's hand and the rhythm of my breathing.

Toby starts pushing me forwards. It's not easy. The way he's got me held, I'm leaning forwards some, but our feet are practically touching. So us moving towards the reception desk is something of a shuffle.

The girl is turning the pages in chunks, her and Toby trying to work out if they should be looking under 'N' for 'news' or 'T' for 'television'. I'm wondering if it wouldn't be a better idea to look under 'C' for 'catering' because I've heard these hostage situations can go on for days, and I haven't eaten breakfast.

So I say to Toby, 'I'm hungry.'

I feel him panic. He tenses, like for a second he was about to go and get me a sandwich. 'Shut up,' he whispers.

'I'm so hungry I might be sick over the Yellow Pages.' This is a lie.

'Shut up,' he whispers, in a way that says he's got no breath left. I hear him swallow. The gun goes back to my temple, and he pushes. 'Shut up!'

'Why don't you let her go, now?'

The way I'm being held, I can't turn my head to see, but I know that voice.

Tremulous from having been sixty-five years in use. It's Thomas.

'She's a child,' he says. 'Let her go. Let the kids go. You've got plenty of us here.'

'I'm a hungry child.'

The gun leaves my temple again, and I know where it's got to be aimed. Chivalry – it's a wonder it hasn't been bred out of us.

'Toby,' I say. 'Toby, you need to put the gun back against my head right now.'

'Be quiet.'

'Put the gun back!'

'No!'

'You put that gun against my head right now or I'm going to do my damnedest to kick you in the balls, and then I'd like to see you aim at anything. So put it back! Put it back!'

Bang. The recoil jars his whole body. The way I'm being held, it jars mine, too. I wait for the screaming, for blood to start spreading on the tile floor and stain the soles of my sneakers. There's just the dial tone. I twist my head to see the gun in Toby's hand, still held out straight, aiming at a totally wrecked piece of bookcase. He's blown a hole clean through the shelf, books from above it falling on to the books below. Books with eviscerated lower halves, and eviscerated upper halves, and spines blown apart. There are little bits of paper floating down. There's a thud as half a dozen hardbacks unbalance, and nosedive to the tiles.

The asystole of the phone finally cuts out, and there's a tinny woman telling us to hang up and try again. Quickly, the receptionist pushes her finger down on the receiver.

'All right,' Toby says. 'No one's going anywhere.'

'You're scared,' I say.

'Please, Jeanette,' he says. 'Please be quiet.'

'If you get your news crews here, the police will come. They're going to shoot you.'

'No they won't,' he says.

'They will. As soon as they get a clear shot. In the back of the neck, so your reflexes fail and you can't shoot me.'

'Then I'll face forwards.'

'Don't count on them being too worried about that. You die, I die; they still save all these people. We can't all be in front of you.'

He turns the gun on the receptionist. 'Get on with it.'

'Back on me, Toby. Put the gun back on me.'

'Once she does her job.'

'Her job is directing people to the fiction section! Her job is to fine people for late returns! Whatever this is, it's not her job!'

The receptionist has her head down again, is back to tearing her hair. Better to concentrate on thin pages than look up at the gun, inches from her head. Her breathing is ragged and it's hard to tell it and the rustle of turning paper apart. Coming back into this place really was the stupidest thing I ever did.

When she's found some numbers, Toby has her put the speaker-phone back on. Has her speak to other receptionists in other buildings, telling them to mobilise their news crews, get reporters down to the library right now.

'Put the phone where I can use it,' he says.

The receptionist complies, holding the handset an inch away from his mouth. She's doing pretty well; it's almost not shaking.

'I've got a gun,' Toby says to the phone. 'And seven hostages. I want my demands broadcast to the public. Tell them I've got a gun!'

'He does,' she gasps. 'He really does.'

There's a gap of five minutes between the time the phone-calling's done and the time we first hear sirens. In that time, the receptionist practically collapses, if you can collapse without moving. She sits back in her chair, then, sort of, settles. Just goes limp and stays perfectly still, staring really hard at a rolodex on the counter-top.

'OK,' Toby says. 'You,' he waves the gun at the people sitting on the floor. 'I want you to take the computers from those tables and start building a barricade. Something we can all sit behind. I want you to wall off the corridors between the bookshelves.'

The door into the library is glass. If we stay where we are, the police have a perfect shot, but crouched in between the stacks it'll be hard for them to get an angle through the narrow basement-style windows tucked up under the ceiling.

The people on the floor are Thomas, who still has his arms around the dark-haired librarian with his eyes closed, and a middle-aged red-head with blue eyeshadow. A woman with grey hair and smooth skin clutching an Agatha Christie, and a boy I think I recognise from school. A year younger than me. Maybe two. I smile at him; he looks terrified.

'Get up.'

Both women move. The one with the Agatha Christie puts it down and reaches out to the schoolkid. 'You're safe,' she whispers. 'You're fine.' The boy gives a quick nod, and pushes himself up without help. Once he's standing, she steers him to the computer access terminals with a light hand against his back. They have the same narrow mouths, the same cheekbones.

The redhead begins unplugging the monitors.

The librarian has begun muttering; his eyes are still closed. Thomas, with his arm around him, says from the floor, 'I think he's in some kind of shock.'

'Well, just...' Toby starts speaking. From where I'm being held, I can see the top of this guy's head as he slumps forwards. 'Just take him over there, put him behind the barricade, then help the others, all right?'

'I think he needs medical attention.' I wish Thomas would shut up. I can't be saving his life twice in one day.

'But I haven't... ' Toby says, motioning with the gun, lifting it up and down like he's drawing a line from the librarian's feet to the top of his head. 'Look at him, he's fine! I'm not going to... ' he stops himself, stills his voice. 'I don't want to hurt anyone.'

'Come on, son,' Thomas murmurs. 'Up you get.'

What I remember of the next few minutes is getting dragged backwards, still arm-locked by Toby, over to the place where the schoolkid and the two women are piling up the desks. I remember more harassing the receptionist to get up and move over to join us. The lot of us, finally, holed up in the library behind plastic and hardboard and paper.

The hostages are sitting. Toby is leaning against a bookshelf, me still in front of him, the gun back against my head.

'You want to shoot me?' I ask.

'No.'

'Sure you do.'

'Stop it.'

'Sure you do.'

At a time like this, what I should be thinking about is how I could have missed Toby being totally nuts. The day we first came here, when we stood by these desks while they were upright, and he showed me those wacked-out conspiracy websites and chatted about planets in outer space, I knew it. I felt it, the way his voice echoed, the way my bones felt cold, it was recognisable. And I had the sense to run away from it, once. At first. This is what I should be thinking about. The mess I've landed these people in because somewhere in that three-day all-nighter I pulled, I lost it – the ability to think. The ability to put myself and a madman into an equation and see the outcome.

This is when I first hear the sirens. And what I'm actually thinking about, at this moment, is how I might have done it anyway. If someone had played me a tape of these minutes, I might have gone with Toby regardless. Perhaps this is the pattern of my life. What I want. Not a mess, but this mess, here, with hostages and a gun, in a wide building used for storage, with death on the tip of a tongue, at the click of a safety.

I wanted, so badly, to find a redeeming feature in the deaths at that warehouse. To find a reason, something that made me the daughter of a man, not a killer, not a fruit-loop with a gun and innocent people at the other end. Perhaps we force repetition into history. It's history tha t can't escape us.

REBECCA SAALBACH is twenty-two years old and has more names than she will ever need. She is from Wales and the USA and is bilingual (*talcen, ceiliog, bwrdd*). This is part of her book. Sometimes she dreams in music.

Contact: rebecca.saalbach@sparksanthology.co.uk

Thursday Night

Kate Cadigan

from a novel

Amongst the earthy-coloured books in the archaeology alcove on the upper floor of the library, Marcus pulled time from his pocket. The immaculately preserved pocket watch, passed down through the family on his mother's side, read seven o'clock. There was a click, then a low buzzing as the lights dimmed.

'I wouldn't leave it all up to you.' Marcy moved away from the switch on the central reading lamps. Her serious face lasted the sentence, then spread into a wide smile as she turned and ran lightly down the worn stairs. Marcus followed the curls and colours of his friend, three steps at a time; he wouldn't run. She reached the door before him. 'Night,' she called looking up from the bottom, then pulled the door open just enough to slip through.

'See you tomorrow.' Marcus smiled as he freed the tassels of her scarf trapped in the door and watched her walk away. He acted out locking the main entrance in case she looked back, then went up the stairs following the grooves of infinite footsteps in the grey stone. From the large Gothic windows he saw the dark outlines of the city, its hills and castle evidence of a time when nature dictated design. He saw Marcy's silhouette step through the pool of a streetlight. Coming up from another alley was a larger figure.

Marcus continued up the stairs to the dimly lit upper floor, he waited before turning on the lamps. The windows reached the ceiling on this level and any light would be seen from some distance away. In a few minutes he knew Marcy would have turned down the road to the station, and the gable of this building would disappear behind her.

It was a Thursday, Marcus' night to lock up. Most jobs have perks, a discount or a status card you can play at some point, no matter how insignificant or irrelevant. Marcus considered this his perk, though neither money nor status came into it. He stood alone in the empty building; in his hand was an oversized steel hoop threaded through brass keys. He enjoyed the shadows of the room. From these windows he saw the back of the castle and the graveyard beneath; nothing of the new city was visible. He waited until he heard the front door pushed open and feet on the stone stairs before turning on the lights. The colours of the room returned and the view disappeared.

The library building was on four floors, the top being the most impressive, with its ornate domed ceiling and balconies, accessible only through concealed stairwells in the bookshelves. A number of wooden ladders maximised the room's height – books towered into a blur of reds and greens. Slender metal rails, low and delicate, were all that prevented browsers toppling backwards. But it was unlikely these rails would save anyone, being more an ornate token gesture; the books came first. Large oak tables filled the floor space beneath the dome – some with reading lights, which were already being used as early as four o'clock. The lower levels offered fiction; beneath that, Scottish history and nature. It was more specific on the fourth floor, beneath the green lamps. But it was not for the openly interested so much as the ones whose research hadn't been sanctioned. Otherwise, they would have a pass for the national library further up towards the Royal Mile.

As the footsteps approached, Marcus heard heavy breathing. Charlie appeared and leant in the doorway, his cheeks flushed. It took him a while to catch his breath.

'All right, Marcus?' he panted.

'Hi, Charlie.' It wasn't a whisper, but neither was it full volume. It wasn't just out of habit. Marcus didn't like the difference in their accents. Charlie's Glaswegian; Marcus was born further north, up past Loch Ness in Nairn. He was sent to an English boarding school at ten, an age at which it was a conscious effort to lose an accent – he had made the conscious effort. He sanded down its rough tones until he had no edges, not from his past anyway. He knew something disappeared and the result was that he couldn't be placed any more. Marcy had asked him once about his childhood, to which he'd replied with a formality she wouldn't have recognised, 'It's hard to think of your child self objectively.' He'd paused, and then, seeing the confusion in her face, he'd brought it to a close: 'I don't think of him at all.' But that had been a half-truth.

Charlie had never questioned the whispering. If anything he enjoyed the sense of conspiracy. Charlie headed straight to his usual table; he didn't take off his coat, but instead pulled a scarf from his brown satchel.

The library officially shut at seven, but on a Thursday Marcus and a few others stayed until they decided to leave. They didn't advertise, the late-nighters; nothing was set in stone. The only downside to the set-up was that the heating was on a timer that automatically turned off at six forty-five. After that, the temperature fell quickly. It was a small price to pay. Marcus, for a reason he hadn't questioned, liked it.

Charlie laid out his pens on the desk, then spread out five sheets of paper. Marcus helped him find the books he had set aside last Thursday. As Marcus pulled them from the shelves, Charlie double-checked each selection, traced its title with his finger, then nodded. It had been the same five books for months.

He was researching Edinburgh, its streets and legends. He had been for the five years Marcus had known him, and probably for many more before that. He called Marcus over sometimes to show him things; Marcus listened. It was incredible what Charlie found, or maybe just believed he had found. Charlie traced back the things others had missed, or grew tired of. He pinpointed what decisions were made, which men ceased to speak, then he followed the alternative route, the ones littered with names deemed unworthy of fame. Marcus was pleased Charlie was on to it; that an area was being given that amount of attention put his mind at ease. There was so much. They stored all Charlie had written so far behind the archaeology shelves.

Marcus pulled on a heavy knitted jumper that he kept beneath the main desk. He had his own research to be getting on with, but he was watching Charlie. He worked in the parks when Marcus was away. He couldn't work at home, he had not said why. He never took books out.

'You think they'll come tonight?' Charlie asked as he looked up, struggling to focus in his reading glasses.

'Maybe,' said Marcus. 'I hope so; it's been a while.'

'Mmmh.' Charlie looked back at the books open in front of him.

He was referring to Roi and Elsa. Roi's Israeli and Elsa was from Musselburgh by the sea. She was a specific type of mystery, or at least the reasons behind her friendship with Roi were. He was more vague altogether. She translated for him, but what was said was never discussed with anyone else. They wrote something together; they took it in turns, though unlike Charlie's work theirs was never left behind.

Charlie liked having them in the room. Their soft voices; wordless music. The door downstairs opened again, both men listened – a single set of footsteps.

'Sarah,' said Charlie, his cheek tinged green from the glass on the lampshade.

'Sounds like it,' Marcus replied. Satisfied, Charlie went back to his work. Marcus left him and climbed up a narrow staircase through the shelves, reappearing on a balcony. He walked past the books, looking down at the wooden floorboards and stopping at one with a large knot in the wood shaped like an eye. He patted his hand along the top of the books, tracing the shape of a slim bound document.

'Hello.' Sarah's coarse whisper brought him down the ladder.

'Good to see you,' Marcus said, now dangerously close to the balcony edge.

'God, it was warmer in the graveyard.' She walked over to Charlie's desk, pulling fingerless gloves from her pockets. 'How are you, Charlie?'

'I'm not too bad. You?' He half stood to greet her.

'Glad to hear it. I'm fine myself. Brought us a little something.' She took the rucksack off her back and started unpacking it on the corner of Charlie's desk, while he parted papers and balanced books to make space for her.

'Irish-ish coffee.' She smiled as she put down a large Thermos flask and an odd assortment of cups. 'Only the three of us tonight?'

'So far,' Marcus answered, his back to them now as he untied the folder. He smelled the coffee as she started to fill the mugs. For Sarah, the Thursday nights were a chance to write up her week's findings. She was tracing her family back as far as she could, convinced if she dug deeply enough she could connect most people she knew. She'd leave via the graveyard, torch in hand.

'I'll leave yours on the desk,' she said, the words tapering out as she became aware of her volume.

'Thanks. Need it tonight.' Marcus returned to the main level. Sat at his desk with Sarah's coffee, he opened the first page of the document and began to read:

> The focus of Plato's teaching, that which more recent investigators have chosen to ignore, was the advanced nature of the civilisation. This has been overshadowed by an obsessive urge to locate and account for the land mass itself. The telling of Atlantis in true oral tradition was a teaching, and not necessarily of a solely religious nature. We know enough of what are assumed to be punishing floods. If they were truly becoming too close to God, the question must be how this threat was construed.'

The document, written by an old friend, had arrived two days before and this was the first chance Marcus had to give it his full attention. It was true. Although his interest lay in the design of the ringed water city, he had become, like many others, caught up in the arguments of its location: Tunisia, the North Sea, somewhere off Ireland. He'd learned how the land had changed, shifted, grown, and sunk. He had considered all the alternative interpretations of the Pillars of Hercules before returning to the Straits of Gibraltar. Now that Higlend's team were so close to a discovery, Marcus could return to the myths, and fill the time before news arrived. Every notebook he owned contained a sketch of the encircling rivers and Moorish palaces. But there was no trace of this people, and only words to build pictures from. The imagination always floundered on the familiar – he could design no true alternative. The document in front of him was concerned with the philosophy of the place, the democracy (or version of it) on which it was built. But Marcus knew that, like him, his old friend was limited by his own life.

His eyes travelled fast over the page. He would reread and annotate sections later, for now he just wanted to take it all in. Every so often he read something that sent shivers through his body, but when he looked up to voice it, he saw only Sarah's woollen hat moving with the speed of her writing and Charlie's balding head frozen behind a wall of books. Both would offer all they knew to anyone who asked, whilst Elsa and Roi would avoid ever being questioned. Marcus placed himself somewhere in between: to the right person he'd tell everything, almost everything. His mind flicked to the girl. He'd not heard her recently. He used to lie on his floor, her ceiling, and listen. He still did sometimes, but now she was quieter, controlling the sounds of her rooms, the taps and doors, invisibly, like a ghost. She'd changed, or was changing.

They left in reverse order to that which they had arrived. Sarah piled all her belongings back into her rucksack, touching Marcus on the arm on her way out, torch in her other hand. Then Charlie, not long after, yawned, satchel tight to his body, offering as always to help lock up. Marcus, as always, turned down his help. They stayed until they decided to leave. It was late that night when Marcus flicked the final light switch on the fourth floor and the castle and graveyard reappeared in the windows. As he turned, he saw torchlight flickering over the stones. He found a new short-cut back to his apartment.

KATE CADIGAN studied English Literature at Stirling University. After graduating, she returned home to Jersey. She worked for a year in a school for children with behavioural problems before taking the MA at Bath Spa. Kate is now back in Jersey again. 'Thursday Night' is an extract from a novel she is working on.

Contact: kate.cadigan@sparksanthology.co.uk

The Garden Dragon

Penny Thomson

a monologue for radio

MUSIC	'THE WAY WE WERE.' OVERTURE AND STRINGS FADING UNDER DIALOGUE.

HERMIONE

I hate being so old!
When I look down at my hands laid on the white sheet, I can hardly believe they're attached to me.
Papery skin stretched over my knuckles.
Fingers curled in.
Parrot claws with brown age spots like splashed gravy.
I spend more time in my memory than ever before.
Retreat into my childhood. Find refuge there.

FX

DAYTIME. HOSPITAL WARD. WE HEAR THE SQUELCH OF FOOTSTEPS COMING CLOSER.

Oh, here comes that new nurse – Shareen, it says on her badge.
What sort of a name's that?
Coming to take my breakfast tray.
Polystyrene cup, plastic cutlery, heavy plates
– ugh!
Whatever happened to silver and china?
No wonder I look back.
'Come along, Hermione.' She says in her hard bright voice.
I think I'd rather she showed me some respect
– called me 'Mrs Carlisle'.
But I can't even communicate that any more.
I guess she's only doing her job.
Now she's pulling me up by my arm.
Ouch!
Another injection.

HERMIONE	*And* she's left me propped like a rag doll so my head lolls.
	(*sigh*)
	A few hours' peace now.
	Close my eyes.
	I can step back into my young body.
	Another lifetime, days full of sunshine.
	The shadows in uniforms who surround me here can go away for a while!
FX	<u>HOSPITAL SOUNDS FADE TO INTRO MUSIC VERY LOW UNDER.</u>
	(*sigh*)
	What was that story I used to tell the grand-children?
	Oh – I know. It was 'The Garden Dragon'
	– with Geoffrey.
	I wonder what happened to Geoffrey?
	If he ever remembers me – or even if he's still alive?
	Let's see – he was nine and a half when I was eight and a quarter.
FX	<u>MUSIC FADES.</u>
	My lovely Geoffrey from next door.
	Their house was called Sherwood, ours was Summerville.
	They had a hard tennis court in their garden and we had stables.
	Hmm. All been pulled down now.
	'An exclusive development of contemporary execu-tive homes,' the sign said.
	Oh dear, Geoffrey. We were so easy together.
	Like that day when we shared our own private lunch.
	School holidays.
	No one in but us, at Geoffrey's house.
	We fibbed. Well, we didn't fib exactly, just didn't tell.

HERMIONE His mummy was going out. Taking his big brother Robert to a doctor in town to see about getting his tonsils out.

My big brother John had his out last year.

Big brothers. They can be a nuisance sometimes. They always force us to be Indians when we play cowboys and Indians.

I get fed up of being tied to trees.

Anyhow – Geoffrey's mummy thinks he's coming to my house for lunch, 'cos their housekeeper Missus Biggin's away on holiday.

But we never pass on the message to my mummy, so we can have a glorious few hours to do just what we want.

My mummy and daddy have a thing about table manners – so do Geoffrey's.

So it'll be good fun to get our very own – our very own – lunch.

We've put all our pocket money together.

It comes to two and sixpence. Half a crown!

Down at Mister Kenyon's shop in the village we buy a tin of baked beans, a tin of peaches and a box of Maltesers.

They're a bit snobby about all those things at home – tinned stuff and chocolate – so that makes it even better.

We even have enough change to buy some chewing gum.

But, 'No – no, that's going too far,' says Geoffrey.

Walking back home, we plan our feast.

We work out that we have to heat up the beans.

But the first problem is to open the tins.

The tin opener's a bit rubbish and we can't make it work.

It keeps slipping off.

So Geoffrey goes to the shed and gets a screwdriver and a hammer. He sits on the back doorstep holding the tin of beans between his sandals.

Ha ha – he looks just like a chimpanzee.

He bashes holes in the lid by hitting the screwdriver with the hammer.

HERMIONE   It makes a right mess of his socks, all that bean
            sauce splashed about.
            It's even dripping off one of the red and black
            tags on his garters.
            Eventually he makes a jagged hole big enough to
            get the beans out.
            I've found a saucepan in the cupboard next to the oven.
            We get the beans into the pan by turning the tin
            over and knocking the bottom of it with the hammer.
            There's loads of them – coming out one or two
            at a time – like sheep poo.
            (*pause*)
            The ring on the cooker pops and bangs a bit and it
            takes four matches to light the gas.
            Nearly takes my eyebrows off.
            The beans don't get hot for ages – then suddenly
            they all bubble like mad and smell of burning, so
            I turn off the ring and announce: 'Der-da-da-der!
            Lunch is served!'
            The kitchen table at Geoffrey's is Formica, so I just
            pour two dollops of beans straight on to it.
            Saves washing up.
            Ooh! They're scrummy! Yummy scrummy!
            We have to scoff them really quick with forks and
            fingers, before they spread out too far.
            When we've eaten all the beans, we rub our fingers
            on the table, then suck them. Geoffrey can get
            more juice up 'cos he bites his nails and that makes
            his fingertips incredibly bendy.
            Only two forks to wash and that gooey pan. Oh
            well, we'll do those later.
            Next come the peaches.
            Geoffrey opens the tin the same way, but the hole
            has to be much bigger to let the peaches out.
            'Yellow – Cling – Peach – Slices', it says on the tin.
            Some of them get a bit mangled.
            When Geoffrey pours those on to the table, the
            gloopy juice runs all over.
            We have a race to see who can eat a whole slice,
            licking up the drips of juice before it slithers off the
            table. It's super-fun. We giggle a lot.

HERMIONE	At the end we make squiggly finger patterns on the table with the orange mix of all the runny bits.

HERMIONE   At the end we make squiggly finger patterns on the
            table with the orange mix of all the runny bits.
            And we still have a whole box of Maltesers to go.
            Time for a break.
            'Bouncing time,' Geoffrey says. 'That'll give the
            table a chance to dry.'
            We go into the lounge to have a bounce on the settee.
            Their settee's great, big and wide and springy.
            If you run at it and jump bang in the middle, you
            can bounce right over the back, then run round to
            the front again for another go.
            We do that for a while, then Geoffrey hits it wrong
            and it tips over backwards.
            It goes with a big crash and he nearly flies through
            the window.
            I'm just coming round for my next go and I run into
            the upside-down bit at the front and fall backwards.
            We sit on the floor laughing and panting. Just say-
            ing each other's name over and over.
            'Geoffrey.'
            'Aitch.'
            'Oh, Geoffrey.'
            'Oh, Aitch.'
            He always called me Aitch.
            The settee's really heavy to get back on its feet
            and it looks a bit wonky and down at one side, *and*
            we've both got sore knees, so we think we'd better stop.
            Then I say, 'Hey, let's have the Maltesers now.'
            Back in the kitchen we have a contest, rolling them
            across the table along the lines in the patterns we'd
            made.
            The rule is to catch them in your mouth as they fall
            off the edge.
            I score three more catches than Geoffrey. He says
            it's because my mouth's so big.
            So then we have a wrestling match.
            He wins.
            I feel a bit sick now. Tummy ache.
            So I get bossy.
            'Time to clear up,' I say, sounding just like Mummy.

HERMIONE   We wash the two forks, but we can't get the mess
off the pan.
'I know what to do,' says Geoffrey. 'Follow me.'
He gathers up the pan, the baked bean tin and the
peach tin and goes outside.
I trail after him up the path as he heads towards the
compost heap.
There's a garden fork sticking out of it.
'Now Aitch, we have to bury the evidence,' he an-
nounces.
The compost heap. It's much bigger than me,
mostly grass cuttings all gone yellow.
It feels warm when I put my hand on it.
Geoffrey yanks out the garden fork and digs a big
hole in the side of the mound.
The hole's ever so stinky.
Smells of damp leaves and rotting socks.
And it's hot!
'Know why it's hot inside there?' Geoffrey says.
'It's because that's where the garden dragon lives.
Grrrr. We mustn't dig too far or he'll wake up.'
'What does he do?'
'He buries you alive.'
I know Geoffrey doesn't really mean it, but I stand
back a long way, just in case.
He throws the saucepan and the empty tins into the
hole.
Geoffrey pulls the top of the mound down with the
fork, so it overbalances and covers the hole.
Then we scoop up the fallen bits of grass and
leaves and throw them back on the top.
To smooth the compost heap over, so it looks like it
did before, we pat on it.
I only pat a little bit.
We stand back and it's very still, so I know the
garden dragon's not woken up.
I'm a bit nervous, though, when Geoffrey sticks the
garden fork back in.
Phew. All done. Just in time.
I can hear his mummy's car turning into the drive.
We'd better run over to my house.

HERMIONE	Pretend we've been there all day. Oh no – it's not his mummy's car.
FX	<u>DAYTIME. HOSPITAL WARD. WE HEAR A TROLLEY AND FOOTSTEPS.</u> It's the lunchtime trolley coming down the ward. Time for those fearful women. The nurses with the cheery voices. They bring trays of grey pap to shovel into my mouth. Bye bye, Geoffrey. Oh, and by the way, the garden dragon's really got me now.
MUSIC	<u>AS INTRODUCTION.</u>

<u>ENDS</u>.

PENNY THOMSON was born and grew up in the Peak District. Occasionally she still misses the grandeur of the landscape and the warmth of its people. After years working in industry, she returned to education as a mature student. Now a resident of Oxford, she writes radio drama, finding the adventure of life interesting, often startling, but never boring.

Contact: penny.thomson@sparksanthology.co.uk

A Blobby Man in a Bath

Paul Dale

Six months ago I bought a picture. It wasn't titled, but the painter, a friend of mine who was strapped for cash, sold it to me as '*A Blobby Man in a Bath*'. I had to take the artist's word on the gender as 'the man' in the bath had an orange featureless head and was not obviously a bloke. He was, however, blobby.

He sat in his freestanding bathtub, blobby hands rested on the sides, blobby head back, completely relaxed. Pale steam rose above the centre of the bath in a solid question mark. A yellow ducky floated at the far end. The bath was red and had a green rim. The bath mat matched the bath. Banana slippers were to the left of the mat. Oddly for a bathroom, the walls were a lemon yellow. At least the bath water was blue. At either end of the bath were two plants on pedestals. One was a fern, the other a broad leaf, probably a rubber plant, and both were green.

On the back wall of the man's bathroom was either a painting or a window, it was not clear which. In it was a purple sea against a traditional sky and beach. A lone palm tree poked from the lemon sand. An orange blob, presumably the sun, was setting at the back of the beach.

All the colours were the vibrant side of prime, uniformly applied on canvas, and gave the painting a childish quality. This was enhanced by the mixture of strong geometric structure and blobby bits. It was fun.

I'd hung it in the living room for when Alison got back from work. I'd already awarded myself a sack load of points for taking an interest in the house decor without her having to prompt me. I should have waited.

She came into the living room. A cup of tea was waiting for her on the Tunisian iron mosaic coffee table (£250 African Arts). I'd heard her efforts to park on our hill and got the kettle on while she ground gears back and forth. In the first week of her having moved in, I had offered on three successive days to park for her – it is a steep and narrow road – but she had refused. For me it wasn't a gender issue. I scratched the front bumper on the wall opposite the house when I tried to swing the car in, until I got the knack. After ten years I was practised, but Ali refused my tips.

She smiled at the sight of the tea, came over, proffered her cheek, and sat down. She picked up her cup deliberately and cast her eye over the room. My silence had already aroused her suspicion. I snuggled in close to her.

'How was class?'

'Interesting.' She continued her appraisal of the room. 'We're looking at Vermeer's *Girl with a Pearl Earring*. Fascinating painting.'

At first all she could see were the results of her efforts to change the house from mine to ours: mirrored Indian wallhanging (£60 Tumi), iron elephant wall pieces (£30 same place), pale yellow printed curtains that continued the subcontinent theme (£23 a yard, 13 yards, work it out), and a sandalwood phone table (£60 forget where) next to my favourite old Chinese sofa (now draped in a throw to hide its tawdriness). Then she came to the previously empty, skimmed plaster wall above the television (anything bigger than 28 inches would dominate the room)

'Brian, what's that?' she asked.

'A bargain,' I replied avoiding the facetious answer that had been lying in wait (a painting). 'Seventy quid from Barney. He might be famous one day and it could become worth a lot more.'

She hated it on first sight. Frown lines appeared on her forehead, lines upon which she waged a daily chemical war. I'm not sure why. I liked the lines in her face. They made her look mature, a woman, not a girl.

Glaring at the painting, her eyes squinted, which reduced them to slits. She had the most amazing brown eyes when you could see them. She tightened her focus as though she were trying to solve 16 down of the Guardian cryptic crossword (completed once, 1986, student on placement, and bored).

'Why on earth did you buy that?' she asked after a minute of consideration.

'Barney needed the cash and, besides, I like it.' I tried to sound confident but already my bravado was in full retreat. Consultation and joint decision-making were a big part of our relationship; Ali told me so, frequently.

'You like it?' she asked.

'Well, yes. It's a little simple in style, I'll admit, but the overall effect is compelling.'

I sat up. Ali's frown suggested my art appreciation was less than perfect. This was her territory. She flicked her shoulder-length hair.

'And it matches?' I said weakly. It did, as well. The living-room walls were a matte yellow – I forget the particular tone that was on the can when Ali chose it.

'Never mind whether it matches. What statement do you think it makes?' she said. 'You don't think you might have asked me first?'

I had not expected this tack at all. It was a blobby orange man in a bath. I honestly didn't see it as any kind of statement.

'Well...' I began.

'You don't think it says you would be happier without me?'

I felt a hot flush followed by the feeling that a small black hole had opened in my stomach. I was headed for its event horizon. It was an inclination I had in those days, to think dramatically in terms of cosmological catastrophe.

'No. I don't see it like that at all,' I said casually, without being dismissive of her opinion.

'Really?' said Ali. She drew breath. The gravity well in my stomach widened and I felt almost beyond the point of no return. 'Well, what do you see?'

'A man enjoying a relaxing bath?'

'And?'

'Plants?'

'You don't think the bath represents your life, or that the question mark—'

'Steam—'

'—question mark represents your contemplation of life, or the picture on the back wall, paradise?'

Ali paused significantly. She always thought I needed time to catch up with her, which was true, but not because I'm stupid; rather, so I could work out the least offensive reply. I went for agreement.

'Well, yes... Now that you mention it, that's quite subtle. I would never have noticed.'

'And you don't see the problem?'

I shrugged. Words could only exacerbate matters.

'This picture is suggesting all you need is a hot bath.'

I was totally lost by this point. Even by Ali's wild standards, she had left me so far behind I had no idea how to catch up.

'A hot bath?' I mumbled.

'Alone in a bath, you arse. Alone. No partner. This painting is a bachelor's painting, you moron. It tells me you'd rather be alone in a bath contemplating your navel. You'll have to take it back.'

'I can't do that. Barney needed the money for rent. Besides, no bachelor would have plants in his bathroom.'

'Oh, shut up,' said Ali. 'I still want it fixed.'

'How?' Our conversations did tend to follow a predictable template of statement and puzzled question.

'He can paint me in at the other end of the bath.'

Barney was less than impressed, so I bunged him another twenty quid for his muse. The painting stills hangs there, a reminder of our togetherness, and we both hate it.

PAUL DALE's first career was in computing and consultancy. He burned out in the dot-com boom and retired himself to travelling, writing and playing poker. His first novel, *Take Me to the River,* examines young-gun poker set against Las Vegas and Hollywood celebrity.

Contact: paul.dale@sparksanthology.co.uk

Lost Time

Samantha Harvey

from a novel

This is an early extract from a novel about a man called Jake, who, over the course of the story, develops Alzheimer's disease. The extract comes after the sudden death of his wife, Helen. It is part of a much larger piece that looks at Jake's past – his mother Sara, and his Austrian grandparents – whilst keeping some hold on the present and his relationship with Alice, his daughter. The piece begins to introduce the theme of memory and its unreliability.

Sometimes – often – the wrong people die, the people who were not meant to. Jake has based his life on this notion. He has predicted that he will die by mistake, embarrassingly, unconvincingly, and this prediction takes the consolation out of dying. On his exit from life he will not be able to say, this is meant to be, I am ready. Life hurls rounds of shit at you; thick skin and readiness are the only defences available, but he will not even have that. In all likelihood he will perish thin-skinned, and surprised.

Readiness in a wholly unpredictable world is too difficult: if he has to start being ready for everything, then he is not actually ready at all. He practises walking in darkness, expecting anything to jump at him. He is so ready for something to jump at him that he isn't ready for the lack of things that jump at him. The house is as vacant as a sunken ship. His heart beats fast for a thing that never comes. Far from being ready, he finds himself preoccupied and paranoid.

Walking in darkness is an inheritance from his childhood. His grandfather, Arnold, told Sara to practise walking in darkness until she could do it without paranoia, and with trust. Sara passed the life lesson on to him. *Jake, learn to sense your way around.* They used to walk around their rickety home in the middle of the peat moors, black in the sky, black in the soil, black in his mother's hair and eyes, a serene darkness. *Anything can happen underfoot,* she whispered. *I want you to be ready, not afraid.* He wondered what he was supposed to be scared of, and wanted it to happen, whatever it was. With some deliberation and triumph he bumped into doors or bedposts or armchairs that he knew very well were there; he and Sara would laugh.

Now Jake fumbles. How life has changed him. Refusing to be this timid and paranoid creature, this creature who only resembles its younger self by being its exact opposite, he practises, once more, walking in the dark.

Darkness is rather difficult to find: true, old-fashioned darkness, anyhow. Televisions flicker, the night sky over the town tends away from black and towards weak red – signs are reflective, spires are illuminated, cats' eyes guide, shoes and socks glow. Humanity staves off darkness, thereby staving off the disastrous things that can only happen in the dark.

But he feels the opposite: for thirty years of nights he slept next to Helen without disaster, and then her death happened in daylight when the sun was supposed to be keeping watch. In the months after her death he sits for hours in the dark; he turns off anything that is on standby, eager and ready. He enjoys the absolute solitude. The lack of light makes him think of his mother, their dark trips around the house and the peat moors, and the way he learned nothing from these so-called lessons in trust, except that he liked his mother more than he liked his father. It seemed to him that his father was precisely the sort of Unexpected Thing they might find in the dark, the thing they had to be prepared for. He was not there much. But on the whole Unexpected Things were not there much either, which is what made them unexpected.

Sometimes he wakes up and is deeply surprised by the fact that he is still living, as if there has been a terrible mix-up of fates. When alone in the dark, he has the sensation that his entire body is swelling out. Without trying to understand or even interpret the sensation, he lets it take hold, and becomes something of an addict of darkness.

In the peat moor house he must have been nine or ten years old and his mother was here, there, over there, always present. He would sit with her; maybe they had a candle or a gas lamp, or maybe nothing. She would tell him things of which he now has a warped recollection, some facts exaggerated and some whittled away.

He supposes she told him things because she was lonely or sick to the teeth with the reality of that flat expanse of peat – a dreamland of cocoa-coloured space and wild flowers in the summer, but a black, wet trauma in the winter. And one thing Jake remembers well enough from her German-accented anecdotes is the story of Luigi Lucheni. Lucheni, Sara told him, had been wandering around Europe looking for someone famous to kill, so that he could make history. Immediately, Jake intuited, Lucheni is the kind of man I want to be.

At the time Lucheni was prowling, 1897, there were so many other deaths that, beyond the initial shock, one more didn't really matter. Austria at the turn of the century was feverishly shedding life in preparation for the 1900s, as if, like a clerk using up all his holiday before the year-end, it didn't know it was allowed to carry lives over from the closing century. Because of Sara's quiet lists of the dead – von Suppé, she would say, 1895, Bruckner 1896, Brahms 1897, Strauss 1899, Millöcker 1899 – he began to picture time like a mountain range, with new centuries at the peaks and all the unfit or tired people, who had been climbing for so long, dropping off into chasms just before they reached the top. Composers especially, with their instruments and batons somersaulting into the air.

Luigi Lucheni was only twenty-six and wasn't set to die, but Jake imagined Lucheni was nevertheless infected with the end-of-century death fever. He was as single-minded as a child when it came to his project of killing someone before the century was out. His victim had to be famous, but other than that Lucheni was absolutely the most easy and undiscriminating of assassins. So he left Italy and wandered from country to country, came to Geneva in the knowledge that the Duke of Orleans was visiting at the time, and decided to kill him.

(Jake remembers Sara clasping her hands in the dark and saying, 'Moron Luigi! Ugly and weasly but, with that much determination, he could have taken over the world rather than kill one meagre queen!')

When the Duke failed to arrive Lucheni had to rethink: he checked the local newspaper, checked his pulse, checked the bright-red anarchist's blood charging through his veins, and saw that Elisabeth, Empress of Austria, Queen of Hungary, was also in Geneva. The beautiful empress, the loveliest woman in Europe. To be able to murder such a wonderful person was like living a fairy tale, and his heart soared at the prospect. He went to the Beau Rivage Hotel, near which she was due to board a steamship, and stabbed her in the heart with a shoddy little blade he had fashioned from a shoemaker's file.

Lucheni went to prison and hanged himself twelve years later. Had he rotted in prison he might have been nothing but a nothing, but his premature death elevated him. No less than a comic book superbeing, Lucheni used to be a hero to Jake, who was a child when Lucheni started squatting in his mind and a young man when he left it. Whilst in situ the criminal rewired his brain and made him see that commitment to an insane cause is better than no commitment at all. Lucheni suggested selfishness and the preservation of one's identity above all else, above even the lives of others.

But then Helen came, and God. Jake married Helen and God, and they told him that selflessness was the way and the truth; that a human being had no identity separate from the Father. And commitment to a cause was not an individual business but a collective one, in which a person decides, according to a law of universal hunches, what is right, and commits oneself to it. And commits oneself not to its opposite.

Piece by piece Jake packs Helen's clothes up into boxes for the attic. Alice tells him he should leave mementoes around the house, that it is unhealthy to eradicate someone you love, and he agrees without saying what he really feels, which is that, far from scattering memory triggers left right and centre, he is loath to remember his wife at all. You only remember things when you no longer have them; memory becomes a way of punishing yourself for all the things you have lost.

There is work to bury himself in: the mammoth Edwardian building to be converted into a new school, and renovation plans for an eighties precinct. He tries to throw himself at it. The precinct project is wholly uninspiring, since the council have too little money to renovate in earnest – they will probably do some patching up and install an elaborately raised figure-of-eight flower bed as an obstacle, more than anything, to the skateboarders. The Edwardian project becomes interesting, however. It gains its first long-awaited approval, though this doesn't yet amount to a go-ahead. There are studies and surveys still pending – costings, soil surveys, research into materials. 'Pending' – what a catch-all word, he thinks. All things would suddenly appear to be pending, as if pending is some incredibly intricate manoeuvre that takes time.

Each day he throws himself at the desk and throws himself back home at six or seven or eight, upon which he makes a drink, a sandwich and throws himself into a dark room in front of a television which is sometimes on and sometimes off. He throws himself into the effort of not reading Helen's most recent diary because then he would have to remember her, which he is loath to do.

One evening, hardly by accident, he finds a picture of his grandfather and grandmother, and another of a cherry tree. They are in his study in a drawer of things pending, having decided to do all the pending things he can find, now that he is throwing himself at life. The photographs are awaiting frames and have been for around fifteen years. So he hacks together two small wooden box frames and seals the pictures inside.

The image of his grandparents comes from the late 1920s, when they were on the cusp of ageing – an odd-looking pair. On the back, in Sara's hand, is written: "Arnold 'the trembler' Cohn and his wife, my mother, Minna."

Arnold was tall– without his straggling beard and nervous look he might have seemed much younger. He was shabbily dressed, too, but maybe that was just a symptom of the time, postwar, when Austria's *krone* had crashed on the rocks and thousands of them would not even buy you a meal. He has symmetrical scars on his left and right cheeks, inch-long diagonals of silver skin. Jake wouldn't have noticed his grandfather's scars had it not been for Sara saying, 'Look, here, scars, see?' The scars are slithers, but invisibly they influence his face into a more aquiline shape than it really had.

Arnold's wife, Minna, was thin and dark-haired, crookedly good-looking with a mole on her right cheek. In the photograph she is standing next to Arnold with a broad closed-lip smile and a straight back, holding a praise ring – an old embroidery hoop with ribbons attached.

Being a wife had given her either poise or rigidity depending on which way you looked at it; Jake thinks rigidity. She cooked her way through marriage. Apfelstrudel, halvah, goulash, triangular hamantasch biscuits, though the food was not always kosher. They picked and chose – some days they were practising Jews, other days not – picking and choosing was part of their prerogative and happiness. They spoke German. They didn't want to be different: they had no Zionist friends, they loved Vienna and the non-Jewish maid who took care of their precious things. The maid used to go through the alphabet forwards and backwards when she worked. Hah, eeh, yot, kah, ell, emm, enn. Enn, emm, ell, kah, yot, eeh, hah. She was fluent both ways. Sara claimed these were the first sounds she ever heard.

Opening tins of fish, Jake announces the sounds to himself, dictating his memory of Sara to the dim kitchen. 'Yot, kah, ell, emm, enn.'

It's peculiar: these people in the picture do not coincide with Jake's idea of them. What he imagines is Minna licking the prune jam off her fingers while making the hamantasches (hamantaschen? hamentaschi? he ponders, toying with his useless German). Maybe she would wave out of the window at people she knew walking past. He imagines Arnold sitting with a newspaper on the brink of the twentieth century, his feet on a stack of books in his so-polished, so-well-stocked Viennese bookshop, a Persian cat in his lap, an empty coffee cup trembling in his left hand and not a whiff of this photographed shabbiness about him.

Probably, he thinks, Arnold 'the trembler' Cohn trembled because he was reading about the flush of death going on around him, the beautiful Habsburg empress killed by a mad Italian, the archduke who had committed suicide, the other archduke who had died before making it to the throne, and the dear old composers falling off life's mountaintop, their somersaulting instruments.

'How can you set about forgetting your wife, *my* mother,' Alice asks, when Jake tells her about the photograph, 'but spend so much time remembering your grandparents, whom you never knew?'

'Because, my dear Alice, because.'

Because he never knew them. Memories are pliable, can be added to, taken away from, controlled, or so Jake had thought. In fact, it is not as simple as that. In fact, it works both ways – he leaving his residue on his memories, his memories leaving residue on him. He learns that memory is fluid and selfish, and capable of shape-shifting. He is aware that this Persian cat, the stack of books, the coffee (which changes from white to black to white) might have no grounding in reality. There are no pictures of Arnold and Minna from this time, and probably they didn't yet have a camera. What he knows comes pieced together from things he recalls Sara saying in the dark, as if talking to herself, and from these two later photographs: a bold, black-haired but slightly impoverished couple, and a cherry tree.

Death, he decides, was on Arnold's mind. Arnold with Minna and the praise ring, or in his imagined state ensconced in his chair, with his (Persian? Siamese?) cat and (white? black?) coffee, has the aura of a man who has lost something and is scheming its recovery.

Maybe Arnold feared his wife's death, and this is why she outlived him. It is right to be cautious, assume the worst. Maybe he went home each evening half expecting to find Minna prone on the bed, blue lips smiling, lured by the same morbid call as everyone else. When the somersaulting instruments clanged in the air they must have made the loveliest death knell. Maybe Arnold thought Minna would follow its sound, too.

Jake hears a sound in the kitchen – no death knell, something falling or dislodging. My wife, he assumes in an off-guard moment, and then realises. No, no, not my wife. That time is gone.

SAMANTHA HARVEY is thirty years old and this is her second novel. She studied Philosophy at York University and then the University of Sheffield, spent two years teaching English in Japan, lived and worked in New Zealand for a short time, and has had all sorts of jobs doing all sorts of things in the gaps between.

Contact: samantha.harvey@sparksanthology.co.uk

Selected Poems

Ellie Evans

Chinese Painting Lesson

My ink stick,
two inches long,
a thumb's width thick,
gleams like coal.

In my dish of stone,
the size of my palm,
with a teaspoon of rain,
I grind it

and grind it and
grind till a black eye of ink,
thick and concave, winks;
then my fat wet brush

stains its tip,
spreads on the rice-paper,
grows mountain-tops,
waterfalls, trees.

Okefenokee

I am in front, paddling
liquid mud. Our canoe nudges
through the reeds;
the air is thick, like butter.
Silence: slop of water,
quiver of insects,
whirr of feathers.
Logs cruise by, and wink.

A gap in the sedge: we slide through –
acres and acres
of white water lilies,
miles and miles
of sky. Silence.
The damp heat
is a second skin, muffling,
while my paddle scrapes the oozy floor.

Back at the wharf, we tie up.
On the bank, beside the gift shop,
an alligator, twelve feet long,
has clamped its jaws around a turtle.
The turtle is the size of a dustbin lid,
its paws bat the air.
Silence: then the splinter crack
of teeth through shell.

*Note: 'Okefenokee' is the name the Seminole people gave to their ter-
ritory in Georgia. It means 'the land of the trembling earth'.
The Okefenokee is now a National Park.*

Sinopia

Venus surfing tiptoe on her scallop shell,
all petals and breeze and wheatsheaf hair,
was unrolled for an exhibition,
like a carpet. There, behind the plaster,
Botticelli's underdrawing on the wall.

All frescoes, underneath that sheeny crust,
conceal their first design: maybe cartoons –
their lines pricked out and pounced in charcoal lace –
or just the rough strokes of sinopia,
the bones of an idea, crayoned in ochre.

Over this the artist's daily dollop:
his giornata. He must work fast, for paint
and plaster fuse, so he will guess or falter
from the sinopia under the wet plaster.

Trip

I have been given a book of vouchers, to use during my stay. I've got choices and can use the tickets for cultural activities, entertainments, restaurants and getting about. There is, however, a caveat: they must all be used up by the final date on the last page, which – unfortunately – I don't have; it seems to be missing, I don't know why, but I'll find out at the end.

I was so eager to get started, I pulled off a green retail ticket and bought a pink cotton souvenir T-shirt, with the logo. So now it shows I've been here. Because I was new, I was careful with my coupons, timid about exploring the twisting, high-walled alleys where I could see, through carved gates, courtyards with hibiscus, smell shrimp-oil frying, hear the cooks chopping leaves, or the clink and snap of mah-jong tiles.

But still I couldn't read the timetables in their dusty frames; the elevator where I stayed, in its black frame and wire sides, looked unsafe; its ropes swung like monkey's tails. I tried to get to know the culture, learn the language; my feet tapped on the parquet in deserted galleries as the dust shimmered and the blinds flapped and the guards dozed beside unlabelled curves of marble; the postcards in their racks were faded and curled.

Ellie Evans

Gradually I got bolder, travelled upcountry, swam in a night sea like silk;
the fish were flakes of light, somersaulting around me, pattering on the water.
Once, in a downpour, I cadged a lift on someone's crossbar. Next morning, on the lake,
the merchants moored beside the houseboat, came aboard, unrolled their carpets: suddenly
the room was filled with light flickering from the ceiling upon silks and twisted brass and gems.

During my stay, I was much too busy to eat. I kept cutting meals, intent on
exploring. I used my vouchers to buy mementoes to take back: embroideries,
carved boxes, beads. I even forgot to be hungry, wrapped up in
listening to the strange words, watching the strange faces.
And now the book is empty. I'm hungry.

Written as a lineation poem in response to 'Tar' by C .K. Williams.

Suits

Mel returned your ashes;
we interred them by the sea.
Later, on the beach, facing the sunset,
the boys stood at the shoreline, skimming pebbles.

I watched our boys,
cut-outs against the sun, in suits,
your suits, in fact, that Mel sent back. That's
what she sent, empty arms and legs, ashes.

I watched our boys
skim pebbles where they learned
to swim, and where you'd forge ahead, on through
that arch of rock to where we couldn't see.

I watched our boys:
one pauses, weighs a pebble.
Against the light, his jacket, pocket flaps,
that shoulder-set, that curve of spine. It's you.

The Paper House

One day we left it out in the rain –
the paper house which we made
from the box the boiler came in. We used Lincrusta
for the roof, which you painted yellow, and I drew
roses up the walls and around the window.
I used a tea cloth as a carpet, made curtains out of dusters.
The boys gave their toys tea there; they played
with it for years until that afternoon

we forgot to bring it in. Out on the lawn
rain splattered it. It wobbled on its base,
the wind fingered the Lincrusta on the roof,
the walls grew puffy and sagged, they began
to curve out. Rain washed the yellow off; the roses ran
into the grass – green ink leaf into real leaf.
I drew the thick red curtains as it collapsed;
red velvet, as the paper sides fell down.

ELLIE EVANS was born in west Wales and educated in Cardiff. She
has taught in London, Austria and China. She now lives in Powys. 'Chinese Painting Lesson', 'Trip' and 'Okefenokee' will appear in issue 167
of *PN Review.*

Contact: ellie.evans@sparksanthology.co.uk

Mister Wight's Test for the Fish Boy

Rebecca Lisle

from a novel for
8- to 12-year-olds

The Curse of the Ravens *is set in 1682 and is due to be published in 2007. It will be the sequel to* The Curse of the Toads, *due to be published in May 2006 by Hodder.*

Reuben leant against the yew tree until his heart had slowed its mad beating and the lump in his throat had gone. He didn't know if he felt sick because the men took Gabriel or because Glory had left him.

Glory chose Gabriel! She did! She likes him best... Likes Gabriel more than me... Cheating, faithless cur! My God, Glory, when you were a tiny pup, I fed you mushed-up bread and milk – by hand! Damn it! I brushed your coat till it was silky smooth. Reuben ripped at the long stalks of grass beside him. I did all that for you...

Good riddance to you!

He turned sharply and began to trudge down the hill, down towards the willow trees and the river. It's just as well, he told himself. I'm better off without them both. I can go faster now.

He pulled an apple roughly off a tree and ate it. Glory liked apples. She'd eat anything. Flighty dog. Spaniels are feather-brained. Glory's head is more empty than a... than a licked-out pudding bowl. Have her then, Gabriel. Take her. You're well matched. Stupid dog. Dimwit. Mangy bloody mongrel...

He stopped by the river. It was shallow, clogged with large mossy stones and the water flowed by slowly. Reuben knelt and washed his face and drank the cool water. Beside him he noticed a patch of spignel, a few pale white flowers still remaining on the tops of the stalks. He imagined his grandmother's delight: *'Spignel, Reuben dear boy, how lucky! Governed by Mercury, excellent for the gripes and easing childbirth.'*

Might it help Lady Egmont? Grandmother had used it for difficult births and colic and wind...

Grandmother.

Reuben let his head drop on to the damp grass; his forehead lay in the cool foliage. Dearest Granny, why aren't you here? Why did you have to leave me? We were so content. Now see me here, weeping by the river like a caw-baby. What am I doing? What have I done?

He heard the wind in the trees and the trickle of water and tried to listen beyond it, hoping for a word, something that would tell him what to do. There was silence, no voices. But still, he knew.

He got up slowly. He stared up at the village.

Reuben began to walk slowly towards it. Halfway up the hill he broke into a run.

Elder trees and brambles and dogwood sped by.

To Gabriel and Glory!

Reuben ran without stopping.

It was a large village. Reuben passed thatched cottages, long barns, dovecotes, gardens full of vegetables and ripe golden fruit. Sheds and tiny cottages clustered together. An abandoned scythe. Hen coops. A pigsty. Stables. A wagon packed with sacks of grain. An alehouse where folk were drinking and chatting. No one paid him any mind.

Where was Gabriel?

Reuben passed down a narrow alley between whitewashed cottages. The blacksmith's doors were open. He was shoeing a fine grey horse. The noise of his hammer on the metal rang out. It was a good solid sound, and for a moment Reuben's worries were eased. These people would not hurt a boy.

He heard voices.

Opposite the blacksmith's was the village green; a soggy patch of grass with a large duck pond. Two massive twisted oak trees shaded it. The pond water was black. Rotting logs and slimy vegetation lumped around its banks. Grubby ducks paddled in it.

A small crowd had gathered on the opposite side. Their voices were raised.

Reuben slipped back between the cottages and circled round until he could get down to the pond and came to the green unseen. He crept up and hid behind the wreck of an old cider mill. The mill's wooden sides had split and its wheels had broken.

Reuben crouched behind the mill. It still smelled of apples.

Now Reuben could see Gabriel clearly. How tiny he was! He stood by the pond, shivering. He was fiddling with his scraps of cloth, covering and recovering his face and his hands. And Glory, the crazy, stupid dog, sat there at his feet.

On the slope of the green, to the right of Reuben, twenty or thirty villagers had gathered. Robert, the big blond man from the chapel, stood with his ham-sized hand on Gabriel's shoulder.

'I've sent Hector to fetch Mister Wight!' he shouted. 'We need Mister Wight to see this.'

'What's wrong with the lad?' a woman asked. 'Why've you brought him here?'

Reuben peeped round to see who was talking. It was an ordinary sort of housewife with red cheeks and kind eyes. A mother? She would not hurt the boy, would she?

'He was trying to steal from the chapel,' said Robert. 'We stopped him right enough. But it's not that, Mistress Cowley... Look up, boy!'

Gabriel shook his head and folded his arms over his face.

'You wait. You'll see – his face is out of kilter,' Robert went on. 'And his hands. It's not godly. He's come straight from hell, this one. He's not right, not no ways.' Robert pulled the boy's arms down. 'Come on, boy. Show them your features there. Show them!' He threw off the hat and tugged off the black satin. 'There now! See!'

The crowd stared at Gabriel's misshapen, bulging head. His flat white face. His big frog eyes. His gaping mouth, dribbling, trying not to cry.

The people shrank back like a wave. They blurted out cries of alarm and horror and disgust. They nudged each other. Whispered. Crossed themselves. Then they crept closer. They can't get enough, thought Reuben. He hated them. He felt sickened by their expressions of disgust and yet such awful interest.

Reuben saw Gabriel's face crease with worry, his chin tremble. He doesn't understand!

Gabriel hugged himself with his little stick arms and rocked backwards and forwards.

'It's horrible,' someone shouted.

'Not surprised he tries to hide *that* plate of stew!'

'Disgusting.'

'Aw, he's just a cabbagehead,' said another woman. 'Leave him be.'

'Yeah, let the child alone.'

A large bird passed overhead. Gabriel glimpsed it and looked upwards. He pointed. 'R'ven. R'ven. R'ven.' Then he returned to rocking and muttering quietly.

Reuben heard a new ripple of whispers in the crowd.

'Devil's child.'

'That raven's his familiar.'

'See that! See him talk to that bird!'

'Evil!'

A thin, pinched-faced woman pushed her way forward; immediately Reuben's stomach tightened. She would not be any help to him. She wore an immaculate white apron over her black dress and the white starched wraps around her hair pulled her skin tight. Not a scrap of hair showed.

'I knew it! I knew it!' she said in a low voice. 'You found him at the chapel, didn't you? I was down at the chapel earlier today, sweeping and I *saw* something.' Her voice trembled with emotion, her hands plucked at her stiff apron. 'A man. Dark, all dressed in dark shining clothes with glaring eyes.'

'Now, Mistress Mary,' said Robert, 'your imagination is—'

Mistress Mary spun round at him. Her lips were drawn into a tight line. 'You always doubt me! But you cannot, now you've found that thing! I saw the Devil and he's left his child behind to do us ill, drive us wild with his lewd ideas.'

'Mistress Mary—'

'She might be right,' said a woman beside her. 'I've seen odd shapes. Last night, looking down the hill...'

'And me!' cried another.

'My pig's got a black mark on its back; it appeared only this morning,' said a man. 'It's like finger marks it is, like the Devil put his hand right on the poor pig's back. That's proof for you!'

Gabriel rocked backwards and forwards. He stared at the sky. He looked round at the crowd anxiously, as if he were searching for someone.

'We should tie him up!'

'We should burn him.'

'Wait. Wait for Mister Wight,' said Robert. He looked up towards a large house a little way up from the pond. It was set back from the muddy path behind a neat garden. The gates opened. Everyone turned to watch Hector and the tall elegant figure of Mister Wight come towards them.

Reuben's heart sank further.

Mister Wight was a finely dressed gentleman, wearing a long grey wig and a green jacket. He picked his way over the muddy ground, trying not to let his dainty blue leather shoes with their sky-blue ribbons get dirty. He nodded to the villagers as they curtsied and bowed.

'What do we have here?' he said. 'Mistress Mary? Robert Hampton, good day. I hope you haven't disturbed my rest for something frivolous, Robert?'

'Begging your pardon, I don't think so, Mister Wight, sir.' Robert bowed. ''Tis this thing we found. 'Twas in the chapel. It's right odd, sir. Thought you'd better see.'

Reuben did not like Mister Wight's hard blue eyes and girlish hands. He didn't like the way his soft red lips were pursed up in disgust as he came closer to the villagers, or how he held a lace handkerchief to his nose.

'Well?' said Mister Wight. 'If it is a vagrant come from another village we'll send him straight back. We shan't be made to keep him. Our coffers aren't deep enough. Or is it a thief? Have you searched his pockets? Where is he? Show him to me!'

Robert stood aside to reveal Gabriel.

'It's just a boy,' said Mister Wight, dabbing at his nose. 'Great heavens! Have you brought me out here to see a boy? A doddy-poll of a boy, at that!'

The crowd sniggered.

Robert pulled Gabriel's hands away from his face and lifted the boy's chin. Reuben winced.

'The Devil has had his hand in this,' Mister Wight agreed. 'Why does he not speak but only stare up into the clouds in that way? What is it that he mutters? Is that dog his familiar?'

Gabriel heard 'dog'. He knelt down and hugged Glory. 'G'ory. G'ory.'

'Ah, see how he loves it!' said Mistress Mary. 'Hear how he talks to it in strange tongues? These are no ordinary creatures. I told you...'

'And why's he wrapped up like a Christmas pudding?' said Mister Wight. 'Get those things off!'

You can't! Reuben cried silently. Don't.

Gabriel screamed. He kicked Robert. He clutched at his rags.

'Now, boy...'

'No! No!'

Hector pulled at the cloths while Robert held Gabriel still.

'Agh! His hands!' someone cried.

'Look at his feet!'

'Monster!'

The crowd shifted and moved, each person trying to get the clearest view.

'Animal!'

Oh, poor Gabriel! Doesn't anybody care? Reuben scanned the watching faces and saw a flash of sympathy in a mother's face. An embarrassed grimace on another. Help him! Reuben begged them. Why don't you help?

Gabriel's hands hung like useless, broken things. He stared at his feet, his awful feet, as if he hated them. He began to wail very quietly, a peculiar mewling sound, so soft that most didn't even hear it.

Reuben did.

'Devil!' screamed Mistress Mary. 'Now! Yes! Now, I recall the man I saw had these hands! Yes, his fingers all joined together just so.'

Then someone said, 'Fish!'

'He's got fins!'

'He's a *fish boy*!'

Mister Wight was the only person who had gone nearer Gabriel. 'What abomination is this?' he said at last, with a sneer. 'In God's name, what is this creature?'

'Maybe his mother ate a barrel of cod 'afore she had him?' someone said.

'We should lock him up,' said Robert. 'Shouldn't we, Mister Wight? And let the church men deal with him? They'll know what to do, Reverend Faulkner over at—'

'No.' Mister Wight held up his hand to quieten the crowd. 'I've a better idea. A fish boy should swim, shouldn't it? Let's see if it can swim!' He clapped his hands together. 'Get it in the water!'

'But Mister Wight, sir,' Robert began, but he was pushed out of the way before he could get any further.

'I don't like to touch him,' said Hector. 'But I will.' Hector met Mister Wight's icy blue eyes. 'I will. Who else?' He turned to the crowd. 'Who'll help me with the fish boy?'

Robert stood back and shook his head. Plenty of others wanted to help. They came forward, rubbing their hands together gleefully, laughing and cheering.

Bravely the villagers took hold of Gabriel's thin, dirty limbs and held him at ankle and wrist.

Gabriel shouted.

'R'bn! R'bn!'

He twisted and buckled in their hold. He screamed and shouted and fought.

'R'bn! R'bn!'

'Calling for his bird,' an old man said with a chuckle. 'Thinks it'll fly down and carry him off, I 'spect!'

People laughed.

An icy coldness flooded over every inch of Reuben's skin. Each hair on his body tingled. He didn't think Gabriel was calling for the bird. It was not the same noise he'd made before. He covered his ears.

Gabriel wriggled like a Devil-child and the crowd booed and jeered.

'Look at 'im go!'

'Like an eel!'

'R'bn!' Gabriel screamed, again and again. 'R'bn!'

'Throw him in!'

'Wet his head!'

They lifted Gabriel up and began to swing him backwards and forwards. Higher and higher. Glory barked sharply and skittered up and down the water's edge.

'One.'

'Two!'

'Three!'

Gabriel flew out of their grasp.

Oh, Lord, forgive me. Reuben crossed himself.

Gabriel sailed through the air. He hit the water flatly with a smacking sound and a splash. The ducks, necks outstretched, flapped and quacked and swam for the bank. The folk laughed and clapped.

Gabriel disappeared, then his head bobbed up again momentarily and the crowd cheered. He gurgled and yelped. He thrashed around. There was a great flurry of swirling water and waving arms.

'We'll let him live if he swims,' said Mister Wight. 'And if he doesn't—'

Reuben jammed his knuckles into his mouth. Gabriel cannot swim, he told them silently. He is not a fish. He is, he is… He is Gabriel.

Glory was yapping and whining. She raced nervously up and down beside the pond, this way, that way, barking at the water.

Glory, Glory, hold your noise, thought Reuben. Stop your stupid…

Suddenly the spaniel jumped into the pond. Reuben bit his lip. She surely couldn't save the boy! Glory!

Glory set off paddling furiously towards Gabriel. Her brown nose pointed skywards.

Gabriel had seen her. He splashed towards her. He caught her and wrapped his arms round her neck.

'G'ory!'

Then they both went under.

REBECCA LISLE's first novel was written when she was six. It was about flower fairies and, strangely, never published. However, her first published novel, *Sparks Will Fly,* was written when she was much older and published in 1988 to enormously small critical acclaim.

Contact: rebecca.lisle@sparksanthology.co.uk
         davidhigham.co.uk/html/clients

Hilary's Party

Judith van Dijkhuizen

from a novel
for teenagers

Chapter One

It was the last day of term, so instead of double Biology and Maths
we went to the church for our carol service. As we filed out, the Wind
Band went straight into 'Ding Dong Merrily'. I hung around at the door
to listen. I could hear the instruments clearly, and I liked the way it was
so upbeat. It made me want to dance. I wished I could join them – it
would be fun, playing in a small group. I thought Hilary was the best
on her oboe.

I knew my parents couldn't afford to buy me an oboe. The only reason we could move to Dulwich, and I got into St Barnabas', is because
Gran is helping us pay for it. This really gets to Dad, and he always
refers to her as 'your mother' or 'your grandmother'. It looks polite on
paper – but it's the way he says it.

I walked out into the grey light. The sky was covered with long
clouds, pale overhead, but dark in the distance, advancing steadily as
if the whole sky were moving. I'd been warm in the church, but now I
was standing alone in a sharp wind that chilled me through my skirt and
blazer. Everyone was talking in groups, and I couldn't work out how to
edge my way in.

I was about to go home when the band came out with their black
instrument cases. Hilary waved and ran down the path towards me.

'Hi, Catherine,' she said. 'I suppose that's it for a couple of weeks.
What are you doing in the holidays?'

'Just – hanging out,' I said.

'Yeah, me too. We persuaded Mum and Dad not to go away this
year. Hey – don't you live in Dulwich?'

'Yes,' I said. 'We're in Kingswood Court, next to the – '

'Do you want to come round some time? We're up by the park.
Dovercourt Place.'

'OK,' I said – I was too surprised to say anything else. I'd often
wished I could be friends with Hilary, but she seemed to live in a different world – a grown-up, together sort of world. She's one of those
people who always hands her homework in on time, and never messes
around, but no one says she's boring.

'Christine told me you were good at the piano,' she said. 'So I thought I'd ask you to come over and play, with me and Pete – that's my brother.'

'I didn't know you had a brother.'

'He's three years older than me,' she said. 'He's getting engaged! They're having their party tomorrow.'

I sighed. 'I haven't been to a party for ages.'

'My parents are going away, so we'll be able to make as much noise as we like.'

'Sounds great,' I said. I'd been looking forward to Christmas with my mum and dad, but now it seemed so boring.

'What I wondered was... The thing is... Pete's got all his mates coming, but he said I could invite some people, too. You're probably doing something already, but...'

Yes! A party, with older boys! But what was I going to wear? I didn't have anything fashionable back then. I used to stare at other girls' clothes, always wanting what they were wearing. And then there was Mum...

'I'd like to,' I said. 'But I don't think Mum'll let me.'

'Why not?' said Hilary.

Wasn't everyone's mum like that?

'Can't you just tell her?' she said. 'Pete's friends are great, but I'd like my friends there, too. Can I have your number? I could ring you later.'

She thought of me as her friend! *Hilary*! I eagerly tore the corner off the carol programme and wrote it down.

By the time I got home, Dad was already in his baggy grey tracksuit, slouching at the kitchen table. I patted him on his bald patch.

'Don't remind me,' he said. 'Happy holidays, darling.'

Mum was stirring the soup, with her back to us. I thought, she must be sweltering in that thick fluffy jumper. She's obsessed with pink – says it goes with her red hair. Unfortunately, she's convinced this applies to me, too.

I sat down opposite Dad.

'That was the longest term ever,' he said. 'Don't be a teacher, Catherine.'

'Why not?' asked Mum. She ladled the creamy green soup into my bowl. Leek and potato – my favourite.

'I don't want my daughter wearing herself to the bone for hardly any money,' he said.

'Maybe you'd enjoy it more if you went for a head of department job,' said Mum, filling his bowl. 'Do you want to stay an ordinary teacher for the rest of your life?'

Dad let out a long, loud breath. 'I – don't – want – to. You *know* I don't.'

I wanted to crawl away, but I studied my soup instead. I could see the strands of leek, but no lumps of potato. They must have dissolved.

'Look,' he said. 'I've said it all before. The school's OK, and Steve's a fantastic head of department. I don't want any more responsibility. You'd be the first to complain—'

'I wouldn't complain if I had a new kitchen,' said Mum. I mouthed the words along with her. 'Look at it! Or how about moving to a proper house?'

I've never been able to work out what's wrong with our kitchen. There are plenty of cupboards, and you can look out into the treetops while you're washing up. I could see why Dad got sick of Mum going on about it.

'Why don't *you* get a job?' I said to Mum.

'Catherine,' said Dad. 'This is none of your business.'

I'd only been sticking up for him, and he'd told me off! I didn't get it.

Mum slumped into her seat. Dad put his arm round her, but she pushed him away – they'd been over this so many times. My mind drifted back to the party. I felt so different now Hilary wanted to be my friend; as if the school had been dark, but someone had opened a door into a warm, brightly lit room.

'Hilary's brother's getting engaged,' I said. 'She said I could come to their party. She wants—'

'Hilary?' said Mum. 'Is that the girl who plays the oboe?'

'Yes,' I said. 'It's tomorrow night. She really wants me to go, because they're all going to be older than her, and—'

'No!' said Mum, sitting up straight. 'It's much too close to Christmas. What are her parents thinking of?'

'She ought to go,' said Dad, as if I weren't there. 'She should be going to parties, at her age.'

'She's got plenty of time for all that when she's older,' said Mum. 'I'm sorry, Catherine. Maybe you could invite Hilary over here one day. That would be nice.'

'But *Mum.*' I'd been so busy worrying about what to wear, I hadn't realised how desperate I was to go.

The phone rang; it was bound to be Hilary. I couldn't face telling her – I was so scared she'd go off the idea of being friends with me.

Dad carried on slurping his soup.

'Oh, I suppose I'll have to answer it,' said Mum. She got up and went into the hall.

'Hello,' I heard her say in a sharp, impatient voice. 'Oh – hi, Elizabeth... I've been wondering how you were... *Tomorrow*? Of course – I'd be delighted, but I'll have to check with John. He's very busy with his school work... I'll check with John. I'll ring you this evening.'

She came back in, looking fed up. 'Honestly. Can you imagine. They've had this holiday planned for months. The Gambia, of all places.'

'Oh great!' said Dad. 'Do they want us to pet-sit again?'

'What do you think?' said Mum. 'It's just to save money, I suppose.'

'Fantastic,' I said. 'Fantastic—'

We're not allowed pets in Kingswood Court. And I'd be able to sleep in Esther's room again, and play their brilliant piano. And, best of all, Lyndsey and Sheena were there, just over the road...

'Of course we'll go,' said Dad. 'Don't you want to help them out? I thought they were your friends.'

'You're being very concerned about them all of a sudden,' said Mum, giving Dad a hard stare.

'Well...' he said. 'It would be nice for Catherine to have a decent piano.'

'Nice for *you*, you mean,' said Mum. 'Anyway, we can't possibly get ready by tomorrow. And I'm not doing the Christmas dinner in a strange kitchen. At least I know where everything is—'

'But you said you wanted to be in a proper house! I'll do all the cooking. Christmas Eve, Christmas Day. *Boxing* Day—'

'You *will*?' She sounded surprised. 'I thought you were exhausted.'

'It's great at the Smythes',' I said.

'I don't know about that,' said Mum. 'I hardly saw you last summer. I don't want you going out with those Darlow girls all the time. I don't think Lyndsey—'

'Surely that's good for a girl of Catherine's age,' said Dad. 'In fact, I think it's vital that she—'

'Please, Mum. It's like having sisters.'

Mum and Dad went silent.

'OK,' said Mum quietly. 'If you promise to take Patch out for walks—'

Dad got up and gave her an enormous hug. 'You won't regret it. We'll have an incredible Christmas. I'll light a wood fire every day. Hey – why don't we invite the Darlows for Christmas dinner?'

'No,' said Mum, breaking away. 'Not the Darlows. Christmas is family time. We'll have enough, with us and Mum.'

Dad ran his fingers through his hair. 'Why can't it be the three of us, for once?'

'You just said to ask the Darlows!' said Mum. 'We can't leave Mum on her own. Think of all she's done for us. We wouldn't even be living here if it wasn't for her.'

'Don't I know it,' said Dad.

Mum folded her arms. 'If we're not having Mum, we're staying here.'

'OK,' said Dad with a sigh. 'If you insist. I'll go and let them know.' He rushed out before she could say anything else, and I heard him being over-the-top-friendly on the phone to Elizabeth.

I spent the whole afternoon going through my things, trying to decide what to take. I couldn't wait to get there and put my stuff in Esther's room. I'd be able to take Patch for a walk in the woods – with Lyndsey and Sheena. But what if they had boyfriends? They might not want to see me this time.

The evening crawled by. I couldn't stop thinking about the party. I knew Dad wanted me to go, but he was at Steve's end-of-term do. He'd be back really late, and Mum wasn't going to listen to him then.

All those older boys. I didn't know anyone else who had a brother the right age. I might miss getting a boyfriend... going out with him all over Christmas... falling in love... I could see my life branching off in two directions. One: stay at home, and put up with the girls in my class going on about boys, maybe for years. Two: go to the party, meet a boy, go out and do exciting things... find out what sex really felt like... tell everyone at school... Even if I had to climb out of the bedroom window, I was going. I wondered how far down it was.

The phone rang. One of Mum's boring friends, I thought. Mum called out, 'Answer it, will you? If it's Elizabeth, tell her I'm in the bath or something.'

I picked up the receiver. 'Hello,' I said, putting on my I'm-busy voice.

'Can I speak to Catherine?'

'*Hilary.*' I dropped my voice to a whisper. 'I'm not sure about the party. It's Mum. The thing is, we're going away for Christmas—'

'I thought you were staying at home.'

Her family always went to exotic countries. Now I had to tell her we were going from one part of Dulwich to another.

'We were,' I said. 'But we're going to cat- and dog-sit for Mum's friends in Eynella Close, and Mum—'

'That's practically round the corner! You've got to come. Please.'

'I want to,' I said. 'I really do. But we had to spend ages persuading Mum to go away. There's no way she's going to give in on the party as well. You wouldn't believe what she's like. She has to have us together all the time at Christmas. She—'

'But Christmas is four whole days away!' said Hilary. 'Surely she'd let you out just for one evening.'

'She so *won't*! And I can't keep on asking her. She's totally stressed out with all the packing—'

'Excellent,' said Hilary. 'That's just what you want.'

'What?'

'When are you going?' she said.

'Tomorrow. About ten.'

'Great,' said Hilary. 'All you've got to do is go on at her. Really get on her nerves. Wait till you're about to leave, then tell her you've forgotten something. That's when you ask her. She'll say anything to shut you up. She won't even know what she's saying.'

It seemed a bit dishonest.

'I'll try,' I said. 'I'll ring you tomorrow, when we get there.'

I went to bed early that night. I lay there wide awake, listening to Mum bustling about. I'd have to watch her moods and pick my moment. Maybe when we were doing our last-minute packing, or just as we were leaving. But I couldn't imagine her getting so stressed she wouldn't notice the word 'party'.

JUDITH VAN DIJKHUIZEN was brought up in London. She now lives in Cheltenham, where she writes, plays in bands and teaches young adults. *Hilary's Party* is her first novel.

Contact: judith@sparksanthology.co.uk

MA Writing for Young People

Between Two Seas

Marie-Louise Jensen

from a novel for
teenagers and young adults

Chapter One
Grimsby, August 1885

I'm heading for the privy across the yard, carrying my mother's full chamber pot when they catch me. Three tall girls emerge from the passageway that leads out to the street. Two of them block my way forward to the outdoor privy, the third cuts off my retreat to the safety of the stairway. I turn to face them, my back to the wall.

'Where do you think you're going, Marianne?' demands one girl.

She's taller than me, hard-featured and scrawny. Her name's Bridget, and she lives downstairs in the same tenement building as I do.

One of her skinny arms shoots out and shoves me hard. I'm not expecting it, and I fall heavily against the wall. The chamber pot hits the stone with a dull *thunk*, and shatters, spilling most of its contents down my dress.

'Oh look what you've gone and done, you filthy slut,' Bridget cries, malicious delight lighting her eyes. 'You've got piss all down your dress!'

She slaps me hard across the face. I lift my arms, covering my face defensively, before she can do it again.

'Where's your mother, the whore?' Bridget's voice rings out, loud and confident.

I don't answer her. If I say anything at all, they'll mock the way I speak. I don't have their broad Grimsby accent.

'Speak up, Marianne,' cries another voice. 'We can't hear you.'

'Marianne?' taunts the second girl. 'Who'd want to marry Anne?'

They screech with laughter.

'No one marries a bastard brat!'

I stand still, waiting for the right moment to make my escape.

'Where's your pa, then?' It's Bridget's voice again. 'Or was your mother so busy whoring that she didn't know which one he was?'

'Bastard! Whore's brat!' the voices cry.

Their words ring in my head, but I'm past being angry. It's mostly lies, and I've heard it so many times before. I'm just desperate to get back to my mother.

She's lying upstairs, dying.

One of the girls is pinching my arm. I look down and see her filthy fingers digging into my flesh. I slap her hand away and it works like a signal. They all close in, pulling my hair, pinching me, yanking at my dress.

I spot a gap and throw myself at it, tearing myself away from their cruel fingers. I knock the youngest girl flying into a pile of horse dung. I can hear the others scream with rage, but I'm free now, fleeing across the yard and up the stairs.

I slam and lock the door of our attic room behind me. Panting, I lean against the door. My eyes seek my mother, lying quietly on her bed in the darkened room. Her rasping breathing is harsher than ever.

With trembling fingers, I wash my hands and remove my dress for washing. I only have one other, besides my best dress. Once I've put it on, I go to sit down by my mother. Her frail hands clutch the blanket. I take one of them in mine and hold it, hoping to comfort her. I can see she's in pain. There is fear in her eyes.

I can't even afford to get a doctor for her. It's always been a struggle for the two of us to manage, and now that she's sick we have barely any money left. I haven't told her, but we are also behind with the rent. How shall we manage? I don't want to think about that right now.

'Can I do anything for you, Mother?'

A slight nod of the head.

'What can I do?' I ask.

Her eyes dart sideways to the slate lying on the chair by her bed. I put it into her hands and help her to sit up a little, propping her with pillows. She's no longer able to speak, and writing is becoming increasingly difficult. She grasps the slate pencil and begins to trace out a word. Her writing is shaky:

Sewing Box

I'm puzzled.

'You can't sew, Mother, and I'd like to sit with you a little before I work some more.'

I can't sew by her bedside; the room is far too dark. I need to sit right over by the window to see what I am doing. My answer isn't what she wanted. I can see her frustration as she slumps back on the pillows.

'Sorry, Mother. My sewing box or yours?'

She jabs at herself with the slate pencil, and I go to fetch her sewing box. Sewing and embroidery are how we make our living, and our sewing boxes are precious possessions.

Mother gestures slightly and I understand I'm to open the box. I lift out the tray containing all her threads and needles. Underneath I find a small heavy package wrapped in waxed paper.

'Should I open it?'

A nod.

When I unwrap the paper, coins tumble out on the bedcovers, gleaming gold. Sovereigns. I'm speechless with amazement. Here is more money than I have ever seen together. I stare blankly, and then pick up a couple of the coins and weigh them in my hand. They feel heavy and rich.

'Mother, we've been going hungry and doing without medicine for you, and all the while you had these hidden!'

There are two letters folded in the package with the money. One is sealed and addressed to Lars Christensen. That's my father. The other has my name on it.

'Do you want me to read this?' I ask, holding up my letter.

Unmistakably, she does. I take it over to the window.

May 1885

My dearest Marianne,

I am writing to you before I become too ill to explain what this money is for. For many years I have been saving so that we can travel to Denmark together and find your father. I never saved enough. Now that I cannot go with you, there will be enough for you to go alone. Travel to Skagen and find him. Give him my letter. Please tell him I have loved him and waited for him through all these years. Seek a better life, Marianne!

Yours Affectionately,
Your mother,
Esther

Tears prick my eyelids. This is not the time for them. I count the money: it seems a fortune to me.

'Mother, let me fetch a doctor and buy some medicine for you with some of this money – I beg you!'

She shakes her head more vigorously than before and a spasm of pain crosses her face. She begins to write again. Slowly, tortuously.

Promise

'Promise what? That I won't get a doctor? That I'll go to Denmark?'

A father I've never met, I think bitterly. A wild goose chase. Wasting a fortune going to find a father who doesn't know I exist and might not welcome me when he does. I can't help thinking if my father had wanted to, he could have returned years ago. Besides, how can I do a journey like that alone? I'm sixteen, and I've never left Grimsby. The very thought is terrifying.

But Mother's eyes beg me, desperate. Silent tears trickle down her cheeks. I drop to my knees and take her hands in mine.

'Mother, I promise to go to Denmark and look for my father if that's what you wish me to do. I swear it to you if that will comfort you. But surely there is more than enough money here for the journey. Please, please let me get a doctor.'

Her face is set and stubborn. She won't give in now. And I've made a promise I must keep. My mother grows more peaceful.

It doesn't last, however. By the early hours of the morning she's no longer able to bear the pain. She is writhing and twisting in the bed, unable to make a sound, wild-eyed and sweat-drenched. I can't watch her suffer like this. My mother has been everything to me all my life; she needs help now.

'Mother!' I try to speak calmly and clearly, though my voice shakes. 'I'm not breaking my promise to you. But I am going to get a doctor!'

I can't tell whether she has heard me. Frantic, I run downstairs to Mrs Forbes. She is the only person in the building who has ever spoken kindly to me. One of the few respectable people who doesn't flinch at the sight of me, as though my illegitimacy were a visible stain. I hammer on her door.

Mrs Forbes appears, candle in hand, nightcap on her head.

'Is it your mother?' she asks.

'She needs medicine,' I tell her, and my voice is hoarse with fear. 'But I can't leave her alone.'

'Of course. I'll send my son for the apothecary at once. Go back to her, my dear.'

I turn and take the stairs two steps at a time. Mother has thrown off the bedclothes. I try to wipe the perspiration from her brow with a cool flannel, but I can't get her to stay still. I let out a cry of despair. But in a few moments Mrs Forbes joins me, and together we are able to hold her more still. It is the first time there has ever been a visitor of any kind in our room, but I'm glad of her company. It seems an eternity until the apothecary arrives. He examines my mother. She is so thin, and an unsightly growth has disfigured her throat. He takes me aside.

'There is little I can do for her but ease the pain. I would guess that she does not have many more hours left.'

I nod, blindly. This isn't news to me. The doctor at the charity hospital told us as much weeks ago. The apothecary administers a dose of morphine. I hand one of our precious coins to him. It is hard to part with it. But he pockets it almost casually, as though he sees such money every day, and then he departs.

Mother's eyes glaze and lose their fear for the first time in days. Her frantic movements slow and then cease. Only her rasping breathing remains. Since yesterday she has no longer even been able to swallow, so I can't give her water. Mrs Forbes returns to her own rooms, leaving me alone with my mother. I sit, holding her hand, and watch her slowly fall asleep.

'I'm scared, Mother,' I whisper quietly. 'I'm scared to lose you.'

She doesn't wake again. Towards dawn her breathing becomes harsher, more laboured, but then begins to fail. By the time the sky outside is turning grey, she has gone. And I am left quite alone.

MARIE-LOUISE JENSEN is half-Danish and her background is in foreign languages and literature. She has lived in both Denmark and Germany, teaching English at the university in Münster, Germany, for four years. She completed *Between Two Seas* during the MA course. Marie-Louise lives in Bath and home-educates her two sons.

Contact: mljensen@sparksanthology.co.uk

Playing It Cool

Matt Dix

from a novel
for teenagers

I knew that Claire fancied Elliott Carter. Well, who wouldn't? Even I had to admit he looked pretty good in the photo.

I'd managed to copy his perfect blond quiff by sticking loads of gel in my hair. And I'd left a couple of buttons of my shirt undone like his, so that you could just about see a hint of my not-quite-so-tanned chest. Then I practised trying to copy Elliott's cheesy grin, although for some reason, no matter how hard I tried to look cool and sexy, I just looked a bit like a chimpanzee with constipation.

OK, I'd never expected to look *exactly* like Elliott Carter's double. Otherwise I would be a hunky American teenage movie star desired by millions of screaming girls. Whereas I'm just Ben Matthews, non-hunky Year 9 English teenager desired by... well, nobody.

'He doesn't half fancy himself as Freddie Mercury,' I heard Mum say as she walked across the landing towards my room. She was talking about Dad, who was downstairs singing along to one of his favourite Queen songs, 'A Kind of Magic'. Freddie Mercury was the lead singer of Queen, some rock band from years ago. Mum and Dad met at a Queen concert years and years and *years* ago and tonight they were going to see a Queen tribute band for 'old times' sake'. Handily, they were also dropping me off at the cinema on the way, for my date with Claire.

I quickly shoved Elliott's photograph into my schoolbag on the bed.

'Well, you look nice,' said Mum as she got to the door. She folded her arms approvingly. 'You must really like this Claire girl.'

'Yeah, well, she's all right,' I said.

To tell the truth I wasn't sure whether I did fancy Claire, which sounds a bit mad seeing as I was about to go on a date with her. It was my mate Josh's idea to set me up with Claire. He seemed to think I was a bit of a saddo because most of the boys in our class were going out with someone. Or had at least *been* out with someone. So, without telling me, Josh had asked his girlfriend Julie whether she thought her best friend Claire would go out with me. And apparently Claire said yes and that she thought I was cute (girls seem to think that saying a boy is cute is a compliment). That's when Josh decided to tell me I was going out with Claire on a date and, even though I wasn't sure about it, I'd just acted all cool and said OK.

So here I was, quietly panicking inside and hoping I could pull this whole going-out-with-a-girl-thing off.

'Is Dad ready?' I asked. 'Or is he staying here pretending to be in Queen all night?'

'Bless him, he's just excited about the concert,' said Mum. 'I'll tell him to get the car started, shall I?'

'Yeah. I'll be down in a minute,' I said.

'Right,' said Mum, going off to round (or shut) Dad up.

I looked in the mirror again.

Hair OK.

Shirt OK.

Jeans OK.

Trainers OK.

All I had to worry about now was whether Claire thought I was   OK.

I quietly checked my phone for messages as Dad drove us to the centre of town in the car. He had his Queen CD on again and Mum was humming along, looking out of the window.

'So, what film is it you're going to see, Ben?' asked Dad. 'Something nice and romantic?'

'Dunno,' I said. I wasn't bothered which film Claire wanted to see. I was more worried about what I was going to do once we were in the cinema. Should I put my arm around her straight away, or wait until she gave me some sign? What would the sign be? And would she expect me to kiss her at some point? How would I know? What if I got it all horribly wrong? Josh would never let me hear the last of it if I messed this up.

'Are you sure you don't want us to give you and Claire a lift home afterwards?' asked Mum, looking back at me. 'The concert should finish about 10.30, so we can easily come and pick you up.'

'Mum, it's OK. We can get the bus,' I said quickly. What would Claire think if she saw my mum and dad in their 'Queen Rocks!' T-shirts and scruffy jeans? There was *no way* I was going to let that happen.

'Don't want us cramping your style, eh?' chuckled Dad.

I didn't bother to reply. We were nearly at the cinema. I could feel my stomach leap every time I thought about meeting Claire. Which sounds as if I was dead excited about it, but actually I felt pretty sick.

Dad turned up the volume on the car stereo. I groaned. Another favourite Queen track; this time 'You're My Best Friend'. I know them all, though not by choice.

Dad sang along, looking at me in the mirror as if he was doing it on purpose just to annoy me. Mum joined in with her usual harmonies on the chorus, and they even looked at each other and *giggled*. It's 'our song', Mum says – whatever that means. Why can't they just be normal like other people's parents? Why do my mum and dad have to be so... I can hardly bring myself to say it... in *love* all the time? They *never* argue or slag each other off. It's like *they're* the ones who have just met on a date, and it feels really awkward to be around them when they're so cuddly and kissy with each other all the time.

The worst thing was that the windows in the front of the car were wound fully down. I could see people's heads turning, wondering where the row was coming from. There was a group of girls just staring towards our car and I sank down in the back seat, cringing.

'Can you drop me off round the corner?'

They were so wrapped up in their duet they didn't even hear me.

'Mum! Dad!' I yelled. 'Everyone's looking. Can you turn it down and drop me off just round here, please?'

'Ooh, keep your hair on,' said Dad, winking at Mum. He turned the stereo down a bit, though. 'It's OK. I'll drop you outside the cinema.'

'No,' I said, feeling myself boil inside. Then, trying to act calm, because I didn't want him to see he was getting to me, 'Just here is fine.'

'Roger,' said Mum warningly to Dad, but with a little smile on her face.

Dad relented and turned the corner into the side street, narrowly missing some drunk bloke staggering across.

Dad pulled over and I grabbed the door and got out as quickly as I could.

'Got everything?' asked Mum. 'Money, key, mobile...?'

'Flowers, chocolates...' said Dad.

'Bye Mum, bye Dad,' I said firmly. 'See you later.'

'Thanks for the lift, Dad. Enjoy the concert,' said Dad sarcastically, rolling his eyes.

'Yeah, whatever,' I said, pulling a face back. I slammed the door and Dad tooted the car horn loudly as he drove off.

I wondered if Claire was already at the cinema, waiting for me, and whether she was as nervous as I was.

Well, this was it. Time to play it cool.

That's what Josh had said when I'd asked him for advice.

Play it cool.

One new message.

Maybe Claire had changed her mind. I took a deep breath.

It was from Josh.

'Hi m8. Good luck on ur d8. Talk l8r.'

Trust Josh to be checking up on me. It was ten to eight and I was getting even more edgy. Claire should have been here twenty minutes ago. I felt as if everyone in the street was watching me, sniggering at the thirteen-year-old skinny kid standing outside Mr Cheesy's Pizzeria on a Tuesday night waiting for his first ever date.

Every time I thought of it, I felt a little shiver go through me.

Don't mess this up, I kept telling myself. Just don't mess this up.

There was a small cough behind me.

'Hello, Ben. Sorry I'm late.'

I shoved my phone in my pocket and turned round.

It was Claire. Looking... well, great. Totally different from how she dressed for school – really funky. Silky pink top, silver earrings, designer jeans. And blonde hair flowing round her shoulders instead of being scrunched up in its usual ponytail. She smelled lovely, too, all clean and fresh and flowery, and looked more like sixteen than thirteen to me.

'Wow! I mean, hi, Claire.'

Then Claire's mate, Josh's girlfriend Julie, loomed up behind her. Also dressed totally differently from school. Huge gold earrings, loads of make-up, glossy lips, tight blue T-shirt so that her chest was pushed right out, short white skirt...

What was she doing here?

'Hi Julie,' I said, shooting a glance at Claire. Claire smiled shyly back.

Julie was grinning, knowing what I was thinking.

'Don't freak. I'm not staying,' she said. 'I said I'd walk Claire here and wait for you in case you didn't turn up. I'm off to meet Josh.'

Huh. I was the one who got here on time, I thought. And why hadn't Josh mentioned that he was coming into town to meet Julie too? But I just smiled calmly.

'Cool,' I said. 'So... Where are you and Josh going?'

'Oh, just hanging around,' said Julie vaguely. She plumped up her frizzy hair and I noticed her armpits were all stubbly. 'Send me a text when you're ready to go, mate,' she said to Claire.

'OK,' said Claire. 'See you later, Jules.'

What was all that about? I thought I would be the one taking Claire home, not Julie. Or at least walking her to the bus stop. That was what I was supposed to do, wasn't it? Maybe it was some unwritten rule that I'd never heard of – that girls always made sure their mates were around on a first date in case they needed to make a quick escape.

Why hadn't I thought of that? No, Josh should have thought of that. He was supposed to be the expert, according to him.

'Laters,' said Julie as she wandered off, already ringing Josh on her mobile.

Me and Claire looked at each other awkwardly. For some reason I felt a little bit better that she looked just as shy about all this as me. And, hey, at least she'd turned up.

'What film do you fancy seeing, then?' I asked casually. It felt strange, a bit like something Dad would say, in fact. My heart was thumping the whole time and my mouth felt dry and sticky.

'Oh, I don't mind,' said Claire. 'As long as it's not sci-fi.'

Suits me, I thought.

'How about the new Elliott Carter film?' I said. It was some trashy chick flick, all about a high-school student who falls for a geeky girl who nobody likes and then the girl turns out to be a stunner once she takes off her glasses and has a makeover… Claire was going to think I was completely weird for suggesting it.

'Really?' said Claire, her face lighting up. 'You don't mind?'

Of course. Claire loved Elliott Carter, didn't she? So she probably just thought I was being dead considerate. Which, deep down, subconsciously, maybe I was.

'No, it's all right,' I said. 'Come on, let's see what the times are.'

Claire beamed back at me.

Maybe I could do this.

We walked off to the ticket desk together, and I imagined that everyone was watching us, thinking what a lucky git I was having such a good-looking girlfriend.

MATT DIX currently lives in his home town of Bristol and *Playing it Cool* is his first novel for young people. He was invited to read an extract from this at the Bath Literature Festival in March 2005.

Contact: matt.dix@sparksanthology.co.uk

Silver Boots

Karen Priest

from a novel for
8- to 12-year-olds

Chapter One

Have you ever found a sport that you're really good at? Football's my thing. I'm so speedy, and I never seem to get out of breath. I can run faster than all the girls in my year, even my best friend Danni. But Danni's really special. She can do things with a football that make the boys shut up. She's the one that got me into all this. I'm trying to sort things out.

It all started when the two of us went to see Mr Evans. He'd already made an announcement in assembly, saying that anyone interested in joining the girls' team this year needed to see him in the hall, at break time. He coaches the boys' football team, as well.

Danni and I raced each other over to the hall as soon as the bell went. I won, just. Then we hung around for ages. But no one else showed up. Mr Evans came into the hall, ten minutes later, dressed in his suit and tie for a change. He looked around, as if he expected a few girls to climb down off the wall bars.

'Claire? Where's everyone else?' he asked.

'It's just us,' I explained. 'Me and Danni.'

'We can't have a team with just two players.' Mr Evans put his books down on a nearby bench and scratched the back of his collar.

'Heather's not back at school yet,' I explained. We all knew that the rest of last year's cup-winning team had gone up to secondary school.

'Three of you is still no good, Claire. We need at least five players if we're going to enter the league.'

Danni and I looked at each other, then back at Mr Evans. He shrugged and put his palms out, as if to say that was that.

'But we've *got* to have a team, Mr Evans.' Danni was actually pleading with him. Not something she normally does with teachers. 'We're Junior Girls Champions for the district. We've got to defend our title!'

'I'm sorry, Danni. I know what a good player you are. But even you can't play in more than one position at the same time.' Mr Evans smiled at his own joke. Danni gave him a look of disbelief, and kicked at the floor with a well-scuffed shoe.

'Look, if you two fancy a game, then come along to the boys' training night on Mondays,' he offered, straightening his tie. After that, he picked up his books and went into the staff-room.

I wasn't too upset. I had my place in the netball team, and I was just starting to run for the county. But Danni was gutted, I could tell. She said nothing for the rest of break, and carried on being quiet all through lunch. We hung around on the edge of the tarmac pitch, watching the boys have a game. Normally we'd be out there with them, but Danni said she didn't feel like playing today.

Eventually, I got bored with our one-sided conversation. 'Look, Danni. I'm just as upset about the team folding as you are, but I'm not having a massive moody.'

'I'm not being moody,' said Danni, her face like thunder.

'Yes, you are!' I insisted. 'You've said nothing to me since Mr Evans told us to forget girls' football this year. As if it's my fault. At least you're good enough to play for the Dynamos on Saturdays. I can't even make their B team.'

'I'm sorry, Claire. I'm just so... disappointed.'

I turned and gave her a hug. As I moved back from her shoulder, my eyes drifted over to the other playground. Some of the girls from our class were playing tag, chasing each other really fast. An idea shot into my head.

'Danni, why don't we recruit some more players? There's loads of sporty girls in our year. If I can talk some of the netball players into coming to the training session, we can easily get a squad of five sorted out by next week. And then Mr Evans will have to run the team, won't he?'

Suddenly Danni's face was alive again. She grabbed the sleeve of my jumper and tugged on it. 'Claire, you're a star!'

But getting a team together wasn't as easy as I had made it sound.

Chapter Two

The next day we had a netball practice after school. It was a windy day, and the ball was going everywhere. Mrs Billings, the headteacher, always takes our practices. I think she was a good player. Once. She's got a very smart navy tracksuit, which she wears in all weathers. But she's a bit too fond of warming up, which means that we never actually get time to play a game. So we end up losing most of our matches.

Charlotte is the star of the netball team. She's so tall that she makes everyone else look like extras from fairyland. And she's got arms like elastic bands that shoot forwards to grab hold of the ball. But Charlotte hates the practice sessions.

Today, after a good ten minutes of being told to run, jump and land, I could see she was getting fed up. Every time Billings blew her whistle, Charlotte scowled at her, and traded a look with her best friend, Becks. Although Becks wasn't too bothered. She was pleased to be giving her new trainers an outing. She kept bending down to rub at the specks of dirt on the white bits, in between the blue stripes. Her new trainers were expensive. I knew that because she'd already told me.

Jasmine is the other star of the netball team. She's also the star of the music concerts, the poetry competitions and the end-of-term play. But that's not why Danni and I don't like her. We don't like her because she treats the two of us like personal slaves. It's always, 'Claire, be a pal and get me some paper towels, I've spilled my water bottle.' Or, 'Claire, you're fast. Run down and tell Miss Sparks that I'm going to be late for my flute lesson.' You'd be amazed how the other girls fawn after her, as if she were some kind of princess. In fact, the only girl who tells her to shove off is Charlotte.

Mrs Billings blew her whistle for the end of the game, five minutes before we were supposed to finish, because the wind was doing mad things to her hair. The early finish suited me. It meant I could drum up some support for the football team, before everyone had to dash off. But I was in a bit of a dilemma. Who should I try to poach for the football team? Jasmine, who would bring a heap of friends along to practice sessions, or Charlotte and trainer-mad Becks?

A few girls were getting changed properly, back into their navy uniforms. Jasmine was one of them.

'Jasmine,' I gushed, as we sat around in the cloakroom, 'you were so fast around the court today. Have you ever thought of using your speed on the football pitch?'

She stopped getting changed for a moment and stared at me, as if I'd just said something really bonkers.

'No, Claire. I don't play football.' She put her head straight down and went back to putting on her tights.

'I know, but I wondered if you'd thought about taking it up,' I persisted. 'Danni and I want to get the girls' team going again this year. We need some more players.'

'Sorry, Claire, but I've got horse-riding.' She smiled at me, revelling in such a swanky excuse. I tried smiling back, but my face just wouldn't cooperate. I wanted to grab hold of her golden hair and wrap it round the coat peg behind her. That would take her fat smile away. But it wouldn't do the football team any good.

So I turned round to find Charlotte. I saw her disappearing out of the door, still in her netball skirt, with her uniform stuffed into her school bag. I raced after her, and managed to catch up with her just as she was about to get into her mum's car.

'Charlotte!' I shouted. She turned round, one hand still on the car door. I sprinted over. 'Danni and I are looking for some more players for the girls' football team. Would you be interested?'

Charlotte paused. I thought for one horrible moment that she was going to get into her mum's car without bothering to answer me.

'What night do you train?' She let go of the car door.

'Thursdays.'

'And it's with Mr Evans, right?'

'Yes,' I nodded.

'Do you want me to ask Becks, as well?'

I hesitated. Becks wasn't a great ball-handler. But we were desperate. I nodded.

'All right. Count us in.'

Charlotte gave a wave, and then flung herself into her mum's car. I hugged myself. One more player to recruit and we might actually have a team.

Chapter Three

The next day Danni and I were surprised and pleased. Heather was waiting for us in the playground. She'd had some kind of problem with her kidneys, and she'd been in and out of hospital all summer. But now she was back at school.

There was a new member of the class as well, which was unusual, as we were already two weeks into the new term. Her name was Rubi. She looked a bit different – more grown up maybe. She didn't have much of a uniform, just a white shirt and some navy trousers. Our teacher, Mrs Miniver, gave us the usual spiel about us making Rubi feel welcome. Then we went to sit in our numeracy places.

At break time, none of us girls bothered with Rubi. Jasmine went off with her gang to play gymkhanas. Charlotte and Becks went down to the field to practise handstands. Danni and I hung around with Heather. We stood over by the PE shed, so that Heather could get away from the sun. She looked very white, but she was still the same old Heather, making us laugh with her stories of injections in her bum.

'So, are you going to play for the team again?' asked Danni, the minute she had Heather's attention.

'I can't.' Heather smiled weakly. 'My mum didn't even want me to come back today.'

Danni looked deflated. I'd already told her the good news about Charlotte and Becks agreeing to be on the squad. She was counting on Heather to be our final member, playing in goal again.

'Mr Evans won't run the girls' football this year unless we can get a team together,' I said, trying to explain Danni's long face.

Heather shook her head. 'I'm sorry, but I think you'll have to count me out for a few weeks.' She looked over our heads for a moment, to where the boys were kicking the ball around on the tarmac. 'I might not be able to play, but the new girl looks like she might be up for it.'

Danni and I turned round. We were amazed.

Rubi was dribbling the little ball right round Gareth and Sam, two good defenders from the boys' team. We watched as she nutmegged the rush goalie, Harry, kicking the ball neatly between his legs. The ball flew dead straight between the two navy jumpers masquerading as goalposts. Rubi ran back up the length of the pitch, throwing a victory fist up into the air. Danni, Heather and I cheered.

The game restarted from the centre. Rubi got a quick toe-hold on the ball and then passed it to Ashok. He pushed it back to her, and she made a terrific charge up the left wing. She was only stopped from scoring again by Sam, booting the ball out of play.

I gulped. Rubi looked fast, very fast.

'Claire, do you fancy a quick kick-around?' asked Danni. She wasn't looking at me. She couldn't take her eyes off Rubi's clean footwork.

'No. You go. I'll stay with Heather.' I didn't fancy being shown up by the new girl in front of the boys.

Danni nodded. Then she ran over to join the game on Rubi's side for the last few minutes of break.

At lunchtime, Rubi collected her packed lunch from the dinner ladies. She was free school meals. Then she came to sit with us.

'So, where do you live?' I asked, watching with interest as Rubi pulled her paper box open.

Rubi didn't answer. She took a cheese and tomato sandwich out, and studied it.

'Have you moved in somewhere round here?' asked Heather, puzzled at her stubborn silence.

'You won't be mean to me, will you?' Rubi spoke quietly, looking at us with dark-brown eyes.

'What are you talking about?' asked Danni.

'Well, in the last few schools people have been a bit mean.' Rubi paused, still not explaining.

I wondered what Rubi was finding so difficult to say. We waited while she took a bite out of her sandwich and chewed thoughtfully for a few moments. Then she cleared her throat, as though she was preparing to make a speech.

'My family, we're Travellers. We're staying at the Torrington site.'

I blinked a few times. I could hear my dad's voice, pinging around inside my head. 'They're just a nuisance, always dumping rubbish. Why can't they live in a normal house like everyone else?' I didn't know what to say.

'We won't be mean to you,' Danni announced on our behalf. 'We think you're a fantastic football player. And we want you to join the girls' team.'

'No way! Are you sure? I've never played for a team before!' Rubi's whole face beamed, making the freckles on her face stand out.

I gave Heather a brief look and then smiled. All we were doing was saying that Rubi could play for the school, and it was like we'd just signed her up for the Premiership. If only it was always that easy to please people.

KAREN PRIEST has worked as a primary teacher for several years, both in Cheltenham and Gothenburg, Sweden. *Silver Boots* is an excerpt from her latest novel for children. She also runs writing workshops and coaches girls' football in her spare time.

Contact: karen.priest@sparksanthology.co.uk

The Birth of Venus

Kelley Townley

from a novel
for teenagers

I wander confidently into the yard although my heart is thumping in my chest. I'm trying to fine-tune my cover story as I walk, something about coming to see my dad – a lie closest to the truth is always best – but the two men unloading the van have disappeared. With not a soul in sight, I grab one of their boxes and head inside. The passageway is thankfully empty; then a woman comes out of nowhere. She frowns at me.

Have to think quickly. 'Where's this going?' I ask confidently.

'Who are you?' she scowls.

'I'm with my dad for the day,' I lie. 'You know, work experience.'

'Child labour, more like it. You Jack's girl?'

I nod.

'Well, he's just gone on break.'

'Why do you think I'm unloading stuff?' I smile.

'Typical Jack,' she tuts. 'Just dump it through there, love. Then go and get yourself some tea and biscuits before he eats them all.'

She walks off.

I dump the box, check behind me, then wander back along the corridor. I need to go up. A sign says 'Service Lift'. Now we're talking. Inside I press the button for the ninth floor. The doors close annoyingly slowly. I get to floor three when it stops. I hold my breath. The doors open to reveal an old Hispanic man in blue overalls carrying a mop and bucket. He nods at me. I nod back. He gets off on floor seven. I breathe again. Floor eight. Floor nine. The doors open. I hesitate, like Dad might be there in the corridor, but it's empty.

I step out of the lift. Now what? This looks just like another service corridor. But if I listen I can hear people talking, telephones ringing, the hum of electrical machines.

At either end of the corridor there are doors. I poke my head out of the nearest. Outside it looks posh. This must be the Fine Art Restoration Trust offices. A pretty but stern-looking woman with bobbed jet- black hair and glasses sits at a reception desk. We make eye contact and I snap the door shut.

I try the other door. Again it's the same plush decor, but this time I can see an open-plan office. Lots of people busy at their desks. But still there's no way I can walk through there dressed in my jeans. I look around and spy a pair of discarded blue overalls. Perfect. I slip them on over my clothes and grab a mop and bucket. Everyone makes way for someone with a mop and bucket.

I can't hesitate. I have to come out this door confident and purposeful. I stop with my hand on the door handle. It strikes me that I'm not entirely sure what I'm doing here. I mean, adrenaline has propelled me so far, but I could stop at any time. Just turn around and go home. But I need to know. What is Dad up to? Is he really a criminal? Is Ollie involved? I push open the door and wander out in a bored fashion.

The open-plan space is teeming with people huddled around various desks and coffee machines. Everything seems normal. Just another day in the office. Nothing criminal going on at all. But then, what did I expect? I'm starting to feel stupid. If there is something criminal going on, they're hardly going to flaunt this publicly. It'd be hidden somewhere. What was I thinking? Going off on some Nancy Drew trip. And now I'm standing in the middle of some posh London office, wearing an old man's overalls and carrying a dirty mop. I'm outta here.

Suddenly there's shouting. A woman hurries out of a door on the other side of the room. I get a quick glimpse of the inside before the door slams shut. Lots of people. A meeting. Dad's face!

Fancy that. He really does work here after all.

'Can I help you?'

Damn. I was concentrating too hard on that room and now I've blown my cover. I turn around to face the stern-looking receptionist and her jet-black bob. She's looking at me from behind her glasses with intensely curious eyes.

'I come clean toilet,' I say in my best Hispanic accent, which, let's be honest, is crap. But maybe, just maybe, I sound foreign enough because she points me in the direction of the toilets.

'*Gracias.*' I nod and move towards it. I can feel her eyes on my back but I don't turn around. I start to whistle a flat tune and knock on the door.

'Cleaning lady,' I say, and enter the ladies' toilet.

Luckily it's empty. I rub a hand over my face. What am I doing? If Ollie was mad at me for risking police attention over a mugger, he'll be livid with me over trespassing. But this is Dad's workplace, right? Surely they wouldn't press charges? Maybe not, but if they really are criminals they'd probably just throw my battered dead body straight into the Thames. I have a desperate need to get into that meeting room and solve this mystery once and for all.

The air conditioning hums above me. I look up and smile. Of course. All offices have a false ceiling containing the wiring and air conditioning, tucked away out of sight. I slip into a cubicle. Standing on the toilet lid I can easily reach the ceiling panel. I push and it glides out to reveal a large hole, through which I easily haul myself. Inside it's dark and dirty, but, hey, I'm in overalls.

From above I slide the panel back into place. If the receptionist comes back looking for me, she'll hopefully think I left already. I crawl on my stomach to spread the weight. I don't know how strong the supports are for these ceilings but I'm not taking any chances. As I inch nearer to the meeting room there's more shouting.

'I don't care! Your first duty lies here,' a man with a big voice shouts.

Dad replies, 'With all due respect, Botticelli, sir, I don't see the problem. The painting was delivered and they paid up. I already did my part of the deal. Mikey and I got *The Offering*, safely and securely...'

My heart skips a beat. I can't believe it. Dad may really work here, but he's also just admitted to stealing the Picasso! I am so gonna to kick his butt.

'Safely and securely? Safely and securely?' booms the man Dad just called Botty something.

I'm right above the room now. I can see him shouting and spitting. He's a big man, probably quite intimidating in his youth but getting on a bit now, with white cropped hair and moustache.

'Do you have any idea how much smoothing over I had to do with Interpol? Do you?' he booms.

'A few bruised egos,' Dad shrugs.

'A few bruised egos equals a lot of cash, Leo. You want to pay for it?'

I move so I can see Dad, too. They're glaring at each other

'That doesn't even have anything to do with last night. You just wanted me here as a PR stunt. It was a waste of my time and you know it.'

'Don't get smart with me, Leo. You may be number one, but that doesn't make you irreplaceable.'

Is he threatening my dad? I am so gonna kick his butt, too.

'I'm fully aware of how replaceable I am, and that's why I couldn't be here last night,' says Dad.

'Oh, really? Do tell.'

'I was training my new apprentice.'

He was what? And there I was, thinking he was having Chinese with his estranged daughter. A liar and a thief.

'Don't tell me you've finally got your elusive apprentice,' the Botty man laughs.

'I have, and she's an excellent candidate.'

'She?' Botty frowns.

'Yes. I would like a bit more time with her and then I want to bring her in.'

Who is Dad referring to?

'What's her style?' Botty asks.

'Earl called her a wildcat and I'd say that covers it quite well,' says Dad.

My heart stops. Earl called *me* a wildcat last night. He can't mean me!

'She's met Detective Earl?' asks Botty, narrowing his eyes.

'Yes. That was the other thing I was doing last night: entertaining Earl and his thugs.'

'Again? He really hates you.' That's Mikey's voice. I twist round even further to see who else is in the room. There's Mikey, grinning like a monkey, and two new people. A tall blond man, smartly dressed in a green suit with floppy hair and intelligent but dark eyes. And next to him, a blond boy, bit older than me, also smartly dressed, who looks strangely angelic with his sparkly blue eyes, delicate features and golden surfer dude curls bathed in sunlight from the window...

My attention snaps back to Botty as he shouts, 'So what can this wildcat do, exactly?' I'm intrigued, too.

'She can fight,' Dad says. 'She's intelligent. Quick learner. Agile. Resilient.'

'And she's a stunner,' adds Mikey.

Dirty old man.

'Anything else?'

I suddenly realise the ceiling has been giving way. A bolt pops and metal bows. The panel I'm lying on slides out of its groove. I slip forwards into the room of people. I let myself fall. Holding out my hands, I hit the floor and roll away from the gathering of people now staring at me. I fall back into a fighting stance. They're all looking at me with bemused faces. Except Botty, who's turning pink with rage.

'She also seems to have just added espionage to her list,' Dad says, smiling at me.

The door swings open and the receptionist comes in. 'Sir, I think we have an intruder... Oh.'

Botty goes beetroot. 'I can see that! What the hell is she doing in my office?'

'I'll have you know, I have police back-up,' I say defensively.

Dad cocks his head at me.

'You're all going to jail for a long time,' I say. Then I add for good measure, 'You are all very bad people.'

'Where's Ollie?' Mikey asks.

I blush. 'Well, we had a bit of a falling out...'

'What have you done to him?' he demands.

'Nothing... much.'

There's some commotion outside and Ollie races in.

'See, he's fine,' I say. God, parents don't half worry. Dad is grinning at me. Botty is going nuclear.

'Oh, good. You are here,' Ollie puffs at me. 'Why are you in overalls?'

'What the hell is going on here, Turner?' Botty shouts.

It takes me a second to realise he's referring to Ollie. Does everyone here have a nickname?

'This is Leo's new apprentice,' Ollie says, like it's really obvious.

'To hell with that!' I storm and jump. I catch the rim of the hole in the ceiling and haul myself back inside. I need to get out of here fast.

Dad's face appears behind me.

'Peachkin?' he calls.

'Don't "Peachkin" me, you criminal scum,' I snap, and blow dust at him. He disappears in a plume of grime.

I'm not inching slowly any more; I'm crawling rapidly. I can actually feel the ceiling bowing under my weight. It's not going to hold out much longer. I might as well as come out. I kick out a panel and jump down on to the desk of a startled worker. He makes a grab for me so I kick him in the face. Harsh but necessary. These people are criminals and I don't really have police back-up.

I need some bargaining time. I grab the phone from his desk and dial 999. Everyone is descending on me. Dad and Mikey at the front of the crowd.

'What are you doing?' Dad asks.

'I'm phoning someone.'

He frowns at me. 'Who?'

The handset speaks to me. 'What service, please.'

'Police,' I answer.

'Sweetie? What are you doing?' Dad says totally bemused.

'Some apprentice,' I hear Botty say.

'Shut up, Botty!' I snarl.

'Botty?' someone queries.

'Or Botty-chello or whatever it was,' I explain.

Mikey bursts out laughing, until Botty shoots him a dangerous look.

I really need to get away from these weirdos before they body-bag me.

'Look, I could have the police here in five minutes,' I snap. 'I want you to clear a path to the fire escape for me.'

'No, you couldn't,' says Dad.

'No. I couldn't what?'

'Have the police here in five minutes.'

'Alright, then – six or seven.'

'No, you see Monnie handles the switchboard. Your call hasn't left the room.' He points to the stern receptionist woman with the black bob.

I glance at her, sitting at her desk on the phone, looking straight at me. If this really was 999, they would have put me through by now.

'Goddamn it.' I slam the receiver down. 'How could you?' I glare at him.

'What's the matter? Why are you so upset?' Dad asks.

Everyone in their smart business suits is looking at me standing on a desk in a pair of dirty blue overalls. My panicked flight begins to flow into something else. If I'm going to get out of here in one piece, I need to rely on my instincts. I can feel a calmness seep through my veins as my brain switches to autopilot. I relax my muscles and feel my eyes go dark and hooded. Dad senses the change because his eyes respond. I'm staring right at him and it's like staring into a bottomless well.

'Wait...' I hear him say, but it's too late.

I do a backflip and land by the wall. When I focus again I notice everyone has spread out more, ready to grab me. These aren't your ordinary office workers. I can spot three horse stances and one man's grabbed a bamboo stick from a pot plant and is hiding it behind his back. I decide I want that stick.

'Catherine, just stop a minute,' Dad says, lowering his hands, palm down, in a calming gesture.

'You lying...' I turn and grab the fire extinguisher off the wall, '... art stealing...' I snap open the hose and spray, mainly at the man with the bamboo stick, '... criminal...' I leap and place my foot squarely in the man's solar plexus just as he's bringing round the stick. I prise it neatly out of his hands. '... son of a...'

The misty haze from the fire extinguisher has cleared. I'm now on the opposite side of the crowd. Near enough to the fire exit that I should be able to make it, no problem. And I have a weapon, in case I don't.

'You and the Fine Art Restoration Trust are history,' I spit venomously and rush for the door.

'We don't steal art,' Dad calls.

The door is open. I can see blue sky and breathe fresh air. I turn back to him.

'We steal it back.'

KELLEY TOWNLEY, twenty-five, is specifically interested in writing for teenagers. She has read work out at the Bath Literary Festival and was a prizewinner in the *Bath Chronicle*'s short story competition 2001. She runs two successful teenage reading groups in the Bath Library and works in Waterstone's in Milsom Street.

Contact: kelley.townley@sparksanthology.co.uk
       www.kelleytownley.com

The Mistletoe Giant

David S. Bull

from a novel
for 9- to 12-year-olds

I crept along the landing and stood outside Mum's half-open door. I listened.

'Is that you, Peter?' Mum's voice was quiet. 'I heard shouting downstairs. What's happened?'

I lowered my head and looked at the metal strip dividing the two carpets.

'I burned some toast, that's all.'

'Why don't you come in? I can't talk to you from the hall.'

I hovered in the doorway.

I used to spend hours with my mum when she was first ill. I'd sit and tell her things: what I'd done that day, what the weather was like outside, what was growing in the garden.

Now I could hardly stand the sight of her. I didn't want to be in the same room as her.

She wanted me to be the same, to be close, but I couldn't do it anymore. I needed to keep away.

My dad thought I was cruel.

'You're hurting her,' he said.

But my sister soon took my place. I told her it was her turn to look after Mum. It was time for someone else to report on the outside world. I'd done my bit.

Mum still asked for me. Sometimes I stood like now, in a doorway, not looking but listening. She tried to coax me into the room, to the window, to sit on her bed. I refused.

Sometimes she smelled like an unmade bed. A sort of damp, musty smell. It hit me whenever I walked into her room.

That was when she smelled like death.

It scared me. It was too much.

Helen said she couldn't smell anything. She said that I was making it up. But I wasn't.

Helen was always in Mum's room now. She'd sit on Mum's bed and they'd talk for hours. Or, cuddled up together, Mum would read to her.

Through the crack between the door and the frame, I could see Mum propped up in bed. She was staring out of the window.

'We saw you up by the trees yesterday,' said Mum. 'What did you find?'

I stood there for a moment staring into her room. From the doorway I could see the forest through the bay window. I didn't know what to say to her.

'What did you see in the forest?'

'Nothing. It's just a forest.'

'Were there any birds? You always tell me about the birds.'

There were only the five dead magpies. And I wasn't going to tell her about them. They were my secret. I said nothing and stared up at the trees.

I knew the five birds were watching me through the window. I knew they were listening. They saw my every movement in this new house, as if the walls were invisible. I couldn't hide from their dead eyes.

'What is it, Peter?' said Mum. 'What's upsetting you?'

I walked into the room. Stopped briefly by the door. Then stood in the bay window.

'That's better,' she said.

I turned to look at her.

She smiled at me.

Several pillows and cushions propped her up. A white nightgown clung to her thin shoulders. She'd hardly been outside for months and her face was pale and thin. She looked like the ghost of herself.

Her long hair had gone, to make it easier to keep clean. Her eyes were sunken like buried treasure. They shone brightly from the shadows of the room. A book rested under the palm of one hand. A pen and paper lay by her side. She stared at me and tried to smile. She was wondering what was wrong with me. Her eyes followed my gaze as I looked around the room.

An old radio was on the bedside table. A large church candle rested on a pink saucer. And a tall bottle of mineral water stood on the dresser. It was surrounded by a horde of little brown bottles, all with big white plastic caps. The bottles stood guard over my mum twenty-four hours a day. Like cowboys and Indians they chased each other around the water bottle. They watched her. Waited for her to wake. Then sent her back to sleep.

I pushed myself away from the window-ledge. I glanced at Mum. She looked agitated.

'There used to be a giant in the forest,' Mum said suddenly. 'When I was a girl. A huge statue of a man. All covered in leaves and ivy.'

I looked closely at Mum's pale face. Was this another one of her stories, her way of keeping me in the room? I couldn't tell.

Mum gazed up towards the ceiling.

'We used to play around it. Some of the boys climbed the outside and sat on the giant's shoulders.'

She turned a small black stone in her fingers. Her face seemed to flicker as her mind raced back to when she was a child. Sometimes she smiled and her eyes sparkled as if she'd had a happy memory.

'We had a special name for him,' she said to herself. She dropped her head and smiled at me. 'The Mistletoe Giant.'

Mum waved a hand at me to come nearer and sit on the bed next to her. I stayed by the bay window. She dropped her hand on to the bed and looked down at the sheets.

'All year round,' she continued. 'Even when all the other trees had lost their leaves, the giant always had a ring of mistletoe running around his neck and shoulders. We used to dance around him. It just felt like the right thing to do. It became our special place in the forest.'

Mum smiled.

'We used to hang bottles inside the giant,' said Mum suddenly. 'Little coloured bottles we'd dug out of the ground. Some were blue, some green, and sometimes we'd find little red bottles.' She grinned at me.

'Those were the really special ones.'

Mum pointed to a tiny red bottle over on a high shelf.

'We used to write messages on pieces of paper and push them into the bottles. Tie string around the necks. Then we'd climb up inside the giant. And hang the tiny bottles from the frame or on pieces of wicker that stuck out.

'We had over a hundred of them hanging in there once. When the wind blew hard through the forest, the bottles used to swing about and knock into each other. It made the most magical sound. Like the giant was singing.' Mum's expression changed.

'But the giant burned down.' She fell silent, and looked down at her hands.

'We ran through the forest to the giant,' she said. 'Birds flew out of his body. The flames were taller than the trees. The giant was destroyed in minutes.

'All our bottles were lost in the fire. We found some. But most were smashed or buried when men came to put out the fire. They beat the giant down with strips of rubber tied to long poles. And shovelled earth on to him to stop the flames spreading. We just stood there and watched. All of us cried. Even the boys couldn't keep back the tears. We loved the Mistletoe Giant.' Mum fell silent again.

I wanted to ask her a question. But I knew that would only encourage her. And be a sign that the story had worked. I decided to play along. To see how much she really knew and if I could catch her out.

'What did you write in the messages?' I asked. I sat down on the window-ledge and leant back against the glass.

'We used to write our dreams, our secrets.'

A smile forced its way on to my face.

'Why are you smiling?' asked Mum.

'What sort of secrets?' I asked.

'Oh the usual stuff of a thirteen-year-old girl. Messages to the boys I liked, dreams that they liked me too. Wishes I had for the future. Things that I hoped to do or become when I grew up.'

'What did you want to be?' I asked.

'I can't remember.'

I knew she was lying. She knew exactly what she'd written. She just didn't want to tell me.

'What was the giant made out of?' I asked.

Mum's eyes sparkled and she sat up. 'He was made from wicker, like that old chair over there.'

Mum pointed to a small low-backed chair in the corner of the bedroom. It was made from long thin pieces of wicker woven together. The chair was light blue. I remembered Dad painting it last summer. We'd had it for years. When Mum felt well enough, she would sit and watch the world from that chair.

I also remembered it from Granddad's garden shed. He used to read the newspaper in it. If it was a sunny day, he'd take the chair out and sit under the apple tree. Grandma would make him a cup of tea. And I'd take it out to him. I'd sit on the ground and listen to him slurp. He'd read out funny stories from the newspaper. And we'd laugh together.

Mum had stopped talking and was watching me closely. I sent the memories away and looked down at the floor.

'Why don't you put that chair in the window and sit down?' she said.

Reality snapped back. I'd been tricked. This was a game. I'd been fooled. There wasn't a wicker giant in the forest. She'd made it all up to make me stay. It was a lie to keep me in the room. I looked away from her. I wanted to get out. Instead I slid backwards into myself.

In my mind I walked up to Mum's bedside. Placed a shoebox down on the bed in front of her. Then I stepped back and watched her study the box. She looked up at me.

'What's this?' I imagined her saying.

I grinned back at her. Shrugged my shoulders. How would she react? What would she think of my special gift? What would she think of me?

'Open it,' I said.

Mum looked down and pulled at the string bow. She slightly lifted the thin lid of the box. Then stopped and looked at me. Did she smell something?

She lifted the lid clean off. A red glow from inside the box lit up her face. Mum smiled and placed the lid on the bed and looked inside. I'd concealed the present in red tissue paper. A nice touch. Mum beamed at me.

I just watched and waited.

The tissue paper moved.

Mum's hand darted away. I heard the sharp intake of her breath. She almost screamed, but held it back. She stared at me, questioning. I smiled.

'Don't worry, Mum. It can't hurt you – it's dead.'

She picked up the lid and slowly placed it over the box. Sensing the change in light, the tissue paper moved violently. A chattering laugh came from inside. Mum slammed the lid down. But it didn't quite fit and the magpie's head burst through the tiny gap. Mum struggled to keep the bird inside the box. But the bird was too strong and leapt into the air.

Mum screamed.

I laughed out loud.

The terrified magpie circled the bedroom. It flew at the window and crashed into the glass next to me. Dazed, it dropped to the windowsill. The magpie sprang back into the air and landed on top of the pine wardrobe. It opened its sharp beak and panted. It looked around for a way to escape. The magpie barked out in alarm, its long tail flicking upright, then dropping after every call.

Mum screamed at me to open a window and let the bird out.

The magpie swooped down over the bed and collided with the window again. It knocked over Mum's glass of water. Her medicine bottles tumbled to the floor. The magpie swung from the light shade, sending a cloud of dust on to Mum's bed. It hung from the curtains. Its claws ripped the flowered fabric.

'… Peter? Are you OK?'

The magpie vanished.

I returned.

'I lost you for a second there. The chair?' Mum pointed at the blue wicker chair. 'Why don't you put the chair in the window and sit down? And then I can tell you more about the giant.'

The magpie reappeared in the room, but only for a few seconds. I made it stop flying around. Told it to keep quiet and keep still. It sat on one of Mum's bedposts and kept watch over her.

I moved towards the door.

'I promised Dad I'd finish unpacking.'

Mum looked behind her to see what I was looking at. She looked confused when she couldn't see anything. She reached out a hand to me.

'You will tell me if you find anything in the forest?'

At the door I quickly looked back at the magpie still sitting on the bedpost. The bird tilted its head to look at me. Somehow it made me feel better to know he was there. He was here to look after me.

The magpie squawked as I left the room.

DAVID S. BULL was born in London in 1966, and spent his childhood in Yorkshire. He studied Film and Television at college, has worked in children's animation for twenty years, and was recently awarded funding for his first live-action screenplay. David lives in Bristol with his wife Sylvi and son Joseph.

Contact: david.bull@sparksanthology.co.uk

A Sheep with Orange Eyes

Anne Hume

from a novel
for teenagers

Chapter One

This thing in the back of my hand is hurting. But I can't move it because it's fixed on with a plaster. And there's a needle stuck right in my vein. Yuk! Just looking at the thing is making me want to puke. My belly's coming right up into my mouth. I can still taste the sick from yesterday. Is that moon or sun shining through the screen round the bed? It's like looking through a dragonfly wing, colours split and rainbowed. Am I crying? Am I breathing? Am I here at all? Maybe if I just turn over and close my eyes, I won't exist any more. Wouldn't that be better for everyone, especially me? And him. Dylan. I don't want him to have any more trouble because of me. Nobody understands him like I do. But he doesn't hurt anyone as much as he hurts me.

My name's Polly. I'm one half of twins. Identical. My sister's Anna – so we're Polly-Anna after some book Mum once read, about a girl who always saw the best in everything. Not like me. Or Anna really. Since we got to be about thirteen, life's been quite shit one way or another. When we look in the mirror, it's hard to see which is which. Same red-brown hair. Same green eyes. Her face is wider than mine, a bit. And she's taller. My face looks kind of closed next to Anna's. She's more ready to smile. She's a lot prettier than me. And she's had a lot more fun.

Anna went mad when she heard what I'd done. She hates Dylan. She says he's revolting. Everyone hates him because of how he's treated me. But he's got problems and I know what that's like. So I understand. She yelled at me when she came in to see me last night. Then she got into bed beside me and hugged me for ages.

'You twat. How could you be so stupid? Don't you realise how much you worry everyone, you idiot?' Nothing about ME, how I could have killed myself. Well, she said if I'd really wanted to die I'd have taken more tablets. Would have done, if I could've found any more. She won't believe me if I say that, though. Anna always reckons I'm just attention-seeking. I don't think she's got time to wonder what it's like being the one with the 'problems'. But when she was beside me in the bed I did feel better. Maybe she understands more than she lets on.

There's a nurse here now, doing my blood pressure and stuff.

'How're you feeling, Polly?' She sounds kind. Some of them are very brisk, annoyed. I'm just a stupid teenager to them, who doesn't consider other people's feelings. Wrong! It's BECAUSE I care about their feelings and always seem to be messing things up that I'm here. This nurse is smiling at me. She's young, with blonde hair in a ponytail. She leans down a bit.

'I think you're gonna be OK. You must have been feeling pretty bad to have done this.'

I nod my head without lifting it off the bed. She's adjusting the drip thing going into my hand and writing stuff down on the chart. She just touches my hair, smooths it back a bit.

'Go on, lovely. Have a little cry. You need to.' She's seen the way I'm biting my lip and now the tears squeeze out, dripping hot and angry on to the pillow. You freak, Polly Thomas. Get a grip.

'The doctor will be round to see you in a bit. And I bet your mum'll soon be here, too. I'll be back later.'

I wish she could stay with me. But she's busy. There's so many of us in here. It's a teenagers' unit in the hospital. The girl in the opposite bed is peering at me where the nurse has pushed the screen back a bit. I shut my eyes so she can't see I'm crying. Will I be glad to see Mum or not? She was pretty amazing yesterday. And I was too out of it to notice how worried she must have been. Now I'm a bit better, she'll probably start shouting at me. I don't want to have to bother about how she's feeling. I was throwing up all over her yesterday and she never moaned once. She helped me to the bathroom, though I wasn't supposed to be out of bed. Then she took my pukey clothes off and got me some clean ones. And she stayed beside me all night on a camp-bed thing.

I was drifting in and out of sleep. I kept seeing Mum leaning up on her elbow to see if I was OK. And nurses doing my blood pressure and pulse and writing it down. I pretended I hadn't woken up at all. Mum'd only ask me WHY I took all the pills. She had to go early this morning to get the others off to school and college and stuff. She said she'd be back after breakfast. Must be thinking I'll be all right now.

Last night they weren't sure. Said it would take a few hours before they could tell if the paracetamol had damaged my liver. Or anything else. So they had to do another blood test in the middle of the night. Frigging pain. I just wanted to sleep. For ages. To escape and forget. Didn't want to talk to anyone. That was one of the times Mum woke up. But I kept my eyes half-shut, even when they stuck the needle into my arm and sucked out the blood. I caught a glimpse of it – dark red and thick in the syringe thing – before I turned my head away and faked sleep again.

I heard them say I wouldn't be 'out of the woods' for a few days, but it was lucky I seemed to be fighting off the effects of all the stuff I took. I could hear Mum sucking in her breath, fidgeting, ready to ask a question.

'Doctor... Um, what about her CP?'

'Cerebral palsy?'

'Yes, you know – does it make all this more serious?'

'No, not necessarily. Don't worry. You just get some sleep. We'll have a fuller picture tomorrow. But we'll be monitoring Polly regularly.'

Poor Mum. She must have stressed all night.

That girl's still trying to peer at me. I put my hands over my eyes, covering them like a mask. The sun shines through, making the edges of my fingers pink-red. My blood. Still flowing. I can feel it vibrating through my veins. Thump, thump, skitter. My heart does its weird uneven throb, like a butterfly trying to escape every third or fourth beat. Now I see Dylan. All untidy and dirty. When I reach out to him he fades into the wedge of sunlight filtering through the sides of the curtains. My lost boy. Disappearing back to Neverland like the boys in *Hook*. Nowhere Land. Anywhere Land. That's just it. He could be anywhere. Foster home. Sleeping rough. Police cell. Prison, maybe. Him in a cell and me in hospital.

Oh God, he looks so thin. Here again now, but melting. Into shadows this time. I can hear him crying, that weird noise he makes deep in his chest. I'm following him into the darkness, dissolving, and as I go the sound of him gets muffled, fading into nothing. Till I'm nothing, too.

ANNE HUME, mother and grandmother to a large family, has written 'bits and bobs' all her life. She started writing *A Sheep with Orange Eyes* at the beginning of the MA in October 2004. She has spent the past thirty years surrounded by young people and thinks they are fantastic.

Contact: anne.hume@sparksanthology.co.uk

Joyrider

Karen Saunders

from a novel
for teenagers

Chapter One
April

A s I sit down on the swing I notice a needle on the ground. It's nestled amongst the blades of grass, glinting in the orange glow from the streetlights. I wish Adam had picked somewhere else for us to meet. The park's creepy at this time of night. Or morning, whichever way you look at it. I'd never been here before I met Adam, but it's a halfway point between our houses. A place that's special to us for all kinds of reasons.

I push back against the earth and let myself rock, backwards and forwards. It's comforting, soothing, sitting on a swing. Reminds me of being a kid. My shoes scuff against the ground and I lift my legs out in front of me. As the swing flies higher, I throw my head back to look up at the sky. There are no stars tonight. The city lights are so strong they block them out. I like to look at the stars. They make you realise how much more there is out there.

My parents would go totally schizoid if they knew where I was. What I'm planning to do. They think I'm in bed, tucked up safely like the good little vicar's daughter they want me to be. But they make it so easy to get out of the house with the porch right under my bedroom window. Almost like they're helping me to go.

The swing slows, and I twist my wrist to check my watch. Where's Adam? I wish he'd hurry up. I can't wait to get out of here now. I wonder how Mum and Dad will react in the morning when they find out I've gone. And when they realise who I'm with. They really hate Adam. Hate the idea of me having a boyfriend. They think I should be hanging out with the church youth club. Like that's going to happen. I mean, as if.

I hear the sound of an engine and a screech of brakes on the road behind me. A car pulls up nearby.

'Becky! Over here!'

Adam's leaning out of the car window. I can't believe he's actually managed to get a car. I suppose part of me thought he wouldn't be able to. I mean, he's only sixteen. But Adam can do anything he puts his mind to, so I shouldn't be surprised. And the fact he's here means it's final. We're really going. I step down from the swing, grab my bag and walk towards him, fuelled by a mixture of excitement and nerves. Adam's head disappears inside and then the passenger door opens.

'All right?' He leans across as I climb in and gives me a long kiss. I relax into him, my fingers winding through the hair at the back of his neck, my nerves melting away.

Adam pulls away and smiles. 'Hey you,' he says softly, looking deep into my eyes and rubbing my cheek with his thumb. 'I'm glad you came.'

My insides dissolve into a puddle of mush. 'Like I wouldn't.' I lean forwards for another kiss. 'So where'd you get the car?' I ask, when we finally let each other go.

'Borrowed it from Tony.'

I frown in confusion. 'Your stepdad? You told him where you were going and he agreed to lend you the car?'

'Becs, don't be stupid. He doesn't exactly *know* he's lent it me. But he will, when he wakes up tomorrow and sees the car's gone.'

It's then a slight doubt races through my mind. Am I really going to do this? It's such a big deal. I'm leaving everything behind. Everyone. Suddenly, I'm not so sure any more. But if I don't, I'll lose Adam. And I can't even think about not having him in my life. Things would go back to how they were before. I'd have to go home. Back to my parents. Back to my dull, boring, pathetic existence. I don't want that. I love Adam. Adam loves me, and I want to be with him. I push my doubts aside. This is what I have to do.

I throw my bag on to the back seat and buckle my seatbelt. 'So, are we still heading to Leeds, then?'

'Yep. You sure you want come?'

'I'm sure.'

'Then let's go,' Adam says, revving the engine loudly. With the tyres screaming, and my heart pumping, we speed away.

I've never gone in a car with someone who wasn't an adult before. It's always been with a parent, or a friend's parent, or a relative. It's fun driving with a mate; someone you know isn't responsible and boring.

I watch out of the window as the familiar houses flash by, along the roads I've travelled so many times before, but never like this. Then I realise my house is just around the corner. What's Adam doing?

'Why are you driving this way?' I ask nervously.

'Come on, Becs. Where's your sense of adventure? It'll be fine.'

The traffic lights in front of us are changing, and Adam starts to speed up, like he wants to get through before the red light comes on.

'Adam...' my voice gets caught in my throat. There's a guy walking out on to the crossing ahead. He's staggering around as if he's had too much to drink, with a six-pack clutched under his arm.

Adam blasts the horn, and the man freezes in shock. Like a rabbit caught in the headlights, he can't seem to move.

Adam twists the steering wheel to one side and the car swerves across the road. We miss him by inches. I see his terrified face looking at mine as we swoop past.

It's only as we speed onwards away from the man, away from my house, that I realise I've been holding my breath. I glance over at Adam and I'm shocked to see he's laughing. He actually thinks it was funny. I'm about to give him hell, when I notice his knuckles on the steering wheel are white. His fingers are gripping on tightly.

'You all right?'

Adam stops laughing and nods silently.

'Be careful, OK? He looked straight at us. What if he calls the cops?'

'He won't. Shut up, Becky. Stop going on all the time.'

I bite my lip and turn to look out of the window. Adam realises I'm upset, and moves his hand briefly over to my side of the car, rubbing my thigh, before grabbing hold of the steering wheel again.

It doesn't take long before the streetlights are thinning and we reach the outskirts of town. Adam accelerates as we head into the countryside. It feels safer out here, darker, with fewer people to see us. Suddenly I can understand why people do this. Finally I'm free, and the buzz is fantastic!

I throw my head back and scream in delight as we go faster and faster.

I need more. I wind down the window and stick my head out, relishing the feel of the wind whipping through my hair, crashing against my face, making it hard to breathe.

It feels so intense, so exhilarating, so alive.

'What the hell are you doing, you daft mare?' Adam laughs. He reaches over and grabs the back of my jacket, pulling me back inside.

'This is amazing,' I say, watching the lights of Slaverton getting smaller and smaller behind us. We did it, and I'm stunned at how easy it was to get away. How simple it was to leave it all behind. I don't know what I was expecting, but I suppose I imagined it'd be harder than this. Perhaps I expected to feel more regrets, or doubts, or worries. I hadn't expected to feel this, well, *great*. Being with Adam is all I've ever want-ed, and we're going to be together for ever.

The road stretches out ahead of us, offering endless possibilities. I can do anything I want now, I think excitedly to myself. *Anything*.

We speed along, cocooned in our blackness, for what seems like hours, enjoying being together. But all too quickly the streetlights invade our private space once more, and the main road appears in front of us.

'Which way, then?' Adam asks, looking over at me nervously. This is my last chance to go back, and he knows if I choose left we go home. Back to Slaverton, our parents, and everything we've finally escaped from. Right is the direction up north, to who knows where, who knows what, which will keep us driving into the night.

'Right,' I tell him firmly, and he indicates carefully before pulling out on to the deserted road. That makes me smile. After everything he's done this evening, he's worrying about indicating. There's not even anyone else around.

I'm gazing across the fields at the full moon, not thinking about anything in particular, when I spot them out of the corner of my eye. They're parked in the lay-by, the reflective strips of their car shining in the glare from our headlights as we drive past.

I look over at Adam in shock. 'That was a police car! Do you think they saw us?'

'Nah,' Adam says confidently. 'I wasn't speeding. It'll be fine.'

For an instant I think he's right, and try to ignore the icy trickle of fear that's run down my spine, giving me goose bumps.

Then comes the sound of the siren.

Adam's face pales and my eyes open wide with panic. Twisting around to look out of the back window, I can see the police car racing to catch up with us.

I crash back down into my seat. 'What are we going to do?'

'I don't know, do I?' Adam yells.

I take deep breaths. I need to be calm. Come on Becky. Think. *Think*.

But I can't seem to get my head to work. It's like my brain's totally scrambled.

'Do you reckon we can get away?'

Adam pulls a face. For a moment, his tough exterior vanishes and all I can see is a scared little boy sitting next to me. That frightens me more than the police do.

'Well I don't fancy stopping. Do you?'

Adam shakes his head and, as if he's come back to life, stamps his foot down on to the accelerator. The car jumps forwards.

We're speeding along, but the police are getting closer, much too close, and soon they're only inches away from our bumper.

Adam's staring ahead, concentrating on the empty road in front of him. My head snaps between watching him, then the police, then Adam again.

Their car tries to pull around us, but Adam swerves out into the right-hand lane to block them.

The police accelerate, and draw level. We're driving alongside each other, parallel on the road.

They're so close I can see their faces. I try not to look, I don't want to be recognised if we do get away, but I can't help myself. A man's driving and a woman is in the passenger seat. She's speaking urgently into her radio.

Going faster and faster, we're still on the wrong side of the road. Fear twists my insides as from nowhere; headlights are coming straight for us.

Adam swears as he brakes hard and yanks at the steering wheel. The car skids across the tarmac. Suddenly we're spinning, spinning, and the world turns into a blur.

KAREN SAUNDERS graduated from Warwick University in 1999 with a BA in English. She has spent her time since doing a variety of jobs, travelling the world, and writing as much as possible. Karen lives in Bath and is working on her second novel.

Contact: karen.saunders@sparksanthology.co.uk

An Interview with Mo Hayder

An Interview with Mo Hayder

Peter Mallett

After learning that Mo Hayder was to be my manuscript tutor for the MA in Creative Writing at Bath Spa University, I went to buy one of her books. The guarantee of graphic descriptions of violence in the publicity for her first two novels didn't suggest comforting bedtime reading, so I opted for her last novel, *Tokyo* – and skipped through the gorier parts of that. What sort of mind, I wondered, could have created such books, probing the darkest recesses of the human soul? It came as a huge relief, therefore, when I met the writer in person for the first time, to discover she was surprisingly, and reassuringly, normal.

As we sat drinking cups of tea over the kitchen table of her home in Larkhall, it was impossible to imagine that the woman opposite me was the author of *The Treatment*, which a *Guardian* critic described as 'the most frightening book I've ever read', and of *Birdman*, which left her own mother so shocked after reading it that she didn't speak for a week.

But this is just part of the paradox that is Mo Hayder. She says she doesn't like talking about her work, but is able to do so very articulately. She maintains that she hates being photographed and yet is extremely photogenic. The glamorous photographs on her website appear to have been chosen to present her for the American market as a 'Queen of Crime' personality with model good looks. In the flesh, her beauty is of a more interesting, Gothic kind, hinting at the complex character within.

Hayder claims not to be well read, saying she is a 'junk-food reader', then goes on to cite Ian McEwan, John Banville and Yukio Mishima amongst writers she enjoys. Contrary to the advice normally given to writers, Hayder says she thinks it's an advantage not to have read too well; 'ignorance is bliss'. Coming from an academic family, she rebelled by not reading any books at all for almost ten years. 'I found that whole atmosphere surrounding academia very dry and books symbolised that,' she says, recognising the irony that she should now be making her living writing books.

She left school at fifteen and worked as a barmaid, security guard, film-maker, hostess in a Tokyo club, educational administrator and teacher of English as a foreign language in Asia before starting to write.

Hayder says that she began writing 'out of desperation: if I hadn't been writing, I would have had children.' Yet, she has had a child, three-year-old Lotte, who throws a tantrum as soon as I arrive for this interview and diverts her mother's attention. 'I wanted something I'd created over which I had complete control,' Hayder says. 'It's quite self-evident that I have no control over my real daughter!'

With no previous writing experience, Hayder then produced two immediate bestsellers, winning in the process the 2002 W.H. Smith Thumping Good Read Award. In spite of this success, she remains remarkably grounded and appears to treat the whole business with a certain irony. Amongst the glowing tributes and reviews listed on her website, she has included for each book a diatribe from a certain Norman Quinn, who describes her work as 'absolute rubbish' produced by a 'dreadful purveyor of filth'. When I ask who this critic is, she replies that it was her cat, now dead.

After the success of the first two thrillers, Hayder turned, in *Tokyo*, to something more literary, choosing an ambitious double first person narrative. The heroine, Grey, arrives in Tokyo in the summer of 1990 to look for the only person who can justify the terrible mistake she made in her adolescence, the Chinese professor Shi Chongming. A survivor of the notorious Nanking massacre of 1937, Shi Chongming provides the second narrative with his diary of the tumultuous days of Japan's invasion of China and the orgy of violence and carnage which followed. Events from this period are to have repercussions in Grey's own life as well as in the Tokyo underworld in which she finds herself. *Time Out*, choosing the novel as book of the week, declared that

> 'The reality of crime is never portrayed in fiction – the real awfulness. I object to that.'

Tokyo 'confirms a major talent that transcends thriller writing', while the *Daily Telegraph* praised it as 'both a fascinating and moving historical novel and a thriller so fast paced I had to sit up until the early hours to finish it'.

Hayder based the heroine's experience as a nightclub hostess in Japan on her own and used the beautiful but creepy old traditional Japanese house she lived in for the setting. The book appeared shortly after the murder of Lucie Blackman, the young English woman who'd been working at a club in Tokyo. It was a crime that shocked the British public into awareness of Japanese hostess bars and their connections with the shady gangster world. 'The Lucie Blackman case didn't influence *Tokyo*; I had the idea long before,' says Hayder. 'But it's a sad fact of life that tragedies that have some parallels with your writing sell your books.'

The parallels between *The Treatment* and the Sarah Payne paedo-philia case were more striking. 'It can be quite frightening when some-thing you're writing about starts occurring in real life,' Hayder says. 'I came very close to scrapping that book because it felt so uncomfort-able. I didn't feel the same with Lucie Blackman because the plot didn't bear any relation to what happened to her.'

Despite being shortlisted for the CWA Gold and Steel Dagger Awards for Novels of the Year, 2004, and on the *Sunday Times* best-seller list, *Tokyo* did not enjoy the same commercial success as the ear-lier books, though it is selling well in the United States and is very popular with the French. Hayder is uncertain of the exact sales figures, but in hardback the book sold in the tens of thousands as compared to hundreds of thousands for the earlier two novels.

Hayder thinks she failed with this book by trying to do two things at once: 'Instead of bridging the gap between two areas [crime and liter-ary], I think it fell between two stools with a loud clunk. The commer-cial success proved that people want one thing or the other. I envisaged a readership out there that isn't really there.'

Tokyo was, however, popular with the critics, showing that this change of style was not altogether a failure. Hayder says that in the fu-ture she may 'just bifurcate, split myself into two people'. With her new novel, *Pig Island*, due for publication in April 2006, she has gone back to the original mould. 'It still had certain challenges for me as a writer, particularly getting the voice of the main character, a journalist – it's in the first person,' she says. 'I was pushing myself as a writer; the stretch was there for me, it's just not as evident [as in *Tokyo*].'

Pig Island, dealing with a secretive religious community on a re-mote Scottish island accused of Satanism, promises to be as terrifying and sensationally violent as Hayder's previous three novels. It is inevi-table, therefore, that our conversation turns to the dark subjects she has chosen as the themes of her novels.

Why did you choose these subjects and where did the ideas come from?

You have to go with the subjects that draw you as a reader. Reading has always been a fantastic form of escapism for me at various points in my life when I desperately needed escapism. The subject matter that I found it easiest to escape into was these dark themes. I read a lot of horror rather than crime. There's always the potential in what I write to topple over into horror.

Do you ever think you've taken something too far, been too graphic perhaps, and do sections get omitted or rewritten as a result?

No. If I'd spent a lot of time describing someone preparing a meal, making love or looking in a shop window, no one would criticise me for it. It's inbred into us today not to look at death and violence, but just a few hundred years ago it was not strange for people to travel miles to watch an execution. It's human instinct to be interested in death.

The reality of crime is never portrayed in fiction – the real awfulness. I object to that.

Do the things you've written give you nightmares?

No, but the research does. Things I've discovered keep me awake all night.

How much research do you tend to do for each novel?

Probably too much. I use about ten per cent of the total research I do. Good research and use of authentic action can bring a scene to life, but if you over-research you tend to bend the story to fit the research. I've used the other approach in my latest novel: I wrote the story and then did the research and found mostly I'd made incredibly good guesses.

I'm just about to write a book about a particular drug that's used in some parts of Africa as a ritual. About one in a hundred people drop dead from taking it. Now I'm having a tug of war with family and friends about taking the drug myself, but I can't write about it if I haven't experienced the effects. This might mean I'm not as imaginative as I should be.

Which writers have inspired or influenced you?

I like people who sit on the slightly uneasy edge between the literary and crime: David Lindsey. Robert Wilson. Peter Dexter. Thomas Harris – he's completely underrated as a literary writer. Ian McEwan – he's not that far removed from Thomas Harris, though he's not quite as sensational. There's a fine line between Ian McEwan and Ian Rankin. A writer everyone sneers at and is perpetually flawed is Stephen King, but I really admire the enthusiasm that shines through. The writing just blasts off the page. I wouldn't find any escapism in, for example, Margaret Atwood. I have a lot of problems with her.

My latest book is a little bit influenced by Peter Dexter and possibly by Chuck Palahniuk. There's a great energy in his writing – you have to read it.

Even though the first novel was a bestseller, you decided to enrol on the MA in Creative Writing at Bath Spa. Why?

Firstly, I wanted to explore the idea of teaching creative writing. Secondly, I felt it was a complete fluke that I'd been published. I was writing in the dark. I finished my first novel by trial and error; I wanted some clarity, some lucidity on my techniques. I'd been writing instinctually: I wanted to formalise it, to find out the tools I'd been using so I could have more immediate access to them.

What did you learn from the course and what do you think are the advantages of such courses?

I learned what the advantages are of getting unbiased advice and criticism from your peers. To get this in such quantities is something you'll never ever have again in your career. As soon as you become published, you realise that all criticism has an agenda attached. There's a purity of the criticism you get in college that you don't get in the real world.

With regard to technique, I learned how to make my writing more textured by, for example, using different tenses. It also enabled me to write in the first person – something I'd never done before.

Would your second novel have been different if you had not written it on the course?

No, it wouldn't have been much different, but the course helped me with *Tokyo*. I already had a vague idea of the themes I was going to be looking at in that book while I was taking the course.

What is the hardest part of the writing process and have you discovered any tricks to making it easier?

It changes. I've just now been doing some proof-editing which I used to hate. It felt as if you'd built a house that was slightly unstable and then someone points out a brick on a lower level and asks you to replace it and you can't without the whole house collapsing. But I think I've changed with that. At the moment, I'm just struggling to put words down. The most important thing I've learned is that you can't mould anything out of thin air. It's far better to have two thousand of the wrong words than nothing at all.

Everyone has periods when they can't write. It's all a state of mind. Until you start writing professionally you don't realise what hard work it is. When you get your first set of notes back from the editor, you feel as though you've been kicked down a mountain and have to climb it again. There's no comfort, no food supplies.

Do you have any tips for writers?

My general advice to writers is be very clear about the type of book you're writing. I'm hoist by my own petard with this in that I think I made a mistake with *Tokyo*.

And something else that sounds obvious: if you don't finish the book, you won't get published! It's hard work.

Mo Hayder's novel *Pig Island* will be published by Bantam Press in April 2006.